NAPOLEON'S
ROAD TO GLORY

NAPOLEON'S ROAD TO GLORY

Triumphs, Defeats and Immortality

J. DAVID MARKHAM

BRASSEY'S

Copyright © J. David Markham, 2003

First published in 2003 by Brassey's

A member of **Chrysalis** Books plc

Brassey's
64 Brewery Road, London N7 9NT

Distributed in USA by:
Casemate Publishing, 2114 Darby Road, Havertown,
PA 19083, USA

J. David Markham has asserted his moral right
to be identified as the author of this work.

Library of Congress Cataloging in Publication Data available

British Library cataloguing in Publication Data
A catalogue record for this book is available
from the British Library

ISBN 1 85753 327 5

Edited and designed by DAG Publications Ltd
Designed by David Gibbons
Edited by Michael Boxall
Printed in Great Britain.

CONTENTS

ACKNOWLEDGEMENTS

When I was a very young lad, my father, James Walter Markham, told me stories about Napoleon. These sparked my interest, and over the years that interest grew. Little could my father have known what he had started!

In 1988, my wife Barbara and I attended a meeting of The Napoleonic Society of America in New Orleans. The following year I gave a talk on Napoleon's Italian Campaigns. In 1991, I gave the Keynote Address. I was hooked! During my years in the NSA, the Napoleonic Alliance, the Consortium on Revolutionary Europe and the International Napoleonic Society, many friends have encouraged me in my writing and lecturing. I cannot begin to list them all, but they all have my sincere gratitude.

In all my work, my sister Sara and her husband Ron have been steadfast in their support. Perhaps I will one day turn my young nephew, Adam David Kent, into a student of Napoleon! My in-laws, Paul and Gerry Munson, have likewise been there with many encouraging words.

Special thanks go to my good friend Gregory Troubetzkoy, who has provided me with important research material. His translation of Russian articles, documents and Denis Davidov's memoirs is a major contribution to the field of Napoleonic studies. Working with him is a pure pleasure.

Jerry Gallaher is a good friend and leading scholar whose friendship and support have enriched my life. Together, we have travelled to many conferences around the world, and he has enlivened them all. His advice and counsel have been invaluable. My appreciation also goes to another good friend, Wisconsin Secretary of State Doug La Follette, for his careful editing. Both Jerry and Doug share in any credit coming to this book.

I wish to pay very special tribute to Proctor Jones, a dear friend and colleague who passed away in 1999. His translations of important memoirs have been of incomparable value. A kind and generous man, he never hesitated to tell me if he thought I was wrong and never failed to help me in every possible way. He and his wife Martha made every conference worth the effort. On his deathbed, he was still giving me words of encouragement. I will ever miss him and ever appreciate all that he meant to me, personally and professionally, for so many years.

Without the following people, none of this would have happened.

Donald Horward is the director of The Institute on Napoleon and the French Revolution at Florida State University and one of the world's leading Napoleonic scholars. It was Don who encouraged me to undertake serious research, to give papers at the Consortium and to research at his university's Napoleonic library as well as in European archives. Don and Annabel Horward are dear friends, and his frequent calls of personal and professional encouragement have made all the difference in the world. If I am a historian or scholar of any merit, much of the credit goes to Don.

In 1995, Ben Weider appointed me Editor-in-Chief of the International Napoleonic Society and later Executive Vice-President. It is largely because of Ben that I have met so many people throughout the world and have become known to them. As editor of the Journal and the INS portion of the Napoleon Series WEB site and as organiser of the INS international congresses, I have gained experience, contacts and credibility that have served me well. I will forever be grateful for Ben's friendship, trust and encouragement.

My wife Barbara must sometimes wonder how it all happened. Our house is a Napoleonic museum: books, snuffboxes, porcelains, prints and posters have taken over. It is frequently a struggle for her to drag me away from my writing for a weekend excursion. We travel extensively, but strangely enough there often seems to be a Napoleonic connection to the places we visit. Even when she thinks she has escaped him, as on a recent trip to Norway, I manage to find Napoleonic museums or monuments. As we both now realise, 'He's everywhere!'

Perhaps it was fate: her birthday is the same day as the Emperor's, and she was born in Waterloo, Iowa. (I, incidentally, graduated from high school and college in Iowa City, whose original name was *Napoleon*.) Whatever the case, Barbara is an active partner in all my activities, encouraging me in my darkest hours, proof-reading and criticising countless pages of writing, giving me ideas for new directions and approaches and gently pushing me into activity when my energy or ambition flag. In the process, Barbara has become a very knowledgeable participant in all that I do, and I owe very much of my success to her love and support.

Any errors or omissions are mine alone. Any merit is shared by those named above.

This book is dedicated to

James Walter Markham
Father
1910–1972

to
Barbara Ann Markham
Wife, friend, partner

and to
Napoleon I
Emperor of the French

All pictures contained in this book
are from the David Markham Collection,
a premier collection of Napoleonic snuffboxes,
prints and small decorative arts

INTRODUCTION

I t is often said that more books are written about Napoleon than about any other person in the history of the world. Clearly, the world has been, is, and will no doubt continue to be, fascinated by this utterly intriguing man.

Napoleon's life is the story of a man who from the very beginning represented the future and struggled against incredible odds to overcome injustices of the past. His struggle led to incredible successes and devastating failures. It was an amazing romance in the classic sense of the word.

How was it that a minor nobleman from Corsica, who was no better than middle class in France, could rise to become Napoleon I, Emperor of the French and so dominate Europe? What led him to those heights? Just as importantly, what caused him to fall, rise again and then fall to lonely exile on an isolated rock of an island? This book will help provide answers to these questions.

Part of the reason he was able to rise is simply the time in which he lived. In the last quarter of the eighteenth century, two events occurred that would forever change the very nature of the world. The War of American Independence built on and expanded the principles of liberty that had been born largely out of the history of England. America altered the political and economic structure of the western world, but its influence would be slow to become a major force. French participation in that war would, however, greatly influence the next tumultuous event.

The French Revolution of 1789 hit Europe like a hurricane hitting a coast. Building as it did on ideas from Locke, Jefferson and Rousseau, and heavily influenced by the events in America, it swept aside all it encountered and threatened to demolish the old order. Coastal residents can only take defensive measures; one cannot really declare war on a hurricane! The old order, however, could declare war on the Revolution, and this is exactly what it did.

This, then, set the stage for Napoleon Bonaparte. Napoleon was a genius. His mind was one of the most fertile in history. He developed a level of understanding of politics and war matched by few in history. The

fundamental reason for Napoleon's success was the quality of his intellect and his ability to seize every opportunity that was presented. He had
an equal eye both for detail and the grand picture.

Napoleon would dictate letters to half a dozen secretaries at a time: a
paragraph to the first, then, on an unrelated topic, a paragraph to the
second and so on to the last secretary. He would then return to the first
and pick up exactly where he had left off, without needing the first paragraph to be read back to him. He would repeat this pattern until the
letters were completed and could keep it up for hours at a time. Such was
the genius of the man.

This alone, however, is not enough to explain all that happened. Even
before he was old enough to have ambition, people were taking actions
that made his career possible. Throughout his career, especially in the
early days, he came to know the right people, who would take the right
actions to push him forward. Some of this was the result of luck, some
from his own design. Regardless of cause, there is no question that at critical stages in his life, Napoleon had some very important friends.

The wars associated with the Revolution set the stage for Napoleon's
rise. The exhaustion created by the Revolution and its wars laid the background for his seizure of power. Instability and incompetence had led to
a cynical view of government, and France was looking for someone who
could preserve the benefits of the Revolution while bringing credibility
back to government. The victor of Lodi, the saviour of Italy and the hero
of Egypt would be their man.

Some students of Napoleon, while acknowledging his brilliance, have
suggested that he simply had incredible luck and was always at the right
place at the right time. The latter was certainly often true: Toulon, the
'infernal machine' and the trip to Egypt come to mind as good examples.
But luck plays a role in all lives; we must look deeper to find reasons for
Napoleon's rises and falls.

In the media-centred times in which we live, we take for granted
advertising and propaganda associated with political campaigns. Self-
promotion has become a science, and consultants are paid large sums of
money to promote one candidate or another. In Napoleon's lifetime, such
self-promotion was not nearly so widespread: kings and emperors did not
stand for election or commission public opinion polls!

Napoleon, however, realised the value of such activities and was quick
to use them to promote his rise to power. His proclamations, bulletins

and letters to the government were all written with his own interests in mind. Before him, perhaps only Caesar with his *Commentaries* had fully understood the power of the written word.

By the time of Lodi in 1796, Napoleon had also realised the value of image control beyond the written word and was encouraging the production of prints, statues and medallions promoting his image and his achievements. His Italian and Egyptian campaigns became, in the eyes of the public, crusades of good against evil, those of an enlightened hero against the barbarians. That there was some truth in this made the images all the more believable. Napoleon never lost his understanding of the importance of what today we call 'spin control'. He spent the last years of his life attempting to 'spin' his image for eternity.

Factors contributing to Napoleon's fall are even more interesting – and troubling – to study than the reasons for his rise. Some historians, especially his detractors, point to what they claim were personal shortcomings. Chief among these is said to be his unbridled ambition, his willingness to put his personal glory over the welfare of the people of France and Europe. They would paint him as a man devoid of compassion and consumed by ambition, the first step toward the ogre, the monster. Yet there is very little evidence to support that. The evidence usually given is his invasion of Russia, his refusal to accept peace in the campaigns of 1813 and 1814 and his supposedly ego-driven return for the One Hundred Days which ended at Waterloo.

While in retrospect it would have been better for Napoleon to stay out of Russia, or to accept peace terms before his first abdication, there were very solid military and/or political reasons why he felt he had to do what he did. It may be that he should have settled for the offer of natural borders and put the burden for peace on Great Britain. Perhaps he should have given up Antwerp and faced adverse opinion in France rather than the constant war that ultimately destroyed him. We will see that, at the very least, these were not simply ego-driven decisions and that Napoleon constantly sought, and was constantly denied, the benefits of peace.

Other personal characteristics are better candidates for explanations of his fall. A good case can be made that he sometimes lost sight of reality, that he believed he could do more than was possible even for him. The Continental System of blocking Great Britain's trade with continental Europe is one of the most common examples for this argument. While the system was actually working to some degree and might conceivably have driven the British to peace, it was a long shot. The costs and dangers to France should have been so obvious, that it does, indeed, show some lack of realism on his part.

The other excellent example of his lack of realism was his invasion of Russia. While it was a success in an extremely limited sense in that Napoleon won all formal battles and captured Moscow, it ultimately had no chance of producing the desired end. We will see that the Tsar himself warned of his scorched-earth policy, but Napoleon did not listen.

Of greater importance to Napoleon's fall, however, was his growing tendency towards delay and indecision. Napoleon was a man of action, quick to follow-up any opportunity, but indecision in Russia and Waterloo was disastrous to his career, and indecision after Waterloo was disastrous to his freedom.

Yet to fully understand Napoleon's fall it is necessary to look far beyond any personal characteristics that might have contributed to it. Napoleon was in many ways the product of events he was powerless to control. Those events helped him rise to dizzying heights, but they also landed him on St. Helena.

If it is fair to point out that a number of people helped him rise, it is equally valid to mention that he was sent on his downward spiral by the treachery of others. If one thinks of the activities of Talleyrand, Fouché, Augereau and Marmont, the point becomes clear. The latter's title of duc de Raguse brought a new verb, *raguser*, ('betray') to the French language for a little while; it having a similar connotation to the Norwegian 'Quisling' from the Second World War.

The French Revolution was the single most important event that set the stage for Napoleon's rise. It was also the single most important event that brought about his downfall. That is, it was the French Revolution and its ideas that so threatened the *ancien régime* (old order). It is entirely reasonable to see much of Napoleon's life as a struggle to defend the most important elements of the French Revolution against the reactionary forces that would never rest until those elements and the government that supported them, were gone from Europe forever.

This leads us to the final and most important reason for Napoleon's fall. From the very beginning, Great Britain was Napoleon's most persistent foe. Repeatedly she financed coalitions against Napoleon and sent her soldiers and sailors into battle against him. It was Great Britain who led the way in the demonisation of Napoleon, who harboured so many of the royalist *émigrés*, who conspired against his life and who ended the one peace that he brought to Europe. That Great Britain was acting in what she considered to be her own best interests is beside the point if we are seeking causes for Napoleon's decline.

There is a great deal of sadness in this struggle to the death between Great Britain and France, or rather between Great Britain and Napoleon. Napoleon's France, especially during the Consulate, was the most enlightened nation in Europe. Napoleon's detractors do not like this fact but there can be little doubt of its truth.

The second most enlightened nation in Europe, before Napoleon brought his reforms to other nations, was undoubtedly Great Britain. It was English law, the *Magna Carta*, the Glorious Revolution, the idea of *habeas corpus* that served as the philosophical foundation for the upheavals in America and France.

The story of this conflict is without doubt the story of how perceived economic and military self-interest gained the ascendancy over ideology and the benefits of peace. That the story of the wars of this period is largely the story of conflict between the two most enlightened nations of Europe is an irony of the highest magnitude.

J. David Markham
Olympia, Washington
March, 2003

PROLOGUE
Early Life and Education

O n 15 August 1769, Letizia Buonaparte gave birth to her second
son. As minor nobles living in a portion of a house in Ajaccio,
the capital city of the small island of Corsica off the coasts of
France and Italy in the Mediterranean, Letizia (1750–1835) and her
husband Carlo (1746–85) could not possibly have imagined the significance of that birth. They may well have thought that their son Napoleon
might become a successful lawyer or even an officer in the royal military.
Little could they have realised that their son would become a great
general, a hero of France, the first leader to bring stability after the Revolution and the man who ultimately would become Emperor of the French
and master of most of Europe.

Nor could they have imagined what lay in store for their other children.

Napoleon's elder brother, Joseph (1768–1844), married Julie Clary, the
sister of Napoleon's first love, Désirée. He would become first, King of
Naples and then, reluctantly, King of Spain. Joseph tried to bring
Napoleonic enlightenment to both Naples and Spain; he had some
success in Naples, but events in Spain overtook him. His lack of leadership in Spain and his unwillingness to defend Paris in 1814 contributed
to Napoleon's final defeat.

Lucian (1775–1840) married against Napoleon's wishes and spent
much of his time in exile in Rome, where the Pope made him a prince.
But he rallied to Napoleon's cause during the One Hundred Days and
even offered to join him in exile on St. Helena.

Louis (1778–1846) married Joséphine's daughter Hortense (1781–1824)
and became King of Holland. He suffered ill health, both physical and
mental and eventually lost his kingdom and retired into exile. Their son
Louis became Napoleon III and established the Second Empire.

Jérôme (1784–1860) defied Napoleon and married an American. But
Napoleon prevailed in the matter, the marriage was annulled, and Jérôme
remarried and became King of Westphalia.

Napoleon's sister Elisa (1777–1820) married a Corsican named Felice
Bacciochi and was made Grand Duchess of Tuscany. There she fancied
herself an heir to the Medici and became a patron of the arts.

Napoleon's sister Pauline (1780–1825) was the most interesting of Napoleon's sisters. Her second husband was a Roman prince named Camillo Borghèse, and she took the title princess. Unlike her siblings, she had little interest in governing and insisted on living in Paris. There she led a social life that some found fascinating and others scandalous. She seduced many men and was well known for posing in the nude. A drinking vessel of the day was said to have been moulded from her breast, and few who knew her doubted it. But she was loyal to Napoleon and joined him in exile on Elba.

Caroline (1782–1839) married Joachim Murat, Marshal of the Empire. They first served as the Duke and Duchess of the Grand Duchy of Berg and later as King and Queen of Naples. They enjoyed their life there so much that in Napoleon's hour of need they, led by Caroline herself, deserted him to try to save their kingdom.

Napoleon's rise to power depended on a number of both personal and external factors. While the French Revolution created a climate that encouraged and allowed men with Napoleon's talents and political leanings to rise to the top, his extraordinary skill and ability were the primary factors in his rise. His knowledge of both warfare and politics served him admirably throughout virtually his entire career and was certainly a major factor in his rise to power. Even so, he also depended on good luck, being at the right place at the right time and knowing – and cultivating – the right people.

A person's family is of paramount importance in the development of many careers and Napoleon's family background was no exception. His mother Letizia's perseverance during times of adversity served as an inspiration to her children. Moreover, she strongly encouraged Napoleon in his career. Napoleon confirmed her importance, saying, '… she deserves all kind of veneration'.[1] We shall also see that her youthful beauty and pleasing personality played a major role in giving Napoleon his critical opportunity for a military education.

Although he died while Napoleon was quite young, Napoleon's father, Carlo, played an important role both in the development of his son's value system and in providing some very specific opportunities for his career development. Carlo was a lawyer and a Corsican patriot whose example taught Napoleon both bravery and common sense. A movement to obtain independence from France dominated Corsican politics during Napoleon's youth. This movement was led by the Corsican patriot

17

Pasquale di Paoli. Carlo was among the first to support Paoli, swearing to die for Corsica's freedom. His willingness to take to the hills and risk all for a deeply held belief must have had a tremendous effect on Napoleon. At the same time, Carlo served as an excellent example of good common sense. When it became clear that the Corsican cause was hopeless, he was smart enough to establish good relations with the French, thus protecting his family and giving himself the opportunity to work 'from within' for the betterment of the Corsican situation under French rule.[2]

The French government, under King Louis XVI, provided a number of royal scholarships to various military schools. As French subjects, Corsicans were eligible and Carlo wanted to take advantage of the opportunity to provide free education for his sons. To do so, he had to provide evidence of four generations on the island, pay a fee to the appropriate officials and provide evidence of *noblesse* (nobility). Carlo set into motion the application process that ultimately enabled Napoleon to attend military schools at Brienne and Paris at state expense. While the Bonaparte family was by no means destitute, this was nevertheless the only way that he could have obtained a military education.

Carlo's success in establishing his family's nobility not only made Napoleon eligible for royal scholarships, but also gave Carlo an opportunity to serve as a noble in government. He eventually became a member of the Council of Twelve Nobles. As is often the case, as a member of the *nouvelle noblesse* Carlo was less than subtle. Indeed, his clothing became so fancy that townsmen often called him 'Buonaparte the Magnificent'.[3]

One of the earliest important players in the development of Napoleon's career was Louis Charles René, comte de Marboeuf, the French civil and military commander who took over when the French gained control of Corsica. He became very popular with Corsicans and a good friend to Carlo, in whose house he had stayed earlier in his Corsican assignment. Carlo's status as a noble no doubt helped make the establishment of connections to people such as the comte de Marboeuf all the easier. More importantly, Marboeuf, at the age of sixty-four, developed a strong attraction to Carlo's twenty-year-old wife Letizia. It seems that this never developed into anything more serious than love from a distance, but it prompted him to go out of his way to help the Buonapartes. Marboeuf and Letizia spent a great deal of time together, and for many at the time there was a natural assumption that there was more to the relationship than just the long walks for which they were noted. While some believe that Marboeuf was Napoleon's father, there is no conclusive evidence that there was even an affair.[4]

Marboeuf told Carlo of the availability of Royal scholarships for boys for the military (Napoleon) or the church (Joseph). Admission required Marboeuf's recommendation, which he very willingly gave. And beyond making a normal recommendation, he made all the arrangements, even putting Napoleon's elder brother Joseph up at the college of Autun (where Marboeuf's nephew was bishop) at his own expense. Joseph could stay there until he was old enough to attend the seminary at Aix. Napoleon was accepted for the military school at Brienne, but first had to wait for certificates of nobility. While waiting, he stayed with Joseph at Autun, again at Marboeuf's expense. The two of them arrived in January of 1779. Napoleon spent his time polishing his French and other educational weaknesses. In addition, Marboeuf paid for the seminary education of Letizia's half-brother, Giuseppe Fesch, the future cardinal.

Before all of this came about, Carlo had planned to have Napoleon and Joseph study law in Pisa. Napoleon as a lawyer would no doubt have ranked with the best, but ironically the *Code Napoléon* might never have been written!

With Marboeuf's influence and financial support, Napoleon entered the *École Militaire de Brienne* (Military School of Brienne) in May 1779. He was nine years old. Intellectually, he was a promising student, but some of his personal characteristics made his time at Brienne somewhat more difficult than might have been anticipated. His distinctive Corsican accent left little doubt as to his heritage. His unusual name, added to the fact that he was a 'foreigner', led to a significant amount of harassment from his fellow students and a fair level of social isolation. He engaged in more than one fight defending his heritage against those whose social standing outranked his own.

The French looked down their noses at Corsicans, considering them to be all but barbaric. Thus, 'ethnic harassment' of the frail Corsican was very much in order, at least to most of the French students. Moreover, Napoleon was not exactly flush with funds, a fact that he found quite disturbing:

My Father,
    If you or my protectors do not give me the means of supporting myself more honourably in the house where I am, let me return

home immediately. I am tired of exhibiting indigence and of seeing the smiles of insolent scholars who are only superior to me by reason of their fortune; for there is not one capable of feeling the noble sentiments with which I am animated ... Should fortune absolutely refuse the amelioration of my lot, remove me from Brienne and if necessary give me a mechanical profession.[5]

These experiences were to have a lasting impact on Napoleon. He reacted by becoming especially proud of his Corsican heritage and of the Corsican 'freedom fighter' Paoli. His relative poverty would haunt him for some time and was no doubt the root source of his determination to stress equality for all people when he obtained power. It also added reason for his pride in his accomplishments, starting, as he did, from not only a relatively low social station but a low economical one as well. His relative isolation also led to a love of reading that would last throughout his life. Towards the end of his career, he once remarked on his frugal life style of 1791, long after his graduation, but a reflection of a life style begun many years earlier:

Do you know how I managed? By never entering a *café* or going into society; by eating dry bread and brushing my own clothes so that they might last the longer, I lived like a bear, in a little room, with books for my only friends and when, thanks to abstinence, I had saved up a few crowns, I rushed off to the bookseller's shop and visited his coveted shelves ... These were the joys and debaucheries of my youth.[6]

His Corsican background and poverty notwithstanding, Napoleon eventually began to show teachers and students alike that he was no ordinary student. He became a leader among his own class and engaged in numerous snowball battles that involved rather elaborate fortifications of his design. Even in his leisure hours, he was honing his military skills!

Napoleon studied hard, excelling in history, geography and mathematics. His historical interests lay mainly in ancient heroes, especially Julius Caesar, on whom he seems to have based many of his later actions, and Alexander the Great. His reading was not restricted to these two men, however; he read the works of a wide range of classical writers. When he graduated, he selected the artillery as his preferred branch of service.

Mathematics and geometry were very important to proper usage of cannon, and Napoleon had excelled at both. After five years of study, he graduated in October 1784. He was only fifteen, but his education was about to take an important move forward.

Napoleon's fine academic performance led to an appointment to the *École Militaire de Paris* (the Military School of Paris), the French equivalent to the United States' West Point or Great Britain's Sandhurst. He arrived at the school in October 1784 at the age of fifteen. He now was among the élite of the Royal Military; Louis XVI himself had signed his nomination. However, his performance notwithstanding, he would soon discover that he had not left his Corsican heritage behind. Indeed, many of the students at the *École Militaire* were of a significantly higher level of French nobility than he had found at Brienne. Napoleon was deeply affronted by their snobbery, but he did not let it deter him from success.

When Carlo died in February 1785, the Bonaparte family fell on even more difficult times financially. Napoleon had little money for food, a fact that was reflected in his thin and pale appearance during this period. He was extremely saddened by the loss of his father, and his attempts to console his mother express his capacity for feeling:

MY DEAR MOTHER,

Now that time has somewhat calmed the first transports of my grief, I hasten to assure you of the gratitude with which your kindness has always inspired me. Console yourself, my dear mother; circumstances require this. We will redouble our solicitude, happy if we can, by our obedience, make up in some degree for the inestimable loss of a cherished husband. I terminate, my dear mother, by imploring you to calm your grief. My health is perfect, and I pray every day that Heaven may favour you in a similar way ...

Your very humble and affectionate son,
NAPOLEON DE BUONAPARTE[7]

Napoleon was an excellent student and graduated in September 1785, two years earlier than normal. He was one of the select few to pass the test for admission into the artillery, and at the age of sixteen was given an appointment as *Sous* (2nd) Lieutenant in the French Royal Artillery's *La Fère* Regiment. He spent the next year at Valence learning his trade, all the while finding time to study history and other subjects. He remained an avid reader for the rest of his life and often discussed military campaigns of the great generals in history.

NOTES

1 Las Cases, *Mémorial*, IV (7), 39.
2 Ratcliffe, *Prelude to Fame*, 7.
3 Cronin, *Intimate Biography*, 25.
4 Carrington, *Napoleon and His Parents*. See especially chapters four and five for very detailed accounts of this period of Napoleon's life. Carrington seems convinced that there was no sexual relationship between Letizia and Marboeuf, though she is forced to admit that it is impossible to be certain. She is much more convinced that Marboeuf could not have been Napoleon's father, because he was out of the country at the presumed time of conception.
5 Bingham, *Letters and Dispatches*, Napoleon to his father, 5 April 1781, I: 5.
6 Bingham, *Napoleon and Caulincourt*, I, 22.
7 Bingham. Napoleon to his mother, 29 March 1785. I, 12–13. The original spelling of Napoleon's last name was Buonaparte. The spelling 'Bonaparte' will be used henceforth.

PART ONE

THE SOLDIER
AND
THE REVOLUTION

THE FRENCH REVOLUTION
New Ideas, Old Governments

The late 18th century saw the gathering of the storm clouds of revolution. France was in turmoil, and social disturbances were common. In August 1786, Napoleon was sent to Lyons to quell such a disturbance. Here he added authorship to his list of skills, writing a prize-winning essay and beginning a history of Corsica.

Revolutionary France offered unique, if dangerous, opportunities for those who would become its military leaders. The officer corps of the Royal Army was comprised primarily of men of noble standing. Such men were becoming increasingly *persona non grata* as the Revolution proceeded. Many of them fled the country; others were, as nobles, given an appointment with the guillotine – known as the 'national razor'.

The conduct of those who remained was under constant surveillance, and if they were ever found wanting they could lose their jobs, or even their heads. Thus, for the politically correct and militarily competent, there were opportunities created by numerous vacancies at the top.

The Revolutionary wars that ensued – wars of which the so-called Napoleonic wars were in many ways simply an extension – were another factor providing promotional opportunities. These wars stemmed from the fact that the leaders of Europe would not accept the French Revolution, seeing it as a threat to their own stability. War brings the need for additional troops and, naturally enough, additional officers. War also produces casualties in need of replacement. Napoleon came upon the scene in what was in many ways a perfect situation for his ambitions to be realised.

The possibilities for advancement were fraught with danger; the wrong move politically, or the changing winds of fortune emanating from Paris, could lead to an abrupt reversal of personal fortune. That Napoleon could combine military, political and social acumen to advance to his ultimate heights provides proof of the extraordinary nature of the man.

In the French military of the late 18th century, it was possible to obtain frequent and extensive leaves of absence for almost any reason. This, too, was an important structural factor that led to opportunities for Napoleon's rise to power; opportunities that he quickly and effectively exploited.

Napoleon had strong feelings about the future of Corsica and took extensive leaves to become involved in Corsican politics and to visit his family. The first of these was taken in February 1787 and would last until June 1788. During that time, he attempted to straighten out his family affairs in Corsica, as well as to study that island's history.

In June 1788 he returned to France and joined his regiment at Auxonne. The commanding officer was Baron General Jean-Pierre du Teil who took an immediate liking to Napoleon and did much to encourage his military development. The two became friends, and this period was critical to Napoleon's career progression. Du Teil and his brother Jean, a noted specialist in artillery tactics, were to have great influence on Napoleon's later career opportunities.

While Napoleon is often seen as a product of the French Revolution, he played no direct role in the great events of 1789. When some citizens of Paris stormed the *Bastille* on 14 July 1789 and began one of history's great revolutions, Napoleon was stationed at Auxonne. He took an avid interest in the events that were taking place in Paris and developed a reputation as a Republican supporter of the Revolution. During the early years most people expected the king to play a role in any new government, and it was therefore quite possible for an officer in the Royal Artillery to support a revolution that still claimed to support the king.

On 15 September 1789, Napoleon returned on leave to Corsica. He finished his history of the island (which was never published) and turned much of his attention to politics. The great issue of the day (in Corsica) was whether Corsica should remain part of France. Napoleon joined those who promoted that idea and wrote a well-received supportive address to the French National Assembly. Soon after, Corsica was declared a part of France and Paoli returned as Corsica's new leader. The young Bonaparte, already on the way to a successful military career, found himself on the winning side of what appeared to be a popular cause.

In February 1791 Napoleon returned to duty at Auxonne, but was soon re-assigned to Valence. He was there when Louis XVI made his ill-fated flight to Varennes on 20 June 1791. The Revolution initially had been supportive of the monarchy, but Louis did not always act in a way as to deserve that support. He and his wife Marie-Antoinette had begun to lose faith in the Revolution's commitment to the survival of the monarchy. They had hoped to sneak out of town, join with royalist and Austrian military forces and bring back at least some measure of his former power.

Unfortunately for them, Louis was recognised by the postmaster at Varennes and was captured and returned to Paris. Now it was the people's turn to lose faith in the king and his support of the Revolution. Anti-royalist forces gained strength: the days of the monarchy – and the royal family – were numbered.

Napoleon's political beliefs reflected the increasingly radical public opinion. On 3 July 1791 he participated in the ceremony of the national oath and evidently took it very seriously.

> Until then, I doubt not that if I had received orders to turn my guns against the people, habit, prejudice, education, and the King's name would have induced me to obey. With the taking of the national oath it became otherwise; my instincts and my duty were thenceforth in harmony.[8]

While it would appear that there was enough going on in France to keep anyone occupied, Napoleon soon became restless. Now stationed in Grenoble, he felt powerless in the large picture of the Revolution but saw potent political opportunities in Corsica. He had been back in military service only some seven months after his lengthy leave of absence that had ended in February 1791, and even in 18th century France it was a bit bold to apply for yet another leave. None the less, he applied for a leave to Corsica.

His immediate commander refused the request, but this was only a minor setback. He appealed to General du Teil, now fortuitously stationed at Grenoble. Napoleon's old friend and supporter gave him permission to leave in September.

While in Corsica with his brother Louis, Napoleon supported the radical Jacobin cause and became politically active in the move to make Corsicans full French citizens. There were several political factions competing for control of the Revolution, and members of the Jacobin Club were the most radical and anti-monarchical. Napoleon overstayed his leave and ran the risk of being struck off the active rolls or worse. To avoid charges of desertion from his French unit, he obtained an appointment from the French Minister of War as an adjutant-major assigned to Corsica and was then elected a lieutenant-colonel in the Corsican military, thereby avoiding court-martial or forfeiture of his French rank.

Paoli was turning against the French Revolution and becoming supportive of royalist and clerical factions. This did not sit well with the revolutionary Bonaparte, but there was little he could do to change the situation. During a religious riot protesting against the Revolution, Napoleon's soldiers were forced to fire on Corsican citizens. Paoli's supporters began to question Napoleon's loyalty, so he made a timely return to France. This return was prompted by the fact that his long absence had led to his removal from active duty and he needed to go to Paris to get re-instated. There he was have a view of the Revolution that would stay with him for the rest of his life.

On 20 June 1792, a mob of thousands crowded into the courtyard of the Tuileries Palace in Paris. Louis XVI watched and listened from a window as speaker after speaker insulted and threatened him. This was a mild shadow of things to come. On 10 August a Paris mob stormed the Palace and Louis fled to the National Assembly for protection. Soldiers of the Swiss Guard, under orders from Louis not to resist, were slaughtered by the mob. Napoleon witnessed this event and ever after feared the actions of the mob. He felt that the mob could have been easily dispersed by rounds of grapeshot from cannon. This concept would serve him well a few years down the road.

Napoleon was able to get his extended absences excused and was promoted to Captain retroactive to 6 February 1792. His precautions taken in Corsica to safeguard his return to French military service had worked. Once again, boldness and political astuteness had worked together to further his career. In yet another audacious move, he again applied for leave to Corsica and was again granted permission to go.

Napoleon, now 23, returned to Corsica in September 1792 and was still there when Louis XVI was executed in Paris on 21 January 1793. He attempted to gain power in Corsican politics but this time ended up on the losing side. He had teamed up with Antonio Cristoforo Saliceti (1757–1809), a Corsican lawyer who was twelve years older than Napoleon and who would resurface frequently in Napoleon's early career. Saliceti was a Jacobin politician who had represented the Third Estate (those citizens who were neither nobles nor clergy) of Corsica at the Estates General convened in 1789. His actions had made it possible for Paoli to return from exile in England and regain control of Corsica. As Paoli's support of the Revolution waned, so too did Saliceti's support of Paoli. The Revolutionary government had sent him to Corsica to bring

Paoli under control and to bolster Corsican support for the increasingly radical Revolution.

Saliceti's mission failed, and in the rapidly changing anti-revolutionary climate, the Bonapartes fast became unpopular and in great danger. Napoleon's brother Lucien was an outspoken critic of Paoli, a fact well known in Corsica. Lucien's strong Revolutionary beliefs hurt Napoleon here, but would help him considerably in a few years' time.

Supporters of Paoli sought to arrest and perhaps even kill Napoleon and his family. After hiding for some time, Letizia and all her children made a hasty departure to France in June 1793. They lost everything but what little they could carry with them in the small boat they used to flee the island. Upon safe arrival in France, Napoleon and his family settled in Marseilles. Meanwhile, Saliceti had also avoided capture and fled to France.

Napoleon's latest, and last, adventure in Corsica had been a disaster. However, it was noted by all concerned that he had taken the side of the Revolutionary government and had supported their representative, Saliceti. Consequently, he and his family were well received in Marseilles and he found that his image as a French patriot had been greatly enhanced by the experience.

Saliceti returned to Paris as a member of the Convention, the ruling legislative body of France. In 1793, he appointed Napoleon's elder brother Joseph as Comptroller of Army Supplies. He also appointed Napoleon's uncle, Joseph Fesch, military storekeeper at Le Beausset, near Toulon, and Napoleon's younger brother Lucien military storekeeper at St-Maximin. Lucien, himself no stranger to politics, became president of the radical Jacobin Club.

In 1793 Napoleon, becoming increasingly secure both politically and militarily, reported for duty to the 12th Company of the 4th Artillery Regiment at Nice. Once again good fortune smiled on him. The commanding officer there was General Jean du Teil, brother of Baron du Teil, Napoleon's commanding officer and supporter while he was stationed at Auxonne. Jean also took a liking to Napoleon, who again found that he had a friend in command authority.

Even the most able can benefit from being in the right place at the right time. So it was when Napoleon was placed under the guidance of Jean du Teil. The technology of warfare changes and requires new tactics. There is often a gap between the two; the technology of the machine-gun in the

First World War was only belatedly seen as the death-knell for the mass infantry attacks of earlier wars.

The technology of war was changing as Napoleon began his career. One of the most important changes was the development of smaller, lighter and therefore more mobile cannon. This development allowed for quick deployment of the guns where they were most needed: hitherto the heavy guns had been relatively stationary tools of massive bombardment. It was now possible to bring to bear the power of cannon to prevent the rout of one's own troops or to pursue with deadly speed and efficiency a disorganised, retreating army. That the retreating army might well be using roads that had also undergone improvements in recent years only added to the potential of this new tactic. The artillery could move even faster on those roads, taking greater advantage of them than was possible by infantry. With the retreating infantry somewhat compressed along the roads, they were even more vulnerable to the firepower of the light guns, whether that of cannon ball or grapeshot canister.

Jean du Teil was one of the first French military leaders to recognise these possibilities. Napoleon, too, was quick to grasp the full impact of du Teil's ideas and to incorporate them into his battle tactics. But before we simply chalk up Napoleon's successes to luck or fortune, we must remember that these new ideas were not readily understood and accepted by the military leaders of other armies. The gap between the two levels of understanding helps account for Napoleon's often overwhelming battlefield success. One mark of an extraordinary leader is the ability to take quick and effective advantage of such opportunities, and in this Napoleon was to prove a master.

General du Teil sent Napoleon to Avignon to organise ammunition supplies. While there, he again tried his hand at writing, this time with a short story called *Le Souper de Beaucaire* (*Supper at Beaucaire*, a town in France). This was a defence of the Revolution and a call for an end to civil war, by which he meant internal opposition to the Revolution. Napoleon's writing advocated support for the radical Jacobin government and a strong military defence against any outside forces that might invade to restore the monarchy. He took the side of the extremely pro-revolutionary Montagnards in the National Assembly against the less radical Girondins and the Royalists. These three political factions were engaged in a struggle for control of the future of France.

Napoleon's writing also promoted the increased use of light cannon, arguing that they were at least as good in the field as the more traditional, heavier guns. This writing did him no harm, as it reflected the opinion of General du Teil, who was a known expert in the use of mobile artillery and who had helped Napoleon develop these ideas.[9] From the standpoint of his superiors, Napoleon was both politically and militarily correct.

The leaders of the Revolution were eager for any support they could find and certainly were pleased with Napoleon's politically supportive writing. Saliceti and his fellow commissioner Stanislas Gasparin had *Le Souper* published and it became a major literary document of the Revolution. It was not only the local representatives of the Revolution, Saliceti and Gasparin, who were impressed with the book. To be published in the name of the Revolution it had to pass the scrutiny of the Committee of Public Safety and the Robespierre brothers as well. This was not just a question of agreement, because writing that was 'politically *incorrect*' could cause more than a little difficulty for the author. Fortunately for Napoleon, his writing found a great deal of support in Paris.

NOTES

8   Sloan, *Life*, I, 89.
9   Wilkinson, *The Rise of General Bonaparte*, 18.

A CAREER BEGINS
Toulon and Beyond

Revolutions seldom have the full support of all the citizens. Based as they are on ideology, it is only to be expected that some, perhaps many, elements of society will not agree with the political opinions of those who would lead their country in new directions. Complacency and comfort are also the enemy of revolution; those who are doing well in the current system may not be overjoyed with the prospect of radical change. The War of American Independence is a case in point. The Founding Fathers faced opposition not only from the British Redcoats but also from substantial numbers of their own citizens.

So it was with even stronger feelings in Revolutionary France. The Jacobin government did not enjoy universal acclaim and support. The anti-religious nature of the Revolution outraged many clerics and conservative Catholics, especially in the Vendée region in the west of France. The execution of Louis XVI and Marie-Antoinette had the nobles fleeing the country and agitating for the return of the Bourbon[10] dynasty. Civil war was rampant in much of the country, as counter-revolutionaries and less radical revolutionaries attempted to regain control from the radical Montagnard faction.

Nowhere was counter-revolutionary action more dramatic than in Toulon, an important port city in the south of France. In 1793 Toulon declared itself independent of the Revolutionary government and admitted the British navy into its harbour. The plan was to seek the protection of the British until the Bourbons were restored, at which time the British would leave.

This was treason pure and simple and in reality a military act by Great Britain in their war against France. The French government, naturally, was unwilling to allow it to take place unchallenged and dispatched an army to dislodge the British and regain Toulon. The action had met with little success, and the government was not amused. Several representatives of the government were in the area keeping an eye on General Carteaux, the commander of French forces at Toulon.

Napoleon had been assigned to join the Army of France in Italy and was sent to Avignon. On 7 September 1793, he left Avignon with an ammunition convoy. On his way to Nice, he stopped to visit friends and family in the community of Le Beausset. His Uncle Joseph Fesch was store-keeper of military supplies there. Napoleon also visited his old friend Saliceti.

Saliceti was a member of France's legislative body, the Convention. Convention members were often sent to regions of France to take personal charge of military affairs, or at least to see to it that the 'will of the people' was being followed. Sometimes the 'will of the people' included removal of a general from command and a one-way trip to Paris and the guillotine. Convention members serving in this capacity were called members *en mission*, Commissioners, or Representatives of the People. To many military commanders they were no doubt called 'trouble'. Saliceti was a good man to have on your side, and he was on the side of the Bonapartes.

Saliceti had a great deal of admiration and loyalty for his friend and was in need of an artillery commander at Toulon. Fully aware of Napoleon's rising star, Saliceti offered him the job. Even at this early stage in his career, Napoleon had begun to make a name for himself in Paris. His revolutionary tract, *Le Souper de Beaucaire*, his friendship with the du Teil brothers and his obvious political and military talent all stood him in good stead. His family connections were also useful, especially the fact that Lucien was serving as president of the Jacobin Club of Toulon. The family was clearly on the right side of the current political situation. Napoleon was on the way up, but no one could have imagined the increase in speed that was about to occur.

Napoleon could see that commanding the artillery against the British at Toulon was more likely to advance his career than accompanying munitions to Italy. He immediately and enthusiastically accepted the position. The main players at Toulon were especially fortuitous for Napoleon. In addition to Saliceti, fellow Corsican Stanislas Gasparin was serving as a commissioner, as was Revolutionary leader Louis-Marie Stanislas Fréron, who had had an affair with Napoleon's sister Pauline. Moreover, gaining his appointment from the commissioners Saliceti and Gasparin gave Napoleon political cover, as well as a freer hand in dealing with other military commanders.

Two other commissioners of note were in the area. Both were very important in the Revolutionary government and both would play a major role in Napoleon's rise to power. Paul Barras, witness to the taking of the Bastille and a friend of the important Revolutionary leader Mirabeau, was one of the most important early members of the Revolutionary leadership. Ever the careful politician, Barras quickly determined where the path to success lay during those turbulent times and was one of the first members of the Jacobin Club.

Napoleon's luck, and his ability to exploit it, was handed a gift in the person of the final 'representative of the people' in the area. The French government, in a perpetual state of crisis, was run by the Committee of Public Safety, which had life and death power over all French citizens. The dominant personality of that committee was Maximilien Robespierre, who had become the most powerful man in France. His brother Augustin was the fourth commissioner in the area. The power and influence of these two men were virtually unmatched.

Augustin was well aware of Napoleon's Revolutionary credentials and became a friend and strong supporter of this promising young Revolutionary captain.

A young sergeant, Andoche Junot, was quite impressed with this new young artillery commander at Toulon. Like Napoleon, he could recognise a rising star when he saw it, writing to his father: 'He [Napoleon] is one of those men of whom Nature is sparing and whom she does not throw upon the earth but with centuries between them.'[11] Junot immediately decided to attach himself to Napoleon's fortunes by becoming his secretary. He could not have known at the time, but he and Napoleon would be together for the rest of Junot's life.

Napoleon had a brilliant military mind and little patience for those who had not. He recognised that the use of artillery was the key to taking Toulon, but the commanding officers did not agree. In October, he was promoted from captain to *chef de bataillon* (major), but his frustration continued to grow. In what would have been a bold move for anyone else, but a natural move for Napoleon, he demanded that an artillery general be assigned to the Toulon campaign. Only a general with training and perspective equal to Napoleon's would understand and support his plans. Napoleon's letter requesting an artillery general officer shows how secure he must have felt. In his letter to the Committee of Public Safety of 25 October 1793, he says in part:

I have had to struggle against ignorance and the passions it gives rise to ... The first step I will propose to you is to send to command the artillery an artillery general who can, if only by his rank, demand respect and deal with a crowd of fools on the staff with whom one has constantly to argue and lay down the law in order to overcome their prejudices and make them take action which theory and practice alike have shown to be axiomatic to any trained officer of this corps.

The Commander of Artillery, Army of the South, BUONAPARTE.[12]

One might have thought that Napoleon was taking a great risk in describing his commanding officers as ignorant and a 'crowd of fools', but his reputation and political support again stood him in good stead. His wishes were accepted and his star continued to shine more than he could have anticipated. The general officer appointed was none other than his old friend and supporter, General Jean du Teil. He was not in the best of health and let Napoleon have more leeway than might have otherwise been expected.

In November, General Jacques Coquille Dugommier was given overall command. A general of some repute, he took an immediate liking to Napoleon, as well as to his plans. Clearly, the days of the British in Toulon were numbered.

Previous plans had called for a frontal assault. Napoleon felt that the key to victory was control of the heights around the harbour. This would force the British fleet to leave, as it could not withstand the ensuing bombardment. With the British fleet gone, Toulon would be retaken.

His plan worked. The heights were taken, and British Admiral Lord Hood had no choice but to leave the harbour. The ensuing assault on Toulon was successful. Napoleon was constantly in the thick of the action and suffered a bayonet wound that could have cost him a leg.

The siege of Toulon was a great military victory for the Jacobin government, and it marked Napoleon's first entry into the limelight. The past and the future came together for him at Toulon. Saliceti, Robespierre, du Teil, Barras and Dugommier, contacts both old and new, gave him the support he needed to succeed. He could not have known it at the time, but his future was there as well: André Masséna, commander of some relief troops, and Sergeant Andoche Junot. Both Masséna and Junot would be important to Napoleon's future campaigns.

Napoleon was praised by all who were involved with Toulon. Not surprisingly, he himself set the tone when he wrote to the Assistant to the Minister of War saying, 'I promised you brilliant successes and, as you

see, I have kept my word.'[13] Saliceti and Gasparin wrote, 'The Representatives of the People, bearing in mind the zeal and intelligence of which
Citizen Buonaparte has given proof, have decided to recommend his
promotion to the rank of Brigadier-General.'[14] That promotion came on 22
December 1793. Napoleon was then only twenty-four. Dugommier wrote
to the Minister of War: 'I have no words to describe Buonaparte's merit:
much technical skill, an equal degree of intelligence and too much
gallantry, there you have a poor sketch of this rare officer ...'[15]
Napoleon's success at Toulon led to his first mention in the French
newspaper *Moniteur* (7 December 1793).[16]

His first appointment as general was as Inspector of Coastal Defences.
In 1794, he gained the more interesting appointment of Artillery
Commander to the Army of Italy under General Pierre Dumerbion.
Napoleon had a plan of action designed to drive the Austrians out of Italy,
but to promote his plan he needed support in high places. As it
happened, Citizen Augustin Robespierre was serving in the area as
commissioner. His support gave Napoleon the chance to implement his
plan and gain another star after his name. Ultimately, however, the
government decided on a defensive policy in Italy, not wishing to launch
a major offensive when a strong drive on the Rhine front was imminent.
Even this reflected Napoleon's belief that victory in Germany was the key
to control of Europe.[17]

In 1794, it suddenly seemed that Napoleon's luck – and political
support – had deserted him. The winds of change were in the air, especially in Paris, and the mighty were about to fall. The government had
finally had enough of the mass killings of the Terror. After the execution
of the popular leader Danton, it seemed that the Committee of Public
Safety's thirst for blood knew no limits. The Robespierre brothers and
other members of the committee were arrested and sent to the guillotine
in what is known as the *coup d'état* of *9 Thermidor* (27 July 1794). Upon
their fall, all who had close association with them were likely to make
a one-way trip to the 'national razor'. Napoleon was arrested and held
for a fortnight at the *Château d'Antibes*, accused of wanting to rebuild a
hated prison in Marseilles and of treason during a secret mission to
Genoa,[18] but his real problem was his closeness to the Robespierres. His
old friend Saliceti was placed in charge of the investigation.

Napoleon was in serious danger. Saliceti was not to be trusted at this
point and the political climate in Paris was volatile, to say the least. His

friend Junot urged him to make good his escape, but Napoleon calmly replied:

> The proposal you make to me, my dear Junot, shows clearly enough your friendship for me; you have long known mine for you, and I hope you rely on it.
>
> Men may be unjust to me, my dear Junot, but it is enough that I am innocent; my own conscience is the tribunal before which I bring my conduct.
>
> When I examine it, that conscience is calm; so do nothing, you will only compromise me.
>
> Good-bye, my dear Junot; regards and friendship.
>
> > Buonaparte
> > *Under arrest* [19]

While imprisoned, Napoleon spent his time studying and writing to family and officials in his own, ultimately successful, defence. To the Representatives of the People he wrote:

> You have caused me to be arrested. I have been dishonoured without trial; or rather I have been tried without being heard ... Since the commencement of the revolution, have I not been seen fighting against domestic enemies, or, as a soldier, fighting against foreigners? I have sacrificed living in my *département* [administrative region]; I have abandoned my property; I have lost all for the Republic.[20]

Napoleon's cause was helped by a report from General Pierre Dumerbion, Napoleon's most recent commander. 'Officers of his ability are rare,' and 'Our success has been due to the intelligent suggestions of the commander of the Artillery,' he wrote after the aborted Italian campaign.[21]

Napoleon also wrote a letter to the French representative to Genoa, saying in part: 'I was slightly affected by the fate of the younger Robespierre, whom I liked and believed honest; but had he been my father I would have stabbed him myself had he aspired to tyranny.'[22]

All charges against him were dropped, and he was released. He had dodged a bullet and had remained calm and optimistic.

In the spring of 1795 Napoleon was ordered to put down an uprising in the Vendée and was given command of an infantry brigade. The

Vendée region was very Catholic and very conservative and had been a hotbed of opposition to the Revolution. Napoleon could easily see that firing on French citizens was a losing proposition. Moreover, he was unhappy with his removal from the artillery and assignment to the infantry. This was not just a matter of preference because the artillery was part of the élite of the army, with far more opportunities for advancement.

Napoleon did not go to the Vendée but instead took an extended sick leave. A sick leave could only last so long, however, and his orders remained. He decided to go to Paris to get the orders changed. At first, he had no luck, his interview with War Minister Aubry being completely unproductive.

Disappointed with his lack of success, he requested assignment to Constantinople, to help modernise the Turkish artillery. This was a possible course of action, but his request was eventually either denied or 'lost in the shuffle'. Napoleon was quite serious in his request, as he wrote to his brother Joseph:

> I am at this moment attached to the Topographical Department of the Committee of Public Safety for the direction of armies, in place of Carnot. If I make the request I shall obtain permission to go to Turkey as General of Artillery sent by the Government to organise the artillery of the Grand Signor, with good pay and a flattering title. I will get you made consul ... Everything is quiet here, but storms are perhaps brewing. I shall take five or six officers with me ... The Committee of Public Safety having charged me with the direction of the armies and with the plans of campaign (which is highly flattering) will not, I fear, allow me to go.[23]

Imagine the effect on history if some War Ministry officer had approved the request in a timely manner!

Times of turmoil bring personnel changes on a regular basis. These changes smiled on Napoleon when Louis-Gustave Le Doulcet, comte de Pontécoulant, was appointed Minister of War. Sensing an opportunity, Napoleon tried his luck again. To bolster his case, he discussed his plans for moving the Austrians out of Italy. Le Doulcet was impressed and appointed Napoleon to the *Bureau Typographique*. This assignment was a stroke of good fortune. He was assigned to a section of the Bureau that dealt with events in Italy, and he was constantly studying and making recommendations for the war effort there. This assignment also brought him into contact with high officials both at work and socially. He frequented the *salons* (cultural receptions) of Madame de Staël and others and may have met Joséphine at one of them.

NOTES

10 The Bourbon dynasty goes back to Henri IV. Married to Marie de Médici, his famous Edict of Nantes ended the religious civil war in 1598.

11 Alison. *History*, 5, 12–13.

12 Napoleon I, Emperor of the French. *Correspondance de Napoléon Ier; Publiée par ordre de l'empereur Napoléon III.* Paris, 1858–69, (Hereinafter *Correspondance*), 25 October 1793, No. 1, I, 1–2. Partially translated in John Eldred Howard (ed. and trans.), *Letters and Documents of Napoleon, Volume One: The Rise to Power.* London, 1961, 40.

13 *Correspondance*, 24 December 1793, No. 12, I, 17–18. 'Je t'avais annoncé brillants succès, et tu vois que je te tiens parole.' Partially trans. in Howard, 44.

14 Ratcliffe, 45.

15 Cronin, 77.

16 Marie Henri Beyle – Stendhal (pseudonym), *A Life of Napoleon.* Trans. Roland Gant. London, 1956, 12 (footnote).

17 Markham, *Napoleon*, 13.

18 Chandler, *Campaigns*, 34.

19 *Correspondance, 12–19 August 1794, Nos. 35,* I, 53–54. Trans. in Howard, No. 44.

20 Bingham, I, 40. France was divided into a number of administrative regions known as *départements*.

21 Ratcliffe, 68.

22 Bingham, I, 41.

23 *Correspondance*, 20 August 1795, Nos. 54, I, 83–84. Partially trans. in *Bingham*, I, 50.

SAVING A GOVERNMENT
AND WINNING A WIFE

By the summer of 1795, the situation in France had become very difficult. The monarchy had been inept and out of touch. Much of its downfall could be traced to its inability to deal with significant economic problems. The Convention had been successful at only one thing: perpetuating itself and its power. Even in this, their success was less than total. As to the economy, the Convention was no more effective than the monarchy. Hyper-inflation destroyed the value of the *livres* (hard currency) and *assignats* (Revolutionary paper money), and people could no longer afford to buy sufficient food.

Economic and political conditions were beginning to approach those seen before the Revolution. The people began to realise this, and the Convention's popularity plunged to a dangerous low. Seeking to assure stability, the Convention proposed yet another in a string of new constitutions. This one replaced the Convention with a legislature that would have two houses: the Council of Five Hundred, which would initiate all legislation, and the Council of Ancients, which would have 250 members who were empowered to accept or reject legislation passed by the Council of Five Hundred. Executive power was given to a Directory of five members chosen by the Council of Ancients from a list of names submitted by the Council of Five Hundred.[24]

In a final Act designed to give its members power in the new government, the Convention decreed that two-thirds of the new representatives to each house must come from the Convention's existing membership. The people were outraged with this self-perpetuating decree, and tension mounted, especially in Paris.

In early September the new constitution and the two-thirds provision was approved by a plebiscite marked as much by a low turnout and disenchantment as by anything else. Cries of fraud were heard, and the city of Paris braced itself for what might develop. Even so, the new constitution was scheduled to take effect on 27 October 1795.

For some, the economic and political problems seemed to open the opportunity for a return to a monarchy, and royalist sentiment flourished in some circles. Some began to support the placing of the comte de

Provence, brother to Louis XVI, on a new throne. When Louis XVII, the young son of the executed king, died in June, de Provence had declared himself Louis XVIII and demanded his right to rule France. All the while, the Paris mob, that collection of workers and radicals, was agitating for decisive action. Anarchy seemed a very real possibility. Royalist and Jacobin factions fought for controlling influence over the government. The royalists, dubbed *'jeunesse dorée'* (gilded youth), openly roamed the streets intimidating the radical Jacobins and flaunting their pretensions to be a new nobility.

By early October 1795, royalist sympathisers, elements of the Paris mob and portions of the National Guard headquartered at the church of St-Roch threatened the Convention, which was still in power until the 27th of the month. More than one hundred of the Paris sections (political subdivisions) had declared themselves in a state of rebellion against the government. The very survival of the government and the Revolution was at stake, and a general was needed to lead the defence.

Meanwhile, Napoleon had suffered a downturn in his career. Through what can only be described as a mix-up with profound implications, he had been removed from active duty and put on half-pay. The official reason for this was the fact that he had not accepted his appointment to serve in the Vendée. Of course this reason made no sense, as he had been assigned to an important post in Paris for some time. The inefficient government did not notice this fact, and Napoleon was out of work. His repeated requests for assignment to Italy had been turned aside. Facing poverty and a very uncertain future, his career appeared to be preparing to take a nose-dive every bit as spectacular as had been his rise. Yet his incredible good fortune held out, and events in Paris led to a revival of his career.

There was no shortage of generals in Paris in 1795, and any one of a number of them might have been selected to protect the government. The first to be approached was General Baron Jacques Menou, who proved to be incompetent. Napoleon's future began to brighten when Paul Barras, friend to Napoleon and one of the Directors, was put in charge of protecting the government.

Barras knew just the man for the job. Although Barras was technically in command, the young General Bonaparte was clearly to be the man in charge. Napoleon must have felt some anxiety about this assignment, because he might be obliged to open fire on French citizens. He had avoided this in the Vendée by refusing assignment there, and his memories of the riots in Corsica must have weighed heavily on him. On the other hand, he recalled the massacre of the Swiss Guard that led to the downfall of the monarchy and was well aware that success might give his career a significant boost. In the end, and without much hesitation, he opted for the chance to save the government and prevent the return of the monarchy. The possible benefits of saving a grateful government outweighed the drawbacks of firing on French citizens who were, after all, attacking their own government. Only if he failed would there likely be negative consequences, and he could not consider failure as an option. His faith in his future was by now most certainly part of his innermost and influential feelings.

The mob far outnumbered General Bonaparte's forces. Indeed, members of the Convention were issued arms to serve as a last-ditch defence. Napoleon sent Captain Joachim Murat, later to be his brother-in-law, Marshal of France and King of Naples, to obtain cannon. Cannon can be the great equalisers, especially when firing canisters of small musket-balls, generally known as grapeshot, that turn them into giant shotguns.

The cannon had been placed some six miles away; both sides were aware of their location, and the race was on. Murat with more than one hundred of his cavalry arrived just as a force of royalists had appeared on the scene. They were no match for Murat's men, and the cannon were taken and emplaced near the Tuileries Palace, where they commanded all avenues of approach.

The outcome was never really in doubt. With his famous 'whiff of grapeshot' Napoleon crushed the revolt on 5 October 1795. The attack by the royalists had begun at four in the afternoon, and by six it was all over. The insurgents were swept from the streets, and his soldiers defeated the royalists' last stand at St-Roch. Napoleon then dispatched troops to disarm Paris and restore order.

In defeating the coalition massed against the government, Napoleon had done something that in many ways marked the end of the Revolution. It had begun in Paris and that city had always harboured its most radical elements. The *sans culottes*, the Parisian workers who had served as the radical engine that maintained the Revolution, and their other radical allies had intimidated the Revolutionary government into action it might otherwise not have taken. This had been possible because the government would never stand up against what was loosely called the Paris mob. Napoleon's action ended that policy.

This assignment had been yet another political gamble, as even in victory he could have earned the enmity of many. But as before, Napoleon's judgement proved correct, the gamble paid off, and his career was enhanced. As a reward for his services, he was made *Général de Division* and given command of the Army of the Interior. He was twenty-six and already at what would be the peak of most careers. Perhaps to symbolise the fact that he was casting his lot forever with France, he dropped the Italian 'u' from his name; he would now and forever be known as *Bonaparte*.[25]

JOSÉPHINE

Joséphine de Beauharnais was a Creole from the island of Martinique. Her family, the Taschers de la Pagerie, had been involved in producing sugar from their rather large plantation. Her real name was Marie-Josèphe Rose Tascher de La Pagerie. Her friends and family called her Rose. Napoleon gave her the name Joséphine based on her name Josèphe. Her middle-class family owned slaves and was generally considered successful. Part of their estate still stands today as a museum devoted to her early childhood.

At the age of fifteen, she married vicomte Alexandre de Beauharnais, the son of a former governor of the French West Indies. They had two children, Hortense and Eugène. A noble in the Revolutionary France of 1794 was in constant danger. The Revolution had begun to turn on itself, and the guillotine was busy separating both aristocrats and less-radical Revolutionaries from their heads. Alexandre proved no exception and lost his in July of that year. Joséphine and her children were likely to meet the same fate, but the timely fall of Robespierre and the end of the Terror saved their lives.

A woman of beauty and charm who was willing to do whatever it took to survive – and survive in style – she became the mistress of Barras. This move brought her into the very highest circles of French society. Barras soon tired of her and wished to relieve himself of what he saw as a rather expensive plaything.

It is unclear exactly how Napoleon first met Joséphine, though it is likely that they had been introduced to each other at one of the numerous social functions frequented by Napoleon. He was now a national hero with an obvious political and military future, and hosts and hostesses throughout Paris sought his presence at their social functions. Hortense, Joséphine's daughter from her first husband, relates the following story:

> Following the riots on the *13th Vendémiaire* a law was passed forbidding any private citizen to have weapons in his house. My brother, unable to bear the thought of surrendering the sword that had belonged to his father, hurried off to see General Bonaparte, who at that time was in command of the troops stationed in Paris. He told the General he would kill himself rather than give up the sword. The General, touched by his emotion, granted his request and at the same time asked the name of his mother, saying he would be glad to meet a woman who could inspire her son with such ideals.[26]

Hortense said that Joséphine then visited Napoleon to express her gratitude at his generosity, and Napoleon fell head over heels in love. This story may or may not be accurate, but clearly Napoleon was ready to take a wife and soon began to see Joséphine as the woman for him. He wanted a woman who would provide financial security and social standing. While stationed in Marseilles he had courted Desirée Clary, sister of his brother Joseph's wife, Julie. Desirée's family would have provided Napoleon with some financial security and social standing, but when he went to Paris they drifted apart. In a touch of irony, Desirée eventually married General Bernadotte, who later turned against Napoleon. They became the King and Queen of Sweden.

Joséphine was reluctant at first, perhaps unsure that this thin young general would provide her with the life-style to which she had become accustomed. Napoleon, on the other hand, was passionate in his love for her. This passion is reflected in his letters to her both before and after their marriage. A letter to her in December 1795, written in Paris on the day after what must have been an interesting evening, leaves no doubt of that passion:

> I awake full of you. Your image and last evening's intoxication have left my senses no repose whatever.
>
> Sweet and incomparable Joséphine, what a strange effect do you produce upon my heart! Are you vexed? Do I see you sad? Are you troubled? ... My soul is crushed with grief, and there is no repose for your lover; but is there any the more when, abandoning myself to

the profound emotion which masters me, I draw from your lips, from your heart, a flame which consumes me? Ah! It was last night I really understood that your portrait was not you!

You are leaving at noon; I shall see you in three hours.

Meanwhile, *mio dolce amor*, a thousand kisses; but do not give me any, for they burn my blood.[27]

Joséphine at thirty-two was six years older than Napoleon and did not have the wealth that he had anticipated. Moreover, the marriage was opposed by most of his family, especially his mother. Letizia wanted only the best for her son, whom she saw as key to the family's success. Joséphine was an older, previously married woman, with little money or connections. She felt that Napoleon was marrying beneath his status, and she would have none of it.

Encouraged by Barras, the romance flourished, and they were married on 9 March 1796, after Napoleon had been appointed General of the Army in Italy. According to her daughter Hortense, Joséphine waited until almost the last minute to make up her mind. 'She did not yield until she saw the General about to leave without her. He had been appointed commander-in-chief of the army in Italy. She loved him and could not bear the thought of giving him up. Finally, she consented to become his wife.'[28]

NOTES

24. Doyle, *Oxford History*, 318–19.

25. His family name had been spelled *Buonaparte*. To the end of his life, his detractors, especially the British, insisted on using this spelling.

26. Hortense, *Memoirs*, I, 26.

27. *Letters of Napoleon to Joséphine*. Ed. Léon Cerf, trans. Henry Bunn. New York, 1931, 21–22.

28. Hortense, I, 27.

A COMMAND OF HIS OWN
Italy, 1796

From the beginning of the Revolution, the rest of Europe sought to limit its success and, if possible, bring about the restoration of the Bourbons. The Austrians had been especially concerned. This was true partly because one of their daughters, Marie-Antoinette, had been the Queen of France and had eventually been beheaded by the Revolutionaries. Furthermore, the Austrian government represented the very essence of the type of government that the Revolution detested. As head of the Habsburg Empire and what remained of the Holy Roman Empire, the Austrian Emperor Francis II was eager to join in the European coalition designed to bring about the fall of France's revolutionary threat to the 'natural order' of things.

Northern Italy was one of the most important stages of confrontation between the Austrians and the French. Italy was not unified as we know it today, but divided into a number of independent kingdoms. The most important of these to the French was Piedmont, whose King Victor Amadeus III had allied himself with the Austrians. The goal of the French was simple: defeat the Piedmontese, drive the Austrians out of Northern Italy, secure the coast and then negotiate a peace that would assure France's security in this region.

The goal was simple, but the French had not been able to achieve any success in the region. Napoleon had just saved France from an internal threat. Now he was given another opportunity to save her from her external enemies. His political and military fortunes thus far had been incredible. Still, this was his first command of an entire campaign: northern Italy was no Toulon. If he succeeded, his future was wide open. It would be his first major test.

Never let it be said that Napoleon was slow to get going. He was given the command of the Italian campaign on 2 March 1796. One week later (9 March), he married Joséphine in a civil ceremony. Napoleon was three hours late for the wedding; the reason is unclear, but it is generally accepted that he was working on plans for the upcoming Italian campaign and lost track of the time. For reasons also obscure, bride and groom each lied about their ages; she claimed to be four years younger

46

than her thirty-two, and he claimed to be almost two years older than his twenty-six.

They were married in a brief ceremony and two days later Napoleon left for his new headquarters in Nice, where he arrived on 27 March. He was fresh, ambitious, confident and anxious to begin the campaign. The same thing cannot be said of his Army of Italy.

Napoleon inherited a ragtag and demoralised army of perhaps 41,000 soldiers facing combined forces of some 47,000. Moreover, the strategic position of his army was not advantageous. Their position was along the crest of the Maritime Alps, an area that was something of a wasteland and could hardly support the food and other needs of the army. The British fleet often interdicted their communications with Nice along the coastline. They had a strong opponent in front and a hostile sea behind; there was little thought of taking the offensive. Supplies were difficult to obtain and they were short of just about everything. But from the very beginning Napoleon proved himself capable of taking that army to the heights of glory.

Even the finest general, the finest military mind, is enhanced by the work of an excellent staff. Napoleon understood this and assembled what was perhaps one of the greatest collections of military minds serving together at one time.[29] Chief of staff Alexandre Berthier was a model of organisational efficiency and would serve him well until Napoleon's first abdication in 1814. Berthier had the difficult job of interpreting his often confusing orders to the rest of the senior staff. An essential component of Napoleon's staff, Berthier died nineteen years later, weeks before Waterloo. Many students of that most critical battle feel that Berthier's absence was the primary reason for Napoleon's defeat.

Colonel *aide-de-camp* Joachim Murat would develop into one of the best cavalry officers in history and eventually marry Napoleon's sister Caroline. He had suggested his own appointment, and, while he is known for his courage and dash, he is known too for his lack of imagination and intellect. Few could inspire men as well as he could and he would prove invaluable through much of Napoleon's career. Also joining Napoleon were Andoche Junot, Auguste Marmont and Napoleon's own brother Louis. Waiting for him at Nice was another future Marshal of France, General André Masséna, as well as General Charles Augereau.

These two generals were none too happy with Napoleon's appointment. They felt that he was too young and inexperienced and that his appointment was strictly political. Worse, they saw the appointment as a reward for relieving Barras of his mistress, Joséphine. Masséna, moreover, had wanted the appointment and felt that he had been unjustly passed over.

Their scepticism would soon vanish, as their young leader made it quite clear that he was no ordinary man, political appointment or no political appointment. Napoleon's depth of knowledge and 'take charge' personality swept aside all doubts. Indeed, even his written words made this clear. A French diplomat in Tuscany wrote:

> I received a first letter from him, in which he announced that he was about to put the army in motion. At the same time he asked me to give him any information I could about the state of Italy. I saw at once by his style, which was concise and animated, although careless and incorrect, that he was no ordinary man. I was struck with a breadth and depth of view on military and political subjects, such as I had not found in any correspondence I had held up to that time with the generals of our army of Italy. I predicted, therefore, either great success or great reverses. My uncertainty did not last long. The campaign was opened, and a series of victories as dazzling as they were unexpected, succeeding each other with surprising quickness, raised the glory of our French soldiers and that of the great captain who led them daily to fresh triumphs, to the highest.[30]

Napoleon believed that his soldiers were better than their opponents' but were discouraged by a lack of supplies, leadership and action. His soldiers were so discouraged that some were being insubordinate and others were expressing loyalty to the king. Napoleon understood that they needed inspiration, and his address to his troops was designed to provide that inspiration:

> Soldiers! You are hungry and naked; the government owes you much, but can give you nothing. Your patience and courage, displayed among these rocks, are admirable, but that brings you no glory ... I will lead you into the most fertile plains on earth. Rich provinces, wealthy cities, all will be at your disposal; there you will find honour, glory and riches ...[31]

The Directory was now the administrative branch of French government, and with Napoleon's encouragement it had determined that the defeat of the Kingdom of Sardinia and control of Piedmont were necessary to challenge the Austrians and relieve pressure on the Army of the Rhine. To Napoleon, this was an opportunity to conquer the whole of Italy.

His strategy was to split the Piedmontese and Austrian forces, opening the 'fertile plains' that would provide a much-needed source of food. With a series of moves, Napoleon was able to lure Austrian General Argenteau to a small fort at Montenotte. There, in what was Napoleon's first victory in Italy, the French soldiers under the leadership of Masséna easily defeated Argenteau's forces, eliminating one wing of the Austrian forces.

Napoleon then turned to the Piedmontese. His forces decisively defeated them at the battles of Millesimo, Ceva and Mondovi in late April and forced them to sue for peace. These battles pointed up the basic difference between the new style of war of the Revolutionary army under Napoleon and the old style of the Austrians. Napoleon's formations were flexible and very mobile. They could change direction and cover a lot of ground in short order. The Austrians were rigid and linear in their formation and had nowhere near the flexibility and speed of the French. Nevertheless, at the battle of Mondovi, it took the personal leadership and bravery of Murat to ensure victory and the defeat of Sardinia.

We must not forget that the French troops were still under-armed, hungry and always on the verge of mutiny, despite Napoleon's inspiration and success. The use of thousands of captured muskets from the battle of Mondovi did make the situation a great deal better. Of equal importance was the fact that the fertile plains of Piedmont were now available to feed the starving troops. Without the muskets and food, it is hard to say how much more fight was left in the French troops. Some contend that the Battle of Mondovi was the most important battle in Napoleon's career, for had he lost it he might have lost the Italian campaign and his future.

Napoleon won his victories using the tactics of concentrating his forces against the centre and then defeating the various elements of his enemy individually. He well understood the importance of topography and moved his men around almost as if they were his cannon. A tireless campaigner, he could work twenty-hour days, pausing only occasionally to sleep. These characteristics served him well for the rest of his career. Here also we see the key to his future military successes, namely the adoption of new and decisively effective military tactics. He was fighting today's battles against yesterday's armies. It was an advantage he would exploit to great benefit in the many battles to come.

Napoleon wanted to overwhelm his opponents in battle, but wanted to be moderate in his treatment of them in defeat. His treaty with the Piedmontese represented that moderation. Numerous proclamations to the army gave them great credit for their victories but admonished them against looting and asked them to respect the people whom they were there to liberate.

He understood that if one does not treat an enemy well in defeat, they will be a constant threat. This was a lesson ignored after the First World War, and the world paid a fearsome price. Moreover, his basic objective was to drive the Austrians out of Italy. His campaign was, in a very real sense, a war of liberation.

The Directory was not quite as interested in moderation. Their primary non-military goal was to loot as much wealth, including works of art, from the Italians as was possible. The Director in charge of the Italian campaign was none other than Saliceti. He arrived on the scene in late April and admonished Napoleon on the generosity of his peace terms. It was hard to argue with success, however, and Napoleon was providing enough wealth to the Directory to keep them satisfied with his efforts.

With the Piedmontese out of the way, Napoleon could turn his attention to the Austrians under General Beaulieu. He crossed the River Po and moved towards Milan and Beaulieu. He managed to avoid a confrontation with the Austrians in that crossing, taking Beaulieu by surprise.

Napoleon would not be so lucky in crossing the River Adda. The only bridge available was a 170-yard long wooden bridge in the small town of Lodi. Beaulieu had left a rear-guard of some 12,000 men and fourteen cannon. Napoleon's advance guard faltered in the face of such opposition, but Napoleon was quickly on the scene and personally restored the momentum of his troops. The date was 10 May 1796, and he was about to set the stage for the rest of his career.

Napoleon decided to storm the bridge. This was an obviously risky manoeuvre with a quite strong possibility of unacceptable losses. The Austrians' guns completely dominated the bridge. To help counter this, Napoleon sent a cavalry contingent up the river to cross and then sweep down on the Austrian right flank. He formed his grenadiers into columns in the shelter of the city walls and gave yet another inspirational speech. His grenadiers, to the cries of *'Vive la République!'* stormed the bridge.

This attack faltered and a new effort was organised. Napoleon's soldiers, led by Masséna and Berthier, again stormed the bridge. The fire on the bridge was murderous, but this time there was success, as many troops jumped off the bridge and opened fire from the river shallows. A counter-attack by the Austrians almost worked, but the French cavalry arrived at the moment when more French infantry were attacking the bridge. The cavalry silenced the Austrian guns and turned the battle into a rout. The Austrians fled, leaving behind their guns, several hundred dead and nearly 2,000 prisoners.

Throughout Napoleon had been a whirlwind of action. Observing from close range and from a church tower, he took personal charge of every detail. He even positioned the cannon along the river, earning himself the title 'the little corporal' for doing work normally assigned to a soldier of that humble rank. Napoleon's strength lay not just in his military skills. He inspired his men to undertake the rather daunting task of getting across the bridge in the face of concentrated fire. He showed his ability at emotional leadership, something that had not been particularly necessary in his previous engagements.

Leadership was not the only emotional attribute Napoleon demonstrated during the campaign in Italy. He was, after all, a young man madly in love with his new bride. He wrote love letters to her daily; even before his arrival in Italy his letters began to pour forth:

I have not passed a day without loving you; I have not passed a night without clasping you in my arms; I have not taken a cup of tea without cursing that glory and that ambition which keep me separated from the soul of my life. In the midst of affairs, at the head of troops, moving through camps, my adorable Joséphine is alone in my heart, fills my mind, absorbs my thoughts. If with the speed of the torrent of the Rhône I separate myself further and further from you, it is that I may see you again the sooner. If in the midst of the night I rise to work, it is to hasten by some days the arrival of my sweet love, and yet in your letters of the 23rd and the 26th *Ventôse* you treat me to a *vous*.[32] *Vous* yourself! Ah, wicked one, how could you have written those letters? How cold they are ... Woe to the man who should be the cause! May he suffer all the agonies that would be mine were guilt proved! Hell has not torments, nor the Furies snakes, enough! *Vous! Vous!*...[33]

Joséphine, however, was not nearly as passionate towards Napoleon, and her letters showed it. While he spoke words of love and loneliness, her letters were much cooler. Their reserve already made him suspicious of her fidelity, a suspicion not altogether unwarranted.

Joséphine found his letters uncomfortable, perhaps even comic. Napoleon found hers depressing and he told her so, to no avail. He became convinced that she was ill, but the Directory refused his request for compassionate leave to see her.

Finally, after his defeat of the Piedmontese, Napoleon sent Murat to Paris to bring Joséphine to him, the Directors having given their permission. Murat arrived in Paris a few days before the battle of Lodi and reported that she was in ill health. Using this as an excuse, Joséphine continued to decline Napoleon's request that she join him in Italy.

The Austrian retreat from Lodi opened the road to Milan and gave the French troops new confidence. Five days later Napoleon took up residence in Milan's palace. The wealth of Milan gave hard currency to the soldiers and great wealth to the Directory in Paris. Lodi was far more important than simply a battle on the way to Milan. Militarily, it was not of overwhelming importance, in that it was against a rear-guard of substantially smaller size than Napoleon's own forces. Of much greater significance, it created a change in Napoleon's attitude toward his future. He always knew he was a good military man. He now knew he was a leader. More importantly, he saw, perhaps for the first time, his star rising far beyond his fondest dreams. Many years later in exile at St. Helena he wrote:

> It was only on the evening of Lodi [10 May 1796] that I believed myself a superior man, and that the ambition came to me of executing the great things which so far had been occupying my thoughts only as a fantastic dream.[34]

Lodi also had an important effect on Napoleon's soldiers. It was at Lodi that they first observed him in action, and it was here that they finally gained complete confidence in him. This was also the beginning of the special relationship between Napoleon and his men, symbolised by his nickname *le petit caporal* (the little corporal). Lodi marked the beginning of their personal devotion to him that would last some 20 years.

In Milan, Napoleon was seen as a conquering hero of almost mythological stature. He was treated as royalty and was invited to a constant round of parties. His generals were also treated well and took full advantage of the romantic opportunities available. Napoleon, however, continued to pine for Joséphine. Then, in July, Joséphine announced that she was coming to Milan. Napoleon was ecstatic, but had he known the entire situation his emotions would have been quite different.

In the past, Joséphine had not been a pillar of chastity; she had been, after all, the mistress of Barras. She was fond of Napoleon and perhaps somewhat in love, but she had not yet reconciled herself to a life of monogamy with him. She was embarrassed by the level of Napoleon's passionate devotion to her and unable – or unwilling – to match that level of emotion in her feelings for him.

Joséphine arrived in Milan accompanied by Lieutenant Hippolyte Charles. Young, handsome and dashing, Charles was able to sweep Joséphine off her feet. Although their affair was evidently torrid, it was as yet unknown to Napoleon. He suspected that Joséphine might not be entirely faithful, but he had no particular man in mind.

Thus, when Joséphine arranged for Charles to travel in the same coach with her for the journey to Milan, Napoleon chose to concentrate on his joy at having her there, rather than on the manner of her travelling arrangements. While Joséphine was in Italy, Charles was ever at her side as an *aide-de-camp*. If Napoleon suspected anything, he said nothing.

In the midst of his new-found glory, disaster struck. The Directory, perhaps concerned at the increasing success and popularity of their burgeoning hero, informed him by letter that he was to share command with General François Kellermann. Napoleon was to take command of a southern Italian campaign, with Kellermann assuming command of the northern campaign. Senior to Napoleon, Kellermann was a living legend, a hero of the Revolution and victor of the battle of Valmy. There was no question in Napoleon's mind that Kellermann would become the dominant leader of the Army of Italy, and Napoleon's road to glory would take a down turn.

As in earlier crises, Napoleon took bold action. He wrote two letters to the Directory. In the first, he outlined his objections to sharing power with Kellermann, pointing out that, among other things, 'one bad general is better than two good ones'. He also wrote that he could only inspire his men to heroic action if they believed that he had the complete confidence and support of the Directory. To share power would be to question this confidence and support and to weaken the effectiveness of the army.

In essence, Napoleon was saying that the concept would not work and that if the Directory insisted on following their stated intentions he would have to resign as commander. Either his arguments or his threat, or both, worked, as the Directory quietly dropped their plans for a dual command.

While the Directory had made Napoleon commander of the army in Italy, they maintained overall control and were constantly sending him directives as to how to conduct the war. While he certainly followed their general instructions, he had little respect for them or their ideas. As at Toulon, he disdained what he considered their interference. The memoirs of Louis Bourrienne, long time friend and private secretary who was ultimately disgraced, are not altogether reliable. His comments on this matter, however, certainly reflect Napoleon's character:

> He one day said to me, 'What gross stupidity is this! It is all very well to say to a general, "Depart for Italy, gain battles and sign a peace at Vienna"; 'but the execution – that is not so easy. I never followed the plans which the Directory sent me. Too many circumstances occur on the spot to modify them. The movement of a single corps of the enemy's army may confound a whole plan arranged by the fire-side. Only fools can believe such stuff.'[35]

Napoleon quickly moved south to neutralise the Papal States and Tuscany. He was almost immediately victorious and began to send an enormous amount of treasure back to Paris. He then marched north to confront the Austrians again.

Two other victories in this campaign have become a part of the Napoleonic legend: Arcola and Rivoli. In November, Napoleon fought a three-day battle against the Austrian forces of Josef Allvintzi von Berberek. The action centred on the bridge near the town of Arcola. Both sides took heavy losses, but eventually Napoleon was able to prevail. He led his troops in action on the bridge, his horse was wounded, and Napoleon found himself in the murky waters by the bridge. He was essentially helpless but his brother Louis and friend Marmont pulled him out and the French carried the day. Napoleon always considered this to have been one of his most dangerous moments.

In January 1797, the Austrians made a determined effort to push back the French and relieve their own troops under siege at Mantua.

Napoleon met them near the town of Rivoli. He was outnumbered and surrounded, but with skilful deployment of his soldiers (and a fair amount of luck) he won a major victory. Almost immediately afterwards, the French totally defeated the armies led by Provera and Allvintzi. With no relief in sight, Mantua surrendered on 2 February. The Austrian fate in Italy was sealed.

Under orders from the Directory, Napoleon again moved against the Papal States. He quickly exacted millions in gold from them and secured his southern flank. Turning his attention to Austria, he marched to within a short distance of its capital, Vienna. Austria quickly agreed to seek peace. The campaign was over.

The preliminary treaty, the Peace of Leoben was finally ratified on 17 October 1797 as the Treaty of Campo Formio. This recognised a number of territorial gains made by other Revolutionary armies. Belgium had been made part of France as a result of the French victory under General Jean-Baptiste Jourdan against the Austrians at Fleurus in 1794. The treaty also gained for France her so-called 'natural boundaries' on the left (west) bank of the Rhine. These gains were not without their dangers, however. One of Great Britain's worst fears was a powerful France that included Belgium and Holland, with their ports just opposite England across the North Sea.

As long as France held that territory, the British government was most unlikely to accept a lasting peace. Any French leader who surrendered them would do so at the risk of his career. This dilemma would prove to be insoluble for the British and for Napoleon. As a result, war to the death between the two countries was virtually inevitable.

The treaty also established the Cisalpine Republic from Milan, Bologna and Modena, areas formerly held by Austria. This was unheard of, a general establishing a new country; it was far beyond the scope of his orders or authority and a direct challenge to the authority of the Directory. Napoleon, however, was never content with simply the expected. As in the past, his gamble worked, and he was seen by French citizens as a liberator of the oppressed and carrier of the Revolution into the rest of Europe. He organised the new republic, provided a constitution and nominated the members of its new government.

Napoleon was quite aware of political developments back in Paris. He held the Directory in general contempt, but had no desire for a return to rule by the Bourbon dynasty. Inept though it was, the Directory was the primary defender of the Revolution in the government and Napoleon was a supporter of the Revolution and, therefore, the Directory. Royalists, however, were gaining some measure of political power in the Council of Five Hundred and the Council of Ancients, and there was considerable fear of a royalist *coup d'état*. This would certainly not be good news for Napoleon, so in the name of defending the Revolution he took measures to defend the very government he despised. In September he sent General Augereau to lend support to the Directory.

In what became known as the *coup d'état de Fructidor* (4 September 1797), Napoleon's troops under Augereau forced most of the royalist supporters out of the legislative bodies. Augereau's actions on behalf of Napoleon eliminated, for the moment at least, the possibility of the re-establishment of a Bourbon government, strengthened the security of the government (thus earning their somewhat reluctant gratitude) and weakened the position of certain potential foes who were implicated in the royalist schemes.

His actions also made it clear to one and all that the army was a major political force that could give – or remove – legitimacy from any particular government. Moreover, he managed to do this by proxy while still safely in Italy. If anything went wrong, he was safely out of harm's way.

It was a brilliant move and shows how astutely he could combine the use of military and political action to his own ends while appearing to promote the fortunes of others. This political astuteness was one of the primary reasons for Napoleon's successes, and the *coup d'état de Fructidor*, while given relatively little consideration by some historians, is an excellent and instructive example of it.

In only one year, Napoleon had completely defeated the numerically superior Austrian army occupying Italy and had achieved the Treaty of Campo Formio. As part of that treaty, he gained the release by the Austrians of General Lafayette. A hero of the War of American Independence, he had become disenchanted with the increasingly radical nature of the French Revolution and fearful for his own safety. In 1792 he had attempted to leave France and seek asylum in Austrian-controlled territory. Instead of asylum, he had been made a prisoner and kept in German prisons. His release could only add to Napoleon's lustre.

Napoleon had preserved the Directory by providing it with riches and, when needed, direct military support. The Directory was not the only beneficiary of the appropriation of wealth from the conquered territories.

Appropriation was, of course, consistent with the time-honoured tradition of armies: soldiers kept a portion of the wealth for themselves, which was how fortunes were made. Napoleon was no different – given his lack of wealth *could* be no different – but now he no longer needed to worry about his personal financial situation. He was careful to see that his mother and other family members were provided for as well.

General Bonaparte was now a true national hero of France and her greatest soldier. More importantly, he had met his first complete military challenge with overwhelming success. He had brought glory and riches to France and great confidence to himself. In Paris he was hailed as 'The young Republican hero, the immortal Bonaparte', and his street was renamed *rue de la Victoire*. In Italy, there were performances of a play dedicated to his glory, *Le Pont de Lodi* (The Bridge of Lodi). His soldiers loved him; he was on top of the world.

The Directory cared more for riches than glory. Its inability to deal with various financial crises left the country in great financial difficulty that was to be partially solved by Napoleon's successes in Italy. Napoleon was politically astute enough to recognise this, and he sent a steady stream of wealth to Paris. He also endeared himself to his men, not only through his great leadership and personality, but by paying them in hard currency for the first time in memory.

Glory, however, also figured in his political and military strategy. Glory helps inspire troops to fight. Equally important, his victories gave him a degree of national popularity that both threatened the Directory and protected him from political harm.

NOTES

29 Chandler, *Campaigns*, 55–57.

30 Melito, *Memoirs*, I, 94–95. An intimate acquaintance of the Bonaparte family, he spent some time at Napoleon's headquarters in Italy in 1796–7. He later served on the staff of Joseph Bonaparte in Naples and Spain.

31 Britt, Albert S. *Wars of Napoleon*, 6. This quote is often used in Napoleonic literature, but there is at least some doubt as to its authenticity, and it may well have been written later, at St. Helena. It does, however, represent the kind of inspiration that Napoleon was to his soldiers.

32 *Vous* is a formal variation of 'you'. The more appropriate informal variation is '*tu*', which is what Napoleon would expect from his wife.

33 *Letters of Napoleon to Joséphine*, 25. He is complaining about her use of '*vous*' rather than '*tu*'.

34 Markham, 28.

35 Bourrienne, *Private Memoirs*, I, 101. A private secretary to Napoleon 1797–1802, his memoirs are self–serving and not always reliable in matters that deal directly with him.

THE NEW ALEXANDER
Egypt and the Holy Land, 1798–1799

Back in Paris in December 1797, Napoleon was given a hero's welcome by both the government and the people. He was just twenty-eight years old, had already accomplished more than many generals older than he and still had the bulk of his career in front of him. He had brought peace to the continent, security to France, riches to the government and fame and glory to himself. The people of Paris showered him with honour. His stepdaughter Hortense remembered the house being filled with generals and the guards having a very difficult time 'keeping back a crowd made up of all classes of people, impatient and eager to catch sight of the conqueror of Italy'.[36] He was elected to the National Institute and was thus associated with the intellectual élite of France. His presence was demanded at exclusive parties and salons throughout the city.

At a reception given by Foreign Minister Talleyrand on 3 January 1798, Napoleon engaged in a conversation with the author Madame de Staël. As his conversation with her has often been quoted as an example of Napoleon's disdain for women, let us read Hortense's version:

> She kept following the General about all the time, boring him to a point where he could not, and perhaps did not, sufficiently attempt to hide his annoyance. It was at this ball that when she asked him, 'Whom do you consider the greatest woman in the world, past or present?' Bonaparte answered with a smile, 'The one who has had the most children.'[37]

Seen in this light, it is unlikely that Napoleon's response was meant to be serious; rather, it sprang from his exasperation at her constant attentions and a desire to put her off in a humorous way. He certainly must have known that her reaction would be negative; he could not have known that two hundred years later his 'off the cuff' remarks would be used by some to accuse him of being sexist!

Against a backdrop of incompetence and instability, this young conquering general had Paris at his feet. There can be little doubt that his ambitions must have tempted him to make a political move then, but he wisely determined that it was not yet time.

Only Great Britain remained in overt opposition to France, and without her continental allies perhaps she could be dealt with once and for all. Her greatest fear had always been an invasion from across the Channel, and this was the next order of business for Napoleon who was put in charge of planning such an invasion. The most critical difficulty was, of course, the complete domination of the channel by the British fleet. While the French navy, joined by Spanish ships, could be a significant force, they were no match for the British.

Napoleon soon realised that the odds against success for such an invasion were long. On 23 February 1798, he wrote to the Directory:

Whatever efforts we make, it will still be many years before we achieve supremacy at sea. To carry out an invasion of England without command of the sea is as difficult and daring a project as has ever been undertaken. It could only be done by a surprise crossing – either by eluding the fleet that is blockading Brest and the Texel, or by landing in small boats, during the night, after a 7 or 8 hours' passage, at some point in the counties of Kent or Sussex ... Our fleet is no further advanced than it was when we mobilised the army of invasion, four months ago ... The English expedition therefore seems to me impossible until next year; and then it is likely to be prevented by fresh embarrassments on the continent. The real moment for preparing this invasion has passed, perhaps forever ...[38]

Convinced that an invasion of England was out of the question, he and the Directory searched for another appropriate campaign. An idle general, who was also popular – and ambitious – was a recipe for upheaval, and the Directory wanted none of that. A way had to be found to get him out of Paris, preferably in a campaign that would benefit France as well as the Directory.

Foreign Minister Talleyrand, whose scheming would be both a boon and a bane throughout Napoleon's career, suggested the ancient French dream of wounding England by conquering Egypt. The Mediterranean was far larger than the English Channel, and the British fleet was not nearly as dominant there. The French had denied a number of ports to the British fleet, most notably some in Italy. France's repossession of the island of Corsica should also be seen as part of this process, for it effectively removed the British threat to the French fleet at Toulon and greatly weakened their position throughout the Mediterranean.[39]

If France could remove the threat of a British presence in Egypt and the Holy Land, it would harm their domination of trade with the Far East and deal them a severe psychological blow. Moreover, it would strengthen French control of the Mediterranean. This possibility had been considered before, most recently in 1769 by Louis XV.

For the Directory, the campaign had obvious advantages. Not only would it wound the English, but it would also remove Bonaparte from Paris. With any luck, he would achieve great success on the campaign and get killed while he was at it. For Napoleon, the advantages were equally obvious. While he was very popular, he was not yet in a position to seize power. An idle general's glory is soon forgotten. He needed additional glory and publicity, and where better than the ancient, mysterious and romantic land of Egypt to find that glory? The aura of mystery surrounding Egypt could only enhance any success he might achieve.

Not surprisingly, then, Napoleon and the Directory quickly approved the Egyptian campaign. Napoleon was given an army of some 35,000 experienced troops. He took with him Berthier as his chief of staff, together with Lannes and Murat. On 19 May 1798, Napoleon set sail from Toulon. His entourage included some four hundred troop transports, thirteen ships-of-the-line and four frigates. The flagship, *l'Orient*, was the most heavily armed ship in any navy at that time.[40]

En route he captured Malta, securing both riches and an important naval base. Lightly defended by the Knights of St. John, the island fortress offered little resistance and within a week Napoleon was ready to leave for Egypt. Before leaving, however, he completely reorganised the island, wrote a new constitution, deported the Knights, initiated a new educational system and confiscated countless treasures. He gave religious freedom to the Jews and abolished slavery and feudal privileges. In six days, he mirrored his reform-oriented approach that had been seen in Italy, was about to be seen in Egypt and soon enough would be seen in France.

Control of Malta, as with control of Corsica and other islands, was not simply a secondary consideration. Any nation that wishes to control the Mediterranean must control the major islands as well. This was the fruit of the Romans' victory in the first Punic War, and it was to be a basic consideration from then on. That ancient goal accomplished, Napoleon sailed on for Egypt.

The political situation in Egypt was complex. Since the defeat of the European armies of the crusades, Egypt had been run by the Mamelukes, former slaves from Eastern Europe, Georgia, Armenia and Turkey. These rulers, known as Emirs, had had military training and were warriors. Since the 16th century, the Ottoman Turks had officially controlled Egypt. The Mamelukes, however, paid little more than lip service to the Turkish control of their country, and the Turks had done little to change the situation.

To Napoleon, this presented an excellent opportunity to justify the invasion. He had long been interested in Turkey and could now claim that he was there on Turkey's behalf to defeat the Mamelukes and restore Turkish control of the region. Egypt under Turkish control, friendly to France, could give the French a decidedly shorter passage to the Far East, than was available to the British.

France had other reasons for wanting to control Egypt and the Middle East, which was their ultimate goal. An African colony just across the Mediterranean could yield riches beyond those involving trade with the Far East. The goal of 'civilising' a backward land and improving their living standards was certainly in the European tradition. Finally, by helping restore Turkish control over the area, they would cement relations with their traditional allies, the Turks.

Unfortunately, the political justifications for the expedition would be sabotaged by political inaction in France. Talleyrand was supposed to travel to Turkey and explain France's pro-Turkish motives for the invasion. The French were sure that Sultan Selim III would understand and support them. For some reason, no doubt including his lack of interest in promoting the fortunes of this ambitious young general, Talleyrand chose not to make that trip. The Turks were never informed of France's intentions.

Because of Talleyrand's inaction – some would say treachery or treason – Napoleon would have to confront not only the Mamelukes but eventually the Turks as well. It is certainly no coincidence that Talleyrand failed to inform Napoleon of this unexpected turn of events. Napoleon had written numerous letters asking if Talleyrand had been to Turkey and he never received a formal reply.

At the very least, Talleyrand's behaviour bordered on treason.

In many ways, Napoleon was a romantic, and he certainly had a good understanding of history. The most famous conqueror of that part of the world was Alexander the Great. He had the goal of unifying the region under one power (his) and then bringing to his new subjects the enlightenment of the Greek world. He also was willing, often to the consternation of his generals, to adopt many of the Persian ways in an effort to keep his new subjects from a constant urge to rebellion. Alexander would learn all he could of these new lands and send back information and plant samples to his former tutor, Aristotle.

Once serious consideration had been given to an Egyptian campaign, Napoleon became even more fascinated with the campaigns of Alexander the Great. He read all he could find on the subject and no doubt began to see himself as the new Alexander who would found a new empire. Thus, it is not surprising that there are numerous parallels between the two campaigns.

In addition to his substantial military force, Napoleon brought a large number of civilians to study every aspect of this largely unstudied land. These included some 167 scholars from a variety of fields. There were linguists, naturalists, mineralogists, painters, surveyors and others, all intent on expanding western knowledge of all things Egyptian. While there, this team would record everything they found, and artists would create images that would become the basis for a virtual Egyptian stylistic frenzy in France that would last for many years.

Napoleon had the Egyptian Institute formed, which provided overall supervision of the scholarly work that was done. Its first director was art historian Vivant Denon. Under his leadership, the groundwork was laid for what would become the crowning glory of the Institute. In 1802, Napoleon ordered the preparation of a publication that would combine all the work done by these scholars and artists (Denon alone produced more than 200 drawings).

During the next twenty years, a team of more than 400 copper-engravers produced *Description de l'Egypt*. Finally published in 1822, this monumental work consists of ten folio volumes so large that a special bookcase had to be designed to hold them. Later two anthologies would be produced. The work contains more than 3,000 illustrations, including 837 copper engravings. It is a sumptuous work of art and considered by many to be the greatest result of the French expedition to Egypt.

The most important accomplishment that led towards a greater understanding of the ancient Egyptian world was the discovery of the Rosetta Stone, found by a French soldier in a wall near the town of Rosetta. On this were inscribed letters in Greek, Egyptian cursive and hieroglyphics, and it was a valuable prompt to the translation of the cursive and hieroglyphic forms. Members of the Institute immediately recognised its importance and made many copies of its text.

The British also recognised the stone's importance and when the French withdrew from Egypt, they took it to London, where it currently resides in the British Museum. Nevertheless, the Frenchman Jean-François Champollion was the first to translate the Rosetta stone, in 1822, thereby opening the floodgates of knowledge that would feed the Western fascination with all things Egyptian.[41]

Napoleon's interest in the study of Egypt offers a fascinating and important insight into the man himself, as it shows the great breadth of his intellectual interests. Having founded the Institute, he played an active role in its work. More important was the fact that he even conceived the Institute and foresaw the importance of the artistic and scientific work that accompanied the military expedition. His love of history and of knowledge allowed him to see the expedition in far wider terms than simply a military conquest. Of course he also fully understood the trade-route possibilities and other geo-political implications of the military action beyond the simple aim of keeping the British out.

Like Alexander, Napoleon recognised the opportunity to make a contribution to history far beyond simple conquest. He saw himself as a modern liberator. He had liberated the Italians from the domination of the Austrians. Here, he would liberate the Egyptians from the centuries-old domination by the Mamelukes and their often cruel leaders, the Beys. Under overall Turkish control, the Egyptians would gain a great deal of self-rule. He would be the founder of a modern Egypt. In this goal he was largely successful.

The British, naturally enough, viewed these developments with alarm. Informed of the mission by spies, they dispatched a fleet under the command of Rear-Admiral Nelson to intercept and destroy the French fleet. On several occasions the two fleets seemed likely to engage, but each time French good fortune intervened and contact was not made. By July, Napoleon's fleet had arrived a short distance from Alexandria and the soldiers faced no opposition in putting ashore. No opposition, but bad weather made the landings dangerous. Delay, however, meant the risk of Nelson's ships arriving before all the troops had disembarked. Nelson had been searching for Napoleon's fleet, and the two had unknowingly passed quite close to each other. Had contact been made, Nelson would almost certainly have been the victor and Napoleon's career might well have ended.

Nelson had been in Alexandria only days before Napoleon arrived and might return at any moment. Haste was clearly essential. Once again, Napoleon exhibited the determination, leadership and bravery that marked his entire career. Contrary to advice given by his admiral and others, Napoleon gave the orders to disembark at once. Captain Shechy wrote in part:

> On the evening of the 1st instant, after issuing the necessary orders for effecting an immediate landing, the Commander-in-Chief threw himself into a Maltese galley, to get nearer the shore; and in spite of the prudent advice of the seamen, who insinuated that a debarkation was impracticable, on account of the violence of the wind and of the reefs which fill the Bay of Marabout, General Bonaparte persisted in his determination to land and actually did land in this very bay. I was one of the staff that accompanied him ... The Commander-in-Chief and his Staff, after sleeping for about two hours on the sand, got up and put themselves at the head of the divisions.[42]

Napoleon's forces quickly secured Alexandria and its vital water supply. Napoleon wasted no time in making clear his intentions. Like Alexander before him, he understood the need to show respect to the religion and culture of those people whom he was, after all, there to liberate. To that end he issued two proclamations; one in Arabic to the people of Egypt and one to his soldiers. The one to the Egyptians was designed to reassure them as to the intentions of the French presence and to whip up antagonism toward the Beys. It reads in part:

> In the name of God, gracious and merciful. There is no God but God; he has no son or associate in his kingdom.
>
> The present moment, which is destined for the punishment of the Beys, has been long anxiously expected ... Bonaparte, the General of the French Republic, according to the principles of liberty, is now

Pen and ink on vellum portrait, *c.* 1797. This shows Napoleon as General of the army in Italy, together with symbols of the French Revolution.

Tortoise shell snuffbox. Original gold painting of General Bonaparte under glass with gold frame, *c.* 1796–1800.

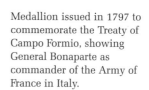

Medallion issued in 1797 to commemorate the Treaty of Campo Formio, showing General Bonaparte as commander of the Army of France in Italy.

I

Nineteenth-century engraving 'Bonaparte'. Signed E. Lechard del. Napoleon in his tent with a map of Egypt on a table and the pyramids in the background.

White on blue Jasperware medallion of Napoleon as First Consul produced by Steel, an early contemporary of Wedgwood, c. 1800. The image of Napoleon is signed W. H. J., and the blue plaque signed STEEL on the back.

Engraving of Consuls Napoleon, Cambacérès and Lebrun designed and engraved by Chataignier, c. 1800. This engraving shows the busts of the three consuls, together with additional allegorical artwork (including Napoleon on horseback) and text indicating that the new government will be good for the letters, sciences, commerce and arts.

Period medallion showing Napoleon as Emperor wearing a laurel-wreath crown in the style of the Caesars.

Nineteenth-century engraving of Napoleon in his study, holding a snuff box.

Mid-nineteenth-century engraving 'Napoleon Premier, Empereur des Français et Roi d'Italie'. Engraved after the design of Tulout, this image shows more of Napoleon's Corsican heritage than most.

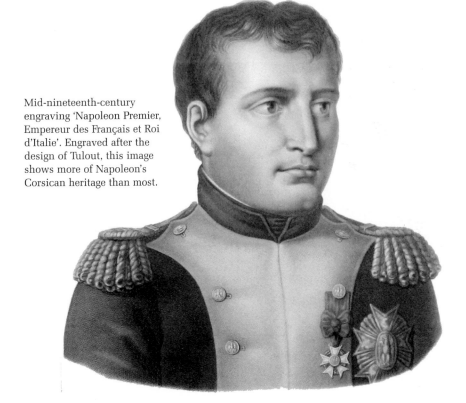

Two First Empire ivory miniatures of
Napoleon and Josephine, signed by
Francois Noël, a French miniaturist of
the late eighteenth century and the
first third of the nineteenth.

Porcelain figure of Napoleon
and Josephine playing chess.
German, c. 1890.

Bronze bust of Napoleon,
signed Colombo, 1885, cast
by the Caranti au Titre
foundry, with an Imperial
Eagle at the base. This bust is
the logo of the International
Napoleonic Society.

Burl wood snuffbox
with signed colour
painting of Josephine
on an ivory medallion,
c. 1810–20.

Limoges Second
Empire plate with
signed painting of
Josephine.

Nineteenth-century
colour painting on
ivory of Napoleon's
son, the King of Rome,
signed by
J. Kozuny.

Lead furniture appliqué showing co-joined
busts of Napoleon and Marie-Louise,
signed ANDRIEU FECIT, *c.* 1810.

Papier-mâché snuffbox with lithograph
showing Napoleon, Marie-Louise, and
Francis I, *c.* 1810.

German or Austrian engraving of Joseph Napoleon 'König von Neapel und Sicilien' (King of Naples and Sicily), by F. C. Boch, c. 1806–8.

Gilded silver statue of the King of Rome with ivory base, c. 1830. Silver label 'DUC de REICHSTADT' (Duke of Reichstadt), his title while being raised in Vienna.

Ninteenth-century engraving of Marie-Louise and her infant son, the King of Rome.

First Empire lithograph of Lucien Bonaparte, by Lacauchie.

First Empire lithograph of Jérôme Bonaparte, by Gaildrau.

Nineteenth-century engraving after Gérard of Queen Hortense de Beauharnais, Josephine's daughter.

Nineteenth-century engraving of
Pauline Bonaparte.

Nineteenth-century engraving of
Prince Eugène de Beauharnais,
Josephine's son.

Nineteenth-century print of
Louis Bonaparte.

arrived; and the Almighty, the Lord of both Worlds, has sealed the destruction of the Beys.

Inhabitants of Egypt! When the Beys tell you the French are come to destroy your religion, believe them not: it is an absolute false-hood, Answer those deceivers, that they are only come to rescue the rights of the poor from the hands of their tyrants, and that the French adore the Supreme Being and honour the Prophet and his holy Koran.

All men are equal in the eyes of God ... Yet are they [the Beys] the only possessors of extensive tracts of land, beautiful female slaves, excellent horses, magnificent palaces!

... Our friendship shall be extended to those of the inhabitants of Egypt who shall join us, as also to those who shall remain in their dwellings and observe a strict neutrality; and when they have seen our conduct with their own eyes, hasten to submit to us; but the dreadful punishment of death awaits those who shall take up arms for the Beys and against us. For them there shall be no deliverance, nor shall any trace of them remain.[43]

Napoleon's proclamation to his men sought to raise their spirits as to the glory of their campaign while also warning them of the necessity to respect the people and customs they would encounter. It reads in part:

You are going to undertake a conquest, the effects of which upon commerce and civilisation will be incalculable.

You will give the English a most sensible blow, which will be followed up with their destruction.

We shall have some fatiguing marches – we shall fight several battles – we shall succeed in all our enterprises. The Destinies are in our favour.

... The people, among whom you are going to live, are Mahometans. The first article of their faith is, 'There is no other God but God, and Mahomet is his Prophet.' Do not contradict them. Act with them as you did with the Jews and with the Italians. Treat their Muftis and their Imams with respect, as you did the Rabbis and the Bishops.

... The Roman legions protected all religions. You will find here customs which differ from those of Europe; you must accustom yourselves to them.

The people among whom we are going treat women differently from us; but in every country he who violates them is a monster!

Pillage enriches but a very few men; and it renders these people our enemies, whom it is our interest to have for friends.

The first city we shall arrive at was built by Alexander, and every step we take we shall meet with objects capable of exciting emulation.[44]

With Alexandria secured, the next phase of the campaign began. Napoleon sent some 10,000 troops, as many as could fit in their transports, with General Desaix up the Nile. He then set out across the desert with about 15,000 troops. Their destination was El Rahmaniya, where they expected to find the Egyptian Mameluke leader Murad Bey with his cavalry.

When Alexander the Great was marching back to Babylon, he and his men suffered untold agony. Water was scarce and was usually bad. The heat was unbearable, driving some men mad and killing others by dehydration. Napoleon's trek across the desert was in keeping with Alexander's experience. He wanted to be the new Alexander, but would no doubt have been quite willing to forego that particular element of his history!

Napoleon's men found little water or shelter but plenty of heat. Worse, unlike Alexander's men who were properly attired for a desert march, Napoleon's army was more prepared for another Italian conflict than for war in the desert. Their heavy uniforms and packs became an intolerable burden. There was an acute shortage of canteens for water. At one point, morale was so low that there was talk of a mutiny. Savary recalled that, 'We all suffered from a parching thirst; several men died of it on the spot.'[45]

Napoleon was determined, however, and the army continued its march. In three days they reached the Nile, and the scenes of the men's jubilation upon finding water for drinking and bathing can only be imagined. It had been a difficult journey, but the French were at the Nile and the real fighting was about to begin.

As predicted and desired, Murad Bey was in the vicinity and ready to give battle. His 10,000 Mamelukes were an impressive sight, but they were unable to break the French formations. Napoleon had deployed his soldiers in squares with cannon at each corner. The Mamelukes were certainly fearsome-looking, but their ancient weapons and frontal assault style were no match for the firepower of the French squares, and they soon gave up the attack. Indeed, this first confrontation was to be mostly between the French and Mameluke gunboats on the Nile. The battle was fiercely fought, but Napoleon's artillery support ultimately made the difference, and the Mameluke navy was no more. Seeing this, Bey and his cavalry hastily retreated.

Two days later, near Cairo, the Mamelukes were again prepared to give battle. This battle, which would become known as the Battle of the Pyramids, took place on 21 July 1798. It is here that Napoleon is said to have told his troops, 'Forty centuries of history look down upon you.' Once again, the tactics of the Mameluke cavalry were no match for the French squares, and in the end the Bey lost several thousand men. The French lost fewer than one hundred. It was a lopsided victory like that of Agincourt,[46] and left Napoleon in control of Cairo.

Cairo was his, but Napoleon's fortunes would soon take a dramatic turn for the worse with the first of three setbacks. The French fleet was anchored at Aboukir Bay. On 1 August, Admiral Nelson arrived with his fleet. French Admiral François-Paul Brueys was in command of the French fleet. In July Napoleon had ordered him either to enter the port of Alexandria or quickly provision himself and leave for Corfu.[47] Had Brueys obeyed his orders, the campaign might well have turned out quite differently. Instead, Brueys lined up his thirteen ships at anchor, near the coast, hoping to force Nelson's fourteen more lightly armed ships to proceed along this line. Unfortunately for the French, Brueys had not positioned his ships correctly and they were too far apart for mutual protection.[48]

The British fleet was able to attack the French ships from both sides, and by the morning of 2 August the fleet had been destroyed. The most dramatic moment came when the French flagship, *l'Orient*, exploded twice and quickly sank with the loss of most of her crew. The battle paused for about ten minutes as sailors of both sides watched in horror and awe.

The battle of Aboukir provides us with an example of the value of modern underwater archaeology. The discovery of the remains of *l'Orient* and two other French ships confirm the poor positioning of the French, which allowed the British to achieve their overwhelming victory.

The implications of this defeat were tremendous. Any hope for French domination of the Mediterranean was now gone. French naval power, such as it had been, was never to recover. Of more immediate concern was the fact that without the French fleet, Napoleon was now isolated from France. This meant that there would be no reinforcements, no supplies and no communication of any great significance. Napoleon, of course, discounted this setback as best he could – he had planned to get most of his supplies from Egypt itself – but he well understood that this had been a major blow to his chances for success. This would soon be followed by additional blows to his mission and his road to glory.

Because Foreign Minister Talleyrand had never informed Sultan Selim II of French intentions, the Sultan was furious when he heard of the invasion of Egypt, and when he learned of Nelson's destruction of the French fleet he decided that the time was right for him to reclaim control of Egypt.

In September he declared war on France. Napoleon, who heard of this from a neutral ship, had thus acquired an additional and unexpected opponent, one that could prove to be more formidable than the Mamelukes.

Napoleon then suffered a second potentially disastrous setback. Cairo was his, but not all Cairo was willing. On 21/22 October thousands of citizens of Cairo engaged in open revolt against the French. Large numbers of French soldiers unlucky enough to be caught alone or in small groups were killed, and the Institute was besieged. General Alexander Dumas, father of the author of *The Three Musketeers* and *The Count of Monte Cristo*, was serving as a cavalry commander, and largely through his leadership the insurrection was put down.[49] Napoleon now turned to deal with the Turkish threat.

As opponents the Turks were a rather different proposition from the Mamelukes, or the 'civilised' armies of Napoleon's European adversaries. They were ferocious fighters with a well-deserved reputation for cruelty. Lopping off heads or other body parts was a normal part of their approach to intimidating subjects and foes alike. Napoleon would have his military abilities tested when he faced them. Soldiers, diplomats, the wounded, women: none would be safe should they fall into the hands of the Turks. The Sultan had declared a holy war against France and there would be no holds barred.

Two Turkish armies were sent to challenge the French, one by sea and one by land. Because of adverse winds, it would be several months before the sea-borne forces would be able to arrive in Egypt, but the army was on the march. Napoleon was determined to defeat it before it arrived in Egypt.

To maintain his control of Egypt and fulfil his dreams of being the new Alexander, he would now have to march north to Syria to fight the Turks.

Napoleon's third misfortune was far more personal in nature, though possibly of much longer lasting significance. Since the very beginning, he had been completely in love with Joséphine. The flames of her love for him had always burned somewhat cooler. During the campaign in Italy he had written to her constantly and ultimately had demanded that she join him there. In Egypt, he had been consumed with military, political and educational (the Institute) matters; none of his letters to Joséphine during the Egyptian campaign are known to exist, but it is reasonable to presume that he had written often and that he had given little thought to taking a mistress as had many of his officers.

Eventually, his friend Andoche Junot provided him with evidence that Joséphine had not resisted amorous possibilities in his absence. She had long since taken up with Hippolyte Charles, now a captain in the French army and her 'escort' when she visited Napoleon in Italy. Napoleon had been aware of their friendship before, but now knew that it had been much more than friendship. Worse, he discovered that everyone in Paris knew of the affair and that he, Napoleon, had become something of a laughing stock.

Furthermore, Joséphine had been engaged in a great deal of profiteering, being heavily involved in the provision of military supplies. Outraged and embittered, Napoleon would never be quite the same again. He wrote to his brother Joseph on 25 July 1798:

In two months I may be back in France. Please look after my interests. I have great private unhappiness; the veil has at last quite fallen from my eyes ... Arrange for me to have a country house when I get back, either near Paris or in Burgundy; I intend to shut myself up there for the winter: I have had enough of human nature. I need solitude and quiet; grandeur bores me; my emotions are dried up. Glory is stale at twenty-nine; I have used everything up; it only remains to become a real egoist ...[50]

When this letter was intercepted and published by the British, Napoleon's humiliation was complete. He became less optimistic and more cynical. He contemplated serious measures, but ultimately settled on only two.

Napoleon decided that he would divorce Joséphine as soon as he returned to France. In the meantime, he was determined to show that two could play at Joséphine's game; he would take a mistress. This was not difficult for a youthful commanding general. He became enamoured of Pauline Fourès, the pretty, blonde, 29-year-old wife of a junior officer, Jean-Noël Fourès. Pauline had been smuggled to Egypt dressed as a soldier, but when discovered lived with her husband in the normal fashion. A beautiful woman with long legs, she was often the centre of attention; Napoleon soon became determined to bed her. He had little use for the local women, whom he found too heavy.

Napoleon arranged to send her husband to France and then began to pay closer attention to Pauline. When she realised his interest, she willingly became his mistress. The two were seen together constantly, and Napoleon no doubt hoped that Joséphine would hear of his having taken this measure of revenge. Unfortunately, Pauline's husband was captured by a British ship and was returned to Egypt; a return probably calculated by the British, who were well aware of the situation, to embarrass the young General Bonaparte.

Fourès' return was marked by outrage and some violence, so the couple quickly divorced. Now Pauline and Napoleon were free to do as they chose. Napoleon called her his 'Cleopatra' and it is entirely possible that had she borne him a son he might have divorced Joséphine and married Pauline. No such thing happened, however, and when he later left for France she stayed behind as General Kléber's mistress. She eventually returned to Paris, where she married and spent the rest of her days.

The divorce from Joséphine would have to wait until his return to France. The Turks needed more immediate attention. Napoleon was determined that they should not be allowed to advance into Egypt, for fear of the effect this would have on the Egyptians. Instead, he would march to Syria to meet them on the battlefield.

The French march across the Sinai Desert with some 14,000 soldiers was reminiscent of the march to Cairo in the nature of the deprivations suffered by the soldiers. Once again Napoleon's force of will led them on. They arrived at the fortress of El-Arish in the Gaza Strip and easily captured the neighbouring town. The fortress, however, delayed them for a fortnight, though they ultimately prevailed, capturing some 2,000 Turks in the process.

This delay was to prove fatal to the campaign. The intention had been to rapidly destroy the Turkish army, followed by a triumphal return to Cairo and an equally quick destruction of the sea-borne Turkish army. After El-Arish, this was no longer possible.

It had taken longer to conquer Gaza than had been expected, and now an even more difficult problem emerged. An army on the march is ill suited to the maintenance of prisoners of war. Moreover, Napoleon was very short of food and could not afford to feed the Turks he had captured. Using his Western sense of honour as his guide, he freed them on condition that they swore not to fight the French ever again. British and other Western soldiers would have adhered to their word of honour. For the Turks, however, Western concepts of honour would prove to have little relevance. They were in a holy war against the infidel, and one does not honour pacts with the devil.

Thinking that problem solved, Napoleon marched north to Jaffa and took the city on 7 March. This was a significant military victory, but it led to one of the more controversial episodes in Napoleon's career. In taking Jaffa the French also captured about 4,000 Turks. Many of these were the very men who had earned their freedom at Gaza by swearing not to fight the French again. Moreover, the problems of food and transportation were now more critical, the French being farther north and the number of Turks doubled.

Napoleon was thus faced with a very difficult situation. He could, of course, release them, but they would eventually rejoin the army and kill more French soldiers. Clearly, Napoleon could not have any faith in their oaths. If he kept them prisoners, they would either starve to death or cause the starvation of French soldiers. Napoleon was torn by the options and consulted at length with his advisers. In the end, reluctantly, he ordered them to be shot.

This incident has been used by some to question Napoleon's character. But a general in the field has as his first responsibility the welfare of his soldiers, and from that point of view he had little choice. It is all too easy to suggest that he could have taken some other action; yet no other action that would protect French lives was available. Henry V had had a somewhat similar horrifying predicament at Agincourt and made the same decision.

Napoleon was unhappy with his choice but defended it to the end. In exile on St. Helena, he wrote:

The reason was, that amongst the garrison of Jaffa, a number of Turkish troops were discovered, whom I had taken a short time before at El-Arish, and sent to Baghdad upon their parole not to serve again, or to be found in arms against me for a year ... But those Turks, instead of proceeding to Baghdad, threw themselves into Jaffa, defended it to the last and cost me a number of brave men to take it, whose lives would have been spared, if the others had not reinforced the garrison of Jaffa. Moreover, before I attacked the town, I sent them a flag of truce. Immediately afterwards we saw the head of the bearer elevated on a pole over the wall. Now if I had spared them again and sent them away upon their parole, they would directly have gone to Ste-Jeanne d'Acre, where they would have played over the same scene that they had done at Jaffa. In justice to the lives of my soldiers, as every general ought to consider himself as their father and them as his children, I could not allow this. To leave as a guard a portion of my army, already small and reduced in number, in consequence of the breach of faith of those wretches, was impossible. Indeed, to have acted otherwise than I did, would probably have caused the destruction of my whole army ... I would ... do the same thing again to-morrow, and so would Wellington, or any general commanding an army under similar circumstances.[51]

Outraged at the deceitful behaviour of the Turks, upon entering the conquered city of Jaffa Napoleon's soldiers sought their revenge by raping the local women and pillaging everything that they could find. Napoleon and his officers were unable to restore order until the following morning.

One reason that the soldiers engaged in such excesses was that a few days before, two French soldiers had been accused of raping a local woman. Anxious to prove to the local populace that such action was intolerable, the French quickly tried the two men, found them guilty and executed them. A few days later, two local Arabs confessed their guilt; the two French soldiers had been wrongfully accused and executed. This incident embittered the soldiers toward the local populace.

The soldiers also remembered the cruel fate of their emissary sent under a flag of truce prior to the opening of hostilities. That breach of what the French considered the international rules of war regarding flags of truce enraged the soldiers and gave them reason to feel that they were not dealing with 'civilised' people and were not, therefore, bound by 'civilised' rules of behaviour themselves.

This was by no means the first nor would it be the last time in history that soldiers have vented anger and frustrations on a local population. It was the horror of war at its worst and it deeply troubled Napoleon. Then, an outbreak of bubonic plague caused death and despair among his troops, and Napoleon was personally struck by their suffering. Their excesses notwithstanding, what greater punishment could he possibly order than that which they were already suffering? He had them given the finest food and had military music provided on a regular basis.

Another heroic image for Napoleon's legend was created when he visited his plague-stricken soldiers. He is generally portrayed as touching their sores. It may be that he did not go quite that far, though on St. Helena he claimed to have done so. All the same by even running the risk of visiting them he earned the love and respect of his solders.[52]

Napoleon continued up the Mediterranean coast to Acre. This port city was defended jointly by Turks led by Djezzar Pasha, known as 'The Butcher' for reasons that are easily imagined, and by some eight hundred British sailors led by Sir Sidney Smith. It was Smith whom Napoleon had defeated at Toulon, and turn about was soon to become fair play.

It was at Acre that the delay suffered at El-Arish proved disastrous. Sidney Smith had arrived only four days before Napoleon. Had Napoleon got there first, it is entirely possible that the city would have been quickly taken. Things turned out quite differently. Smith was anchored just off the coast, where he could bring his guns to bear in support of Acre. Worse, he had captured the siege guns that Napoleon had sent to Acre by ship. Napoleon was therefore without the means to batter down the walls and was up against a significant defence.

After an unsuccessful siege of some six weeks, Napoleon was forced to abandon his efforts. He came close on several occasions, actually breaching the wall, only to find an inner wall blocking any advance. Ironically, the defences had been augmented by fortifications designed by the royalist Frenchman Phélippeaux. Without his efforts, Napoleon might have been successful, despite the untimely arrival of Sidney Smith's ships.

Acre provides us with another irony. Napoleon had observation balloons, which could have informed him of the nature of the inner fortifications. His spies on the ground and soldiers who had managed to penetrate somewhat into the fortifications had given him incomplete and somewhat inaccurate information regarding the inner defences. Just one observation from a single balloon would have made all the difference in the world, but that never happened. Napoleon seems to have had an aversion to the new aerial technology, a rather amazing fact given his genius and use of modern tactics, and he refused to use it. This was a critical mistake.[53]

He did achieve one important victory during this six-weeks' period. General Kléber had been guarding his flank near Mount Tabor and was in danger of being overrun by the Army of Damascus, which was attempting to encircle Napoleon's encampment at Acre. Napoleon personally led a rescue mission and was able to defeat a far larger force. This removed a threat to his forces and reduced the danger of an attack on Cairo.

Indeed, the Battle of Mount Tabor was a major redeeming feature of the campaign in the Holy Land. Napoleon's forces routed the large Mameluke contingent of the Turkish forces, inflicting thousands of casualties on them. The French also captured their entire baggage train, including all their tents, ammunition and, most importantly, their spare horses. After Mount Tabor, the Mamelukes were finished as an effective fighting force for the remainder of the campaign.

Napoleon had sent to France for reinforcements, but they had not been forthcoming. With his soldiers stalled at Acre and their ranks decimated by plague, he had little choice but to return to Cairo. Acre had been a disappointment, but the basic goal of preventing an attack from the north had been accomplished.

The return passage was long and painful; there seemed as many sick and wounded as healthy soldiers. They were forced to throw many of their cannon into the sea. Nevertheless, after leaving most of the sick and wounded in outlying villages, Napoleon led the troops in a triumphal return to Cairo, giving the impression that his trip to Syria had been a great success.

For some two hundred years, Napoleon's detractors have spread the story that he poisoned a large number of his sick and wounded soldiers, rather than leave them behind in Jaffa. Even if this were true, it might have been a humane action given the torture that undoubtedly awaited them at the hands of the Turks.

However, eye-witness accounts lend no credibility to this story and Napoleon himself always denied it. Nathan Schur concluded that Napoleon might have left a small amount of poison for any of the wounded who wanted it, but that most of those who died evidently died of their illnesses.[54] The fact of the matter seems to be that Napoleon left a rear-guard to protect a handful of soldiers so sick that they would die in a matter of hours. The rear-guard left and Sir Sidney Smith arrived on the scene, the Turks evidently staying away from the hospital for fear of infection.

Smith, whose dislike for Napoleon is evident in his writing, never claimed that Napoleon had poisoned any of the soldiers. Indeed, he notes:

> The heaps of unburied Frenchmen, lying on the bodies of those whom they massacred two months ago, afforded another proof of divine justice, which has caused these murderers to perish by the infection, arising from their own atrocious act. Seven poor wretches are left alive in the hospital; they are protected and shall be taken care of.[55]

Another Turkish army was arriving by sea in some 60 transports protected by the British Navy under Sidney Smith and on 11 July 1799, they landed near Alexandria at Aboukir. Napoleon had pulled together all available resources and was ready for them. Led by the dashing General Joachim Murat, the French cavalry defeated the larger Turkish force and drove it into the sea; of the 9,000 Turks, 7,000 were killed and the rest captured.

This second Battle of Aboukir, on land, resulted in a far better result for Napoleon than had been experienced in the prior year's sea battle by the same name. Napoleon was now, at least for the moment, secure in his position in Egypt. He had defeated the Mamelukes and both Turkish armies sent to dislodge him.

It should be pointed out that Napoleon had actually done quite well in Egypt, contrary to the feeling among some historians. He had faced the tremendous environmental difficulties of fighting in a waterless desert, a naval disaster due at least in part to the disregard of his orders and a Syrian campaign made necessary by political treachery in Paris. Yet in spite of these obstacles, only Acre was a defeat for him personally.

This level of achievement must be attributed to Napoleon's ability to inspire his men and organise them in whatever way he deemed necessary to achieve success. In the final analysis, it was his sheer will, combined with his abilities, that prevented a major disaster and, indeed, allowed a considerable amount of success.

Success in Egypt or not, Napoleon began to hear of French defeats in Germany and Italy. A new coalition had formed against the Revolutionary government and had achieved some significant military victories against French interests. Not the least of these was the retaking of Italy, including the Cisalpine Republic, by the Austrians, thus undoing the good that Napoleon had done.

Napoleon longed to be where the real action was. Now, perhaps, the time was ripe for a triumphant arrival in Paris, followed by either a take-over of the government or another heroic defence of the nation. Either way, his personal fortunes and those of France, would be little served by his continued presence in Egypt. He made secret plans to depart, and in October he and a handful of men left for France. His letter to General Kléber, whom he left in command, tries to put the best possible spin on the situation:

Accustomed to look for the recompense of the toils and difficulties of life in the opinion of posterity, I abandon Egypt with the deepest regret! The honour and interests of my country, duty and the extraordinary events which have recently taken place there; these, and these alone, have determined me to hazard a passage to Europe, through the midst of the enemy's squadrons. In heart and in spirit I shall still be in the midst of you! Your victories will be as dear to me as any in which I may be personally engaged; and I shall look upon that day of my life as ill employed, in which I shall not do some-thing for the army of which I leave you the command; and for the consolidation of the magnificent establishment, the foundation of which is so recently laid.

The army I entrust to your care, is entirely composed of my own children. I have never ceased, even in the midst of their most trying difficulties and dangers, to receive proofs of their attachment; endeavour to preserve them still in those sentiments for me. This is due to the particular esteem and friendship I entertain for you and to the unfeigned affection I feel for them![56]

Stopping in Corsica for one week, Napoleon got a taste of his enormous popularity, as he was the constant subject of visits by those wishing to see the great man in person. Indeed, he was sometimes forced to escape his home through a trap door in a bedroom floor, simply to achieve some privacy! It was a gratifying homecoming but when he left Ajaccio, it would be for the last time.

NOTES

36 Hortense, I, 32.

37 Ibid., I, 33.

38 *Correspondance*, No. 2419, III, 644–648, 53–54.

39 McErlean, J. 'The Napoleonic Recapture of Corsica in 1796: A Necessary Preliminary for the Egyptian Expedition.' Paper delivered to *The International Congress: Napoleon and the French in Egypt and the Holy Land 1798–1801*. Tel Aviv, 5 July 1999.

40 Connelly, *Blundering*, 52.

41 For an excellent discussion of the Institute of Egypt see Melanie Byrd 'The Napoleonic Institute of Egypt', in J. David Markham, ed. *Napoleonic Scholarship: The Journal of the International Napoleonic Society*, I, 2, December 1998, 33–40.

42 Captain Adjutant Shecy to Citizen Doulcet, rue St-Piacre, at Paris, in *Copies of Original Letters From the Army of General Bonaparte in Egypt, Intercepted by the Fleet Under the Command of Admiral Lord Nelson Part the Second*. London, 1799, 16–18.

43 *Copies of Original Letters From the Army of General Bonaparte in Egypt, Intercepted by the Fleet Under the Command of Admiral Lord Nelson*. London, 1798, 235–36.

44 Ibid., 237–38.

45 Savary. *Memoirs*, I, 53.

46 On 25 October 1415, British soldiers led by Henry V defeated Charles VI's French army at Agincourt. The French lost 7–10,000 men, the English only about one hundred.

47 Howard, No. 336.

48 Battesti, M. 'La bataille d'Aboukir et ses implications'.

49 Gallaher, *General Alexandre Dumas*, 115–17.

50 Howard, No. 329.

51 O'Meara, *Napoleon in Exile*, I, 212–13.

52 For a good discussion of the taking of Jaffa, see Mordechai Gichon, 'Jaffa, 1799', in *Napoleonic Scholarship*, I, 2, December 1998, 23–32. This issue has a number of other important articles on the Egyptian campaign.

53 Gichon, M. 'The Peculiarities of Napoleon's Near Eastern Campaign', paper presented to *The International Congress: Napoleon and the French in Egypt and the Holy Land 1798–1801*. Tel Aviv, 4 July 1999.

54 *Napoleon in the Holy Land*, 158–61. Schur is a leading expert on the campaign in the Middle East.

55 Smith to Admiral Lord Nelson, 30 May 1799, 313.

56 Bonaparte, Commander-in-Chief, to General Kléber, Alexandria, 22 August 1799, in *Copies of Original Letters From the Army of General Bonaparte in Egypt, Intercepted by the Fleet Under the Command of Admiral Lord Nelson, Part the Third*. London, 1800, 25–27. Also *Correspondance*, No. 4374, V, 734–38.

SEIZING A GOVERNMENT

O n 16 October 1799, Napoleon arrived in Paris. His status was
somewhat ambiguous, to say the least. The Directory gave him
a cool reception because, technically, he had deserted his army.
On the other hand, they had sent a message suggesting that he return,
though Napoleon never received it.

The general populace, however, considered him a great hero. News of
his great victory over the Turks at Aboukir had recently arrived, and to
the French people Napoleon had been an enormous success in Egypt. The
government was in no position to take action against a general who had
the support of the army and of the people. Napoleon's combination of
luck and determination had again held in his favour.

He had returned to France determined to divorce Joséphine. She, on
the other hand, was determined to save their marriage. She rushed to
intercept him before he reached Paris and his family, all of whom would
have been delighted to see them divorce. As fate would have it, their
paths crossed on different roads and Napoleon returned to an empty
home. He ordered her belongings to be removed. Within two days
Joséphine returned. After a difficult evening, Joséphine and her children,
Hortense and Eugène, were able to convince him to abandon his plans.
He had never truly lost his love for her, and she had never lost her political and social connections to the power structure. Besides, Napoleon
had important moves to make and he did not need the very public and
embarrassing diversion that would accompany a divorce.

More than one observer has remarked that Napoleon's disillusion-
ment with Joséphine while he was in Egypt was a watershed in his
development. His correspondence to his brother Joseph would seem to
indicate that. As a result, he drew on what was already an incredible
reservoir of energy and poured it into his work, his ambition. In Italy he
had sent a constant stream of letters to his new love; no matter what the
military situation, he always had time for affairs of the heart. Now,
while his love for Joséphine remained real, he was far more focused on
affairs of state. For the rest of his career, it seemed that he never stopped
working: it was after Egypt that his reputation for nonstop activity was

made. It may well be that his opinion of women took a turn for the worse as well, though he showed a more liberal attitude towards them than was common for the time.

France's continental enemies, led by Austria and Russia and encouraged and financed by the British, had formed the Second Coalition against her, and the internal affairs of the government were in turmoil. The economy was in a shambles. The value of the currency was said to be less than the expense of printing it. Industry had declined to the point of disaster. The infrastructure – roads, public buildings, ports – was in a state of rapid decline, largely due to the combination of a lack of funds and a lack of interest by the government.

In short, the Directory had failed in that most fundamental of responsibilities – the provision of economic prosperity. Unemployment was high, farmers could no longer obtain prices for produce that would assure their own survival, and international trade was virtually at a standstill. The people were tired of war, tired of the poor economy, tired of a corrupt government. They longed for peace and prosperity. They were ready to be led into a new and better era; they were ready for their hero, Bonaparte.

The instability of the government led to a decrease in public safety. Brigands roamed the countryside, much as they had in the days before the Revolution. Napoleon's own baggage train had been pilfered on his way back to Paris.[57] Regions such as the Vendée, never happy after the fall of the Bourbons, were again agitating for the monarchy's return. Despite Napoleon's efforts in the *coup d'état de Fructidor* (4 September 1797), where he had used the potential power of the army to counter Bourbon supporters in the government, another monarchy was considered a very real possibility. This alarmed the heirs to the Revolution. There was a series of destabilising *coup d'états* as the Republicans attempted to strengthen their control over the government.

One can argue whether or not the Revolution had or had not already ended. Its message of hope, however, to say nothing of the nation, was in great danger. Stability was needed, but not necessarily Bonaparte.

The political structure of the French government had taken an unexpected turn. During the Revolution itself, the country had been run more or less by an executive branch headed by a committee, though at his peak Maximilien Robespierre was a virtual dictator. It was the legislative branch, spurred on by the Paris mob, which provided the revolutionary fervour that kept the Revolution going. The Revolution had been, of course, in part a reaction against an executive branch, the king, which had drifted out of touch with the needs of its subjects.

By 1799, however, an interesting reversal of that situation had occurred. The legislative branch had come under the influence of forces whose ideology was less revolutionary and more conservative. Indeed, there were strong royalist forces in the legislative branch and it was entirely possible that these forces would gain the upper hand. Already they had managed to repeal some of the laws that had been passed during the Revolution itself. The legislative body had become the stronger of the two branches of government, and that fact was not good news for republicans.

The executive branch, on the other hand, was now the defender of the principles of the Revolution. Corrupt and self-serving though they were, they were also the only governmental force that seemed committed to maintaining the gains of the Revolution. Odd as it may seem, it was the appointed executive branch that was more in touch with the people than the elected legislature.

The army had become another force of republicanism. Made up as it was of those very people for whom the Revolution was at least in theory intended, they were not happy to discover that the forces of reaction might regain the upper hand. Napoleon's use of the army in *Fructidor* had demonstrated the potential use of that body to preserve republicanism. Anyone who would overthrow the government in the name of the republican principles of the Revolution would need the support of the army.

Emmanuel Joseph Sieyès, a former priest who had voted for the death of Louis XVI, had become a Director. French society was organised into three Estates (somewhat similar to social classes). The First Estate was the clergy, the Second was the nobility and the Third was everyone else, mostly peasants and city workers. It was Sieyès who, in a pamphlet he published in early 1789, had given words to the concerns of the Third Estate: 'What is the Third Estate? Everything. What was it until today? Nothing. What does it want? To become something.'

Sieyès was greatly concerned for the stability – indeed, the survival – of a government that could withstand the forces of both the left and the right and sought to install people whom he felt he could trust. In June 1799 he organised the removal of three Directors, preventing a quorum and thus, in essence, removing the executive branch of the government from any effective action.

For his next step, to gain complete control of the government, he needed someone who could ensure the support of the army. He called this unnamed general his 'sword' and had hoped to recruit General Joubert, an older general he felt he could control. Joubert, however, died in Italy. A new 'sword' was needed, just as Napoleon, his luck ever intact, arrived on the scene.

Sieyès was idealistic, a shrewd politician and determined to save the nation from itself. Napoleon was ambitious, an astute politician and convinced that only he was capable of saving the nation. They were a political pair made for each other, and they each knew it immediately. Napoleon was far more than a sword. The reception he had received during his return to Paris, and in Paris itself, confirmed his status as a true hero of the people. He would add a level of legitimacy and popularity that no one else could approach, least of all the corrupt politicians who surrounded Sieyès and whom he hoped to supplant. More importantly, Napoleon would provide a shield against which the forces of royalism could not advance.

That Napoleon had already proved to be an excellent administrator with republican tendencies was a bonus. In Italy, in Egypt, even in Malta, he had shown extraordinary administrative abilities. His republican credentials could not be questioned, and he had twice (thrice actually, if one includes *Fructidor*) saved the government and thus the Revolution. He was, in short, the perfect man for the job.

Plans were made and the appropriate people brought into the picture: Joseph Fouché, Roger Ducos and Talleyrand, who had been instrumental in bringing together the two principals. The Directors were to resign and be replaced by Bonaparte and two others. In what would become known as the *coup d'état de Brumaire* (9–10 November 1799), Napoleon was to become one of three ruling Consuls.

This was a *coup* that very nearly didn't take place. The plan had been for all the Directors to resign. Two of them refused, and two agreed. A minimum of three was necessary, and the swing vote was Barras. Reluctant to give up his power, he finally agreed and the stage was set.[58]

Now, all appeared to be in order, with the appropriate troops commanded by loyal generals (including Murat) and with Napoleon's brother Lucien, long active in Jacobin politics, installed in October as President of the Council of Five Hundred. The legislature had been persuaded to move out of Paris 'for its own safety'. This isolation from the citizens of Paris made it easier for the leaders of the *coup* to influence its members.

Delays and confusion led to a tricky situation. Napoleon ultimately attempted to appeal to the Council of Elders in person, but made the mistake of suggesting that if necessary he would resort to the use of force. Indeed, his normal gift of oratory completely deserted him and he left the room in disgrace. When he later attempted to address the Council of Five Hundred, he was physically attacked and had to be rescued by several of Murat's soldiers.

Napoleon had been determined to avoid the use of force. The use of soldiers would put him at their mercy in the future and would tarnish his actions as being a military *coup* rather than a political rescue of the government. But the débâcle at the Council of Five Hundred convinced him that he must use soldiers to complete his *coup*.

He sent a group of them to bring his brother Lucien to address the troops. Lucien spoke of the Council being terrorised and of Napoleon being attacked. Indeed, his face had been bloodied, a fact noticed by his soldiers. After appeals for loyalty from Napoleon and Lucien, the soldiers were ready to act. Under Napoleon's command, they moved on the Council, many of whom took the opportunity to depart by way of the windows! Those that were left acted to install a provisional executive government of three Consuls, including Napoleon, Sieyès and Ducos. The President of the Council, Lucien Bonaparte, then addressed the three new Consuls and the members of the Council of Five Hundred:

> Citizens! The greatest people upon earth entrust you with their destinies: within three months, public opinion will judge you. Domestic happiness, general liberty, the direction of the armies and peace itself, are all entrusted to you. You must have courage and zeal to accept such an important trust and high functions. But you are supported by the confidence of the nation and its armies; and it is well known to the legislature, that your souls are entirely devoted to the welfare of the people.[59]

The coup was a success, but its methods had been unexpected and might have led to problems of legitimacy among the population in general. Count Miot de Melito sums up the situation quite well, in explaining why there was no outcry:

We are struck, above all, with the small share taken by Bonaparte in the events of a day that founded his immense power. Although the truth was known to numerous eye-witnesses and suspected by many others, by the time of my arrival in Paris success had justified the means. The contempt into which the Directory had sunk, the fear of falling once more under the rule of the Jacobins, the hopes awakened by Bonaparte's talents and the fame he had acquired, rendered the Parisians very indulgent to the means which had brought about a result from which increased happiness and increased glory were alike expected.[60]

The *coup* had taken place, but the French people, who were constantly exposed to rumours of every variety, were not sure exactly what had happened. Minister of Police Fouché sought to explain the situation to the public through the following bulletin-like pamphlet distributed two days later, on *20 Brumaire* (11 November):

THE MINISTER OF THE GENERAL POLICE OF THE REPUBLIC,
TO HER CITIZENS.

20 Brumaire, Year 8 of the French Republic,
One and Indivisible

CITIZENS,

The government was too weak to sustain the glory of the Republic against foreign enemies and guarantee the rights of the Citizens against domestic factions; it became necessary to think about giving it strength and greatness.

The national wisdom, the Council of Elders, conceived the idea and manifested the will for it.

It ordered the transfer of the Legislative Corps out of the precinct where too many passions rumbled in its midst.

The two Councils were going to propose measures worthy of the Representatives of the French People.

A handful of rebels wanted to prevent these measures; they engaged in spreading a furor that was rendered powerless by the great majority of the Council.

This liberating majority met after dispersing the rebels; it entrusted two Commissioners, taken from among the Councils, with the legislative power.

It placed the executive authority in the hands of the three Consuls who have been endowed with the same power as the Directory.

It chose citizens SIEYES, BONAPARTE AND ROGER-DUCOS, and today they entered upon their duties.

From this moment a new order is beginning. The government has been an oppressor because it has been weak; the one that succeeds it has made it its duty to be strong in order to fulfil the duty of being just.

It calls, for assistance, all the friends of the Republic and of Liberty, *all of the French people.*

Let us unite in order to make the name of *French Citizen* a great one, so that each one of us, proud to carry it, might forget the disastrous designations by the help of which the factions prepared our misfortunes in dividing us.

The Consuls will reach this goal because they strongly want it.

Soon the banners of all the factions will be destroyed; all French people will be united under the Republican standard.

Soon the works of the government will ensure the triumph of the Republic in foreign lands by victory in our land, prosperity by justice and the happiness of the people by peace.

The Minister of Police, Fouché[61]

Napoleon was to have been the *coup* instigators' tool, but he quickly moved to consolidate his power. Sieyès may not have fully realised just how brilliant – and ambitious – Napoleon was. At St. Helena, Las Cases reported:

Sieyès, who was one of the Provisional Consuls together with Napoleon, astonished to hear his colleague, at the very first conference, discussing questions relative to finance, administration, the army, law and politics, left him quite disconcerted and ran to his friends, saying 'Gentlemen, you have got a master! This man knows everything, wants everything and can do every thing.' [62]

Napoleon and Sieyès had primary responsibility for writing the constitution that would establish the new government. Both wanted to ensure a stable, reasonably conservative government. Napoleon, however, wanted to expand the popular base of the government. This was at least in part to help counteract the image of his leading troops against the Council of Five Hundred. He therefore insisted on universal male suffrage at the age of twenty-one and a system of plebiscites to approve the new constitution and the new members of the government. Sieyès had wanted three legislative assemblies – A Council of State for the origination of laws, a 100-member Tribunate and a 300-member legislative body – each of which would consist mainly of landed males who had been members of previous assemblies. Thus it was that Bonaparte, the general who used troops to take power, became known as the true republican, while Sieyès, the man of the Revolution, was seen as defender of the old order and landed gentry.

Both men wanted the executive function split among three men. Sieyès first argued for a Grand Elector who would stay in Versailles and thus remain above the fray in Paris. This position would have two assistants, called consuls. One of the consuls would handle external affairs, the other internal. Sieyès wanted the Elector's position to be well paid though largely powerless. He quickly offered the position to Bonaparte, who just as quickly rejected it. Napoleon was not interested in ceremony; he wanted real power and rightfully believed he had it coming to him.

When Bonaparte rejected the position of Elector, Sieyès proposed a system of three equal consuls. Napoleon agreed with the three consuls, but insisted that one of them be clearly in charge. After lengthy consultations with various committees, Napoleon's version of the new government was adopted. Having originally been chosen to be the Grand Elector; it would now be difficult to argue against his becoming the First Consul, with the Second and Third Consuls reduced to a consultative role. All males of majority age would be allowed to vote. The initial assemblies might well represent the old order, but after that, the people would have a more direct say in the composition of their government.

During the competition that arose between the two men, Sieyès accused Napoleon of wanting to be a king. Given what had happened to the former king, this was a dangerous charge. In the final analysis, however, Napoleon emerged as the true republican, the true defender of the Revolution. Indeed, by insisting on universal male suffrage he put France ahead of even the United States, which initially had a property requirement for voting and excluded slaves. Women were still excluded from direct participation, as they were in the United States and other

European countries, but Napoleon was on the cutting edge of what we would now call the expansion of voting rights.

It was not just an empty gesture or publicity stunt when he ordered the army to observe ten days of mourning when George Washington died on 14 December 1799. The Order of the Day read, in part:

> Washington is dead. This great man fought against tyranny. He established the freedom of his country. His memory will ever be dear to the French people, as to all free men of the two worlds, and especially the soldiers of France who, like him and like soldiers of America, fight for equality and liberty.
>
> The First Consul orders that for a period of ten days all flags and colours of the Republic will be draped in black.
>
> BONAPARTE [63]

Washington's bust joined those of Napoleon's other heroes in the Great Gallery of the Tuileries Palace.

The new constitution called for three legislative bodies. The Senate, headed by Sieyès as its first president, had as its only defined duty the selection of the initial members of the two-house legislative branch. The lower house, the 100-member Tribunate, discussed all legislation but could not vote on it. A 300-member Legislative Body served as the upper house. It had the power to vote on all proposed legislation, but could not discuss any of it. It was an odd arrangement, to be sure. The executive branch was to consist of three consuls, with most of the power residing in the First Consul. This role was reserved for General Bonaparte, and he personally selected the other two consuls. As Second Consul he selected Jean-Jacques Cambacérès. A well-respected lawyer of moderate politics, he would eventually become Napoleon's surrogate while Napoleon was away on campaigns and one of the most important men in Napoleon's government.[64] His Third Consul was Charles François Lebrun, another moderate with an excellent knowledge of finances.

The new constitution was adopted on 14 December 1799. Napoleon was now the new leader of France. As he would again in 1815, he had seized power without firing a shot. He was thirty years old.

To seize power during such a period of instability was risky. This was, after all, just the latest in a string of governmental takeovers. Napoleon had agonised over the decision:

It was a service that I did not like; but when I considered that if the convention was overturned, *l'étranger* [the foreigner] would triumph; that the destruction of that body would seal the slavery of the country and bring back an incapable and insolent race, those reflections and destiny decided that I should accept it.[65]

Napoleon's rise to power resulted from many factors. His determination, intelligence and sheer force of will were certainly important personal characteristics. Additionally, family, luck and the influence of powerful friends also played important roles. Of great importance was his willingness to take significant risks – political as well as military – and his ability to foresee the consequences of his actions. Yet perhaps as much as anything else, Napoleon was a product of the Revolution and the turbulence brought about by a decade of instability, constant change and war. Such a situation is ripe for the advancement of those who are willing to seize opportunities and exploit them. Napoleon proved capable of this from the very beginning. His road to glory now lay open before him.

NOTES

57 Bainville, J. *Napoleon*. Boston, 1933, 89.

58 There are many accounts of these events. One of the most detailed, though biased against Napoleon, is that of Isser Woloch's *Napoleon and His Collaborators*.

59 La Bédoyère, *Memoirs*, I, 210.

60 Melito, I, 307.

61 Original document in the David Markham collection.

62 Las Cases, I, 142.

63 Howard, No. 473.

64 For a very detailed discussion of Cambacérès' role in Napoleon's government, see Woloch, *Collaborators*, 120–55.

65 O'Meara, II, 228. The French word *l'étranger* is in the text.

PART TWO

THE YEARS
AS CONSUL

FORMING A GOVERNMENT

It is not as a general that I am governing France: it is because the nation believes that I possess the civil qualities of a ruler.

Napoleon, 1800

To many historians, Napoleon's years as First Consul were the finest of his career. During this time he instituted many of the most important reforms of his tenure as leader of France. He had the full faith and trust of the French people and, for a short time, a period of peace. It is during this period that, the Battle of Marengo excepted, his reign was known more for its domestic accomplishments than its military glory. This notwithstanding the fact that France was still at war, and Napoleon was destined to excel in war as well as in domestic accomplishment.

Now Napoleon's full political abilities were brought to bear. Secure in the knowledge that his army would support him and that he was a national hero, he convinced the rest of the government that only he could save the nation and the Revolution. At St. Helena he told Las Cases, 'I closed the gulf of anarchy and cleared the chaos. I purified the Revolution ...'[66] In February 1800, by a vote of 3 million to 1,500, the people of France confirmed him as First Consul when they ratified the new constitution. His takeover was now complete and France was about to enter a new era.

If the rhetoric of the Revolution concentrated on the misery of the lower classes, the resulting government under Napoleon and its reforms were decidedly directed toward the advantage of the middle class. The rhetoric was still that of the Revolution, but the stability, the financial, legal and educational reforms, all were worthy of a member of the Institute and were to the great benefit of the new dominant middle class.

Napoleon brought many things to France; perhaps the greatest, and certainly the thing that made all others possible, was stability. No more would there be revolving leadership, *coups* and intrigue. Napoleon brought a level of unity and stability that had been absent in France for many years.

To ensure this Napoleon needed to eliminate the remaining internal conflicts in France. The Paris sections were quiet, but there was still the question of the Vendée, that ultra-royalist, ultra-religious region of west central France that had never accepted the Revolution. Napoleon made it clear that he would not tolerate any further rebellion against the central government and sent troops to back up and make clear his intentions. With the stick, however, came the carrot. Napoleon negotiated with the leaders of the region, gave assurances of religious tolerance and pardoned individual members of the opposition. He wrote to d'Andigné, a leader of the Chouan, a counter-revolutionary group:

Only too much French blood has flowed during the last ten years ... Be sure, then, to tell your fellow-citizens that never again shall revolutionary laws devastate the fair soil of France, that the Revolution is over, that consciences will be utterly and absolutely free, that protection will be given equally to all citizens and relieved from any taint of prejudice and that, for myself, I shall appreciate and know how to reward any services rendered on behalf of peace and quietness.[67]

He did not give all that the most extreme royalists would have wanted; he did not bring back the *émigrés*, so hated and feared by the very middle class on whose behalf Napoleon governed. They wished to return to their old properties, but many of those properties had been confiscated by the state and then sold to the middle class. The ultra-royalists would never accept him; they would forever dream of the restoration of the monarchy. Indeed, Napoleon directly refused their plea for him to personally restore the monarchy, a move they claimed would lead to his everlasting glory. This he could not and would not do. It would betray the Revolution and lead to the destruction of the middle class.

When the Count of Provence, Louis XVI's eldest surviving brother and the future Louis XVIII, made moves to return on his own, Napoleon wrote him to stay away, saying 'You must give up any hope of returning to France: you would have to pass over one hundred thousand dead bodies. Sacrifice your private interests to the peace and happiness of France.'[68] Louis responded:

I am far from being inclined to confound M. Bonaparte with those who have preceded him. I think highly of his valour and of his mili-

tary talents. Neither do I feel ungrateful for many acts of his administration; for whatever is done for the benefit of my people, shall
always be dear to my heart. He is deceived, however, if he imagines
that he can induce me to forego my claims ... [69]

Thus the royalists would continue to be a thorn in his side; they would
attempt to kill him, and they would eventually get both an emperor and
a king.

For the majority of France, however, Napoleon offered a government
that could be accepted by all factions. By force of arms and skilful nego-
tiation, Napoleon brought almost everyone into at least uneasy support of
his government. Even the *émigrés* were given some consideration; their
property would not be restored, but many of them would ultimately be
allowed to return and be afforded the protection of the state.

The coming months and years would see a whirlwind of activity.
Napoleon unified the nation, restored financial integrity to the govern-
ment and reformed all levels of government. And everywhere, there was
Bonaparte, hard at work, usually upwards of eighteen hours a day.
Herbert Fisher in his book *Bonapartism* tells us:

> Napoleon brought to the task of government exactly that assemblage
> of qualities which the situation required, an unsurpassed capacity
> for acquiring technical information in every branch of government,
> a wealth of administrative inventiveness which has never been
> equalled, a rare power of driving and draining the energies of man,
> a beautiful clearness of intellect which enabled him to seize the
> salient features of any subject, however tough, technical and
> remote, a soldierly impatience of verbiage in others combined with
> a serviceable gift of melodramatic eloquence in himself; above all,
> immense capacity for relevant labour.[70]

Herbert Butterfield, a sharp critic of Napoleon, concurs with Fisher:

> [Bonaparte] collected in the service of France a greater assemblage
> of talent, working in a closer collaboration, than had perhaps ever
> been known before; while he himself, more capable of unremitting
> work than any of the rest – moving from one topic to another with a
> mind always in focus and in a state of high comprehension – would

range through the various activities of government, giving his stamp
to all and revivifying all.[71]

Napoleon worked hard, and he expected all those under him to work
equally hard. In 1799, Henri Beyle (1783–1842), later known as Stendhal,
was given a position as one of several hundred clerks in the War Ministry
under Secretary General Pierre Daru. Stendhal, who would one day be
one of France's greatest writers, gives us a flavour of what it was like
working for Bonaparte:

> In a vast room with gilded panels at the War Ministry, the younger
> Daru toiled night and day; Napoleon roared at him, and Pierre Daru,
> in turn, roared like a bull at the people who worked under him ...
>
> All day long he [Henri Beyle] sat at a desk in the office of the War
> Ministry writing letters for Daru ... Daru bore down hard upon his
> assistants. Soon Henri was infected with the general terror of the
> 'wild bull', and his fear of a blistering reprimand from his chief
> never left him.[72]

In order to bring calm out of chaos and reform out of despotism, it is
necessary for a nation to have strong leadership. Napoleon certainly
provided that. Some have suggested that this was a reflection of his lust
for power, but it is hard to imagine how France would have survived,
much less thrived, under any other kind of leadership. The United States
tried a weak system under the Articles of Confederation and got eleven
years of stagnation and futility for her efforts. Later, George Washington
was able to take advantage of a strong central government that grew out
of the Constitution, and only then was America able to embark on her
path to greatness. Napoleon, not surprisingly, was a great admirer of
George Washington.

Some contend that Napoleon ran the government without regard for
democratic principles or procedures. To the contrary: he established principles of democracy important to the ultimate development of the
modern French democratic state. Although he would ask penetrating
questions focusing on the justice and usefulness of an issue and its
history, the Council of State, a group of advisers chosen by him, would
usually make the final decisions. All who wished could speak, and
Napoleon would often question those who had been silent but whose

opinions he wished to hear, even if they were likely to be contrary to his own. Jean Rapp, one of his *aides-de-camp*, relates:

> Napoleon, whatever his detractors may say, was neither overbearing nor obstinate in his opinions. He was eager to obtain information, and he wished to hear the opinions of all who were entitled to hold any. Among the members of the Council, the wish to please him sometimes superseded every other consideration; but when he perceived this, he never failed to restore the discussion to its proper tone. 'Gentlemen', he would say to his lieutenants, 'I summoned you here, not to bring you over to my opinion, but to let me hear your's [sic]. Explain to me your views; and I shall see whether the plans which you propose are better than my own."[73]

Napoleon almost always abided with the majority vote, though he was not required to do so. His only real requirement was hard work; they would often meet all night, and the sleepy received little sympathy from the First Consul! He would often preside from ten in the evening until five in the morning, take a bath and be ready to go again.

It may be that his greatest strength was that once he had established a goal he never wavered in his pursuit of it. This could on occasion lead to excess but it is one reason for his tremendous success.

The Consulate, and later the Empire, may seem to some to have been strong centralised rule, but compared to previous governments they were reigns of freedom. They gave France a government of regular, scientific and civilised administration in place of near anarchy. Sacrifices of liberty were balanced by gains in equality and safety and in the restoration of economic stability. Liberty did not have the importance then that it does in the Western democracies of today. Censorship, for example, was widespread and accepted throughout Europe, as governments were determined to reduce public criticism of their policies. In any event, liberty is dependent on equality and safety for its very existence. Napoleon established the principle of popular sovereignty through the repeated use of the plebiscite.

It is important to remember that France had a long history of centralised government (at least in theory), and that centralisation continues today. *Liberté* under Napoleon was far greater than liberty under the monarchs of the rest of Europe. In February 1807, Napoleon wrote to his brother Jérôme, King of Westphalia, saying, 'What people would wish to return under the arbitrary Prussian system after having tasted the blessings of a wise and liberal administration? The people of Germany, of France, of Italy and of Spain desire equality and liberal ideas … Be a constitutional king.'[74] Later, he wrote that had he won the war against Russia in 1812 his own constitutional reign would have begun.

Napoleon provided more *égalité* than was provided anywhere else in Europe. Indeed, of all the principles of the Revolution, guarantees of equality were given the highest priority. Baron Fain writes, 'Equality of rights was everything in Napoleon's eyes. He saw all the good of the French revolution expressed there in a single phrase, and he brought great honour on himself by keeping this vital principle safe and sound.'[75] This is not surprising, as it was the system of the Three Estates and the hated privileges of the first two that had most outraged the people of pre-Revolutionary France. The inequality of that period included, of course, huge inequities in the ownership of land and the payment of taxes. Therefore, the Revolution had redistributed the land, and taxes were universal and based on the ability to pay. The middle class, concerned that the *émigrés* would return to claim their land, were reassured by Napoleon's actions that continued both the spirit and the letter of policy in this area. Revolutionary laws on the matter would not be repealed. Equality was further promoted by the provision of government scholarships for the middle class. Compared with the despotic rule of other continental nations, whose commitment to equality was marginal at best, Napoleonic France was a model to be emulated.

Napoleon was totally committed to the provision of equality in the 18th-century meaning of the word, namely equality of opportunity. He believed that every man could rise as far as his ability could carry him, and it was the state's job to give its citizens the ability to do just that. His oft quoted belief that 'in every soldier's knapsack is found a Marshal's baton' represented his attitude in civil as well as military spheres. In civilian life, he defended the rights of peasants and *émigrés* alike and granted all men the opportunity to excel. He initiated the Legion of Honour, which reinforced the idea that all men could rise as far as their talents would take them. He removed the benefits of caste and privilege, granted religious freedom and established a new economic order. These actions sent terror into the hearts of the monarchs of Europe, a terror that led to the vilification of the man and to a series of efforts to eliminate him.

As for *fraternité*, Napoleon re-unified the French. By solving many domestic problems and restoring law and order, he re-established confidence in the government and in the process made the French proud to be French.

Vincent Cronin, one of Napoleon's best biographers, sums up numerous statistics that show how France was better off under Napoleon than under previous governments. He points out that this improvement was far more than just a question of statistics, that France saw a change of attitude, a new optimism, as a result of Napoleon's rule. Before the *coup d'état de Brumaire* an official had written of 'Crime with impunity, desertion encouraged, republicanism debased, laws an empty letter, banditry protected.' By 1805 another official was writing of people paying their taxes, the law being enforced, brigandage no longer a fear and economic prosperity for all. 'Fifteen years ago there was only one theatre in Rouen open three times a week, now there are two, open daily ...' In Cronin's words, 'The wheels, in short, were turning, the machine worked. And Frenchmen ... were thankful. In 1799 there had been "disgust with the Government"; in 1805 Beugnot [a prefect] found "an excellent public spirit".'[76]

The Consulate is best known for Napoleon's domestic accomplishments, and much more on that will be said shortly. It should not be forgotten, however, that France continued to face a significant military threat. Great Britain had again used her considerable diplomatic and financial resources to get Russia and Austria to move against France in what was called the Second Coalition. Diplomatic efforts and internal squabbles removed Russia from active participation and the British were content to finance the war from the sidelines. Thus, while the rest of Europe seemed content to see what would develop with this new French government under its fascinating new leader, the Austrians, unwilling to accept the newly won natural borders on the Rhine and the Alps of the French state, were determined to move against the French.

From the beginning, Napoleon had wanted peace. He had written to King George III:

Called by the wishes of the French nation to occupy the first Magistracy of the Republic, I have thought proper, in commencing the discharge of its duties, to communicate the event directly to your Majesty.

Must the war which, for eight years, has ravaged the four quarters of the world be eternal? Is there no room for accommodation? How can the two most enlightened nations in Europe, stronger and more powerful than is necessary for their safety and independence, sacrifice commercial advantages, internal prosperity and domestic happiness, to vain ideas of grandeur? Wherefore is it that they do not feel peace to be the first of wants as well as of glories? These sentiments cannot be new to your Majesty, who rules over a free people with no other view than to render them happy ... France and England may, by the abuse of their strength, long defer the period of utter exhaustion; but I will venture to say, that the fate of all civilised nations is concerned in the termination of a war, the flames of which are raging throughout the whole world.[77]

King George did not deign to answer directly but sent his response to Talleyrand by way of Lord Grenville. The King, wrote Grenville, would not negotiate

with those whom a fresh revolution has so recently placed in the exercise of power in France ... For the extension of [aggressive war] and the extermination of all established governments, the resources of France ... have been lavished and exhausted ... [The King would rejoice when] all the gigantic projects of ambition and all the restless schemes of destruction which have endangered the existence of civil society, have been finally relinquished ... The best and most natural pledge of the reality and permanence of such change, would be the restoration of that line of princes which, for so many centuries, maintained the French nation in prosperity at home and respect abroad ... It can, for the present, only remain for His Majesty to pursue, in conjunction with other Powers, exertions of just and defensive war.[78]

All France needed to do to have peace was give up all her territories gained since the Revolution and restore the Bourbons to the throne. That Great Britain had often fought with the Bourbons and that the Bourbon King Louis XVI had hardly maintained France 'in prosperity at home and respect abroad' was of little consequence to George III and Grenville. The response was insulting to Napoleon, France and the army. It was clear that England felt she had the upper hand and had no interest in peace. Those who accuse Napoleon of desiring war might instructively read this exchange of correspondence. In any event, peace was not at hand; as far as England was concerned, the war, financed but not fought by her, would proceed.

In his memoirs, General Jean Jacques Pelet, *aide-de-camp* to Marshal Masséna during the campaign in Portugal, gave a very good summary of the situation between Great Britain and France:

> I have always considered the War of the Revolution [1792–1815] to be a continuation of the old rivalry existing between France and England – an endless struggle between a continental and a maritime power. Initiated by an avaricious desire to seize our disorganised provinces, rather than by a need to protect or avenge the throne, this war was later carried on to contain the ideals of the Revolution. The conflict no longer had any actual object after the exhausted and often dissident powers saw a stable government established in France. However, England recognised that her eternal rival was growing considerably more powerful as a result of the prodigious activity that follows all revolutions. In her future she could foresee the loss of her maritime preponderance, her [economic] monopoly and with them her complete ruin. From that time on, she decided to fight until the death, prepared to employ without hesitation all the schemes at her disposal.[79]

Napoleon, ever the masterful politician, understood that continued war presented both a challenge and an opportunity. The challenge was simple; the people of France wanted peace along with their new frontiers. If the new government could not give them this, they would likely find a new government that could. With this in mind, Napoleon had written not only to King George III of Great Britain but also to Emperor Francis I of Austria asking for peace.

The necessity of war, however, also presented Napoleon with a much-needed opportunity. He had risen to power in large part on his reputation as a general. If his lasting accomplishments were to be domestic reforms, there must be a period of peace to allow them to take hold. Moreover, reforms of the legal, financial and educational structures, to name a few areas into which Napoleon would delve, would take time. Even after enactment, it would be months, and more likely years, before the people would begin to see concrete results. In the meantime, Napoleon needed something spectacular to keep his star in the ascendancy, to maintain the enthusiastic support of the people. Napoleon knew this very well. He also knew that military action against an old foe would capture the imagination of people and add to his glory, from which he gained his real power.

His star was still rising, and the name of its latest incarnation would be Marengo.

NOTES

66 Las Cases, II, 3, 102.
67 Thompson, No. 54. Also *Correspondance*, 30 December 1799, No. 4488, VI, 78–79.
68 Thompson, No. 58.
69 *New-England Palladium* (Boston) Tuesday, 20 September 1803, vol. 22, 1. Also, Bédoyère, I, 284.
70 Fisher, H. *Bonapartism: Six Lectures Delivered in the University of London*. London, 1913, 41–42.
71 *Napoleon*, New York, 1966, 40.
72 Josephson, *Pursuit of Happiness*, 53–54.
73 Rapp, *Memoirs*, 22.
74 *Correspondance*, 15 November 1807, No. 13361, XVI, 196–97; Thompson, No. 153; partially trans. in Bingham, II, 346.
74 Fain, *How He Did It*, 199.
75 Cronin, 208–9.
76 Bussey, *History*, I, 264–65.
77 Ibid., 266–67.
79 Pelet, *Campaign in Portugal*, 1973, 10.

THE PAST STRIKES BACK
Italy, 1800

France and Austria faced each other in two major areas. In the north, along the Rhine, General Jean-Victor Moreau led the main French army. Napoleon created a new Army of the Reserve and placed it under the command of Louis-Alexandre Berthier. As First Consul, Napoleon was constitutionally unable directly to command this new army, so he selected his close friend and confidant, currently serving as Minister of War, to take formal command. This army would attack the Austrians where they least expected it; they would cross the Alps through the Great Saint Bernard Pass into Italy, move quickly on Milan and then on to face the main Austrian forces led by General Michael Friedrich Melas. Napoleon hoped that French forces currently in Genoa, led by General André Masséna, would tie up enough Austrian forces to allow the French an easy victory.

On 15 May 1800, the Army of the Reserve began its march through the Great Saint Bernard Pass. This passage through the Alps has captured the imagination of historians, writers and all others who read of Napoleon's life. Perhaps the single defining painting of Napoleon is Jacques-Louis David's painting of Napoleon crossing the Alps on his rearing white horse, his cape blowing in the wind, with the names of Hannibal, Charlemagne and Bonaparte inscribed on the stones at his feet. It was Hannibal, of course, who some two thousand years earlier had passed through the Alps with his army and elephants to invade Rome. Charlemagne, too, had crossed the Alps in defence of the Pope and had been rewarded with the title of Holy Roman Emperor. No one could accuse David – or Napoleon – of not having a sense of history!

The reality of the crossing was somewhat less heroic, however. The painting by Delaroche showing a more sombre Napoleon riding on a mule is a much more accurate representation.

Stendhal followed Napoleon through the Alps as a second lieutenant in the 6th Dragoons. He tracked Napoleon's footsteps, only slightly behind Napoleon's own passage through the Alps, even including a stop for refreshment at the Hospice of Saint Bernard. His experience of most note centred on the only real military problem encountered by the French army during the crossing, Fort Bard. This fort, to the south-east of the Great Saint Bernard Pass, threatened serious delay to Napoleon's progress. The defenders refused to surrender so Napoleon simply went around them. While this move was successful, there was a danger, as the soldiers were forced to pass within range of the fort's cannon. They had to pass along a platform, with cannon-balls bouncing fairly close at hand.

In *The Life of Henri Brulard*, Stendhal describes his experience:

> I can remember that I went close to the edge of the platform so as to be more exposed, and when he [his companion] started off along the road I lingered a few minutes to show my courage. That's how I came under fire the first time. This was a kind of virginity which had weighed as heavily on me as the other sort.[80]

Stendhal would write to his sister Pauline:

> All I can tell you is that its [Saint Bernard Pass] difficulty has been extraordinarily exaggerated. There is not a moment's danger to the troops. I passed by the fort of Bard, a much more difficult mountain. Imagine a steep valley like that of the Vallée de Saint-Paul, near Claix. In the middle, a hillock; on this hillock, a fort and passes beneath it within pistol-shot. We left the road at the distance of three hundred feet from the fort and climbed the hill under continual fire from it. What troubled us most were our horses, which bounded five or six feet at every whistle of a bullet or cannon-ball. [81]

Stendhal was not alone in finding humour in the difficult pass through the Alps. Napoleon himself wrote of his trip down the eastern side of the Saint Bernard, 'The First Consul descended from the top of the Saint-Bernard by sliding on the snow and water-courses and leaping over precipices.'[82] He also wrote, 'We are fighting against ice, snow, gales and avalanches. Astonished at being so rudely attacked, the Saint Bernard is putting certain obstacles in our way.'

To Stendhal and to the world, Napoleon's gambit was the stuff of which the romance of history is made. Stendhal expresses this wonderment in the opening lines of *The Charterhouse of Parma*, where he notes (referring to an earlier campaign), 'On 15 May 1796, General Bonaparte made his entry into Milan at the head of that youthful army which but a short time before had crossed the Bridge of Lodi and taught the world that after so many centuries Caesar and Alexander had a successor.'[83] The new Caesar and Alexander wrote to his brother Joseph, 'We have come down like a thunderbolt. The enemy was not expecting it at all and can scarcely believe it.'[84]

Incidentally, while passing through the Alps, Napoleon continued to write his typical romantic letters to Joséphine. One might think that she would now be writing more frequently, but in his letters he often complains that she is not writing to him.

Napoleon swept out of the Alps and into Milan, entering that city on 2 June 1800. He immediately declared the re-establishment of the Cisalpine Republic; the glory days of 1796 were being relived, and Napoleon was to make the most of it. Napoleon then moved to cut off General Melas' supply lines from Austria. He was now prepared to meet the forces of Melas, whom he presumed would have been reduced as a consequence of the siege of Genoa. But on 4 June Masséna surrendered Genoa, giving Melas open supply lines to the British fleet in that seaport city. So Napoleon needed to move south quickly and defeat the Austrians before the two elements of their army could re-unite. He advanced swiftly towards the small town of Marengo, unaware that more than 30,000 Austrian troops were nearby.

His plan seemed simple enough, but on 13 June he sent two units of his army out to discover the Austrians' whereabouts, thereby significantly reducing his remaining forces. One of these units, more than 5,000 strong, was commanded by General Louis Charles Desaix. When, on the 14th, the Austrians appeared in strength near Marengo, Napoleon's main force of fewer than 24,000 men was surprised and greatly outnumbered. The battle began. By mid-afternoon the French appeared to be defeated and he prepared to retreat. Napoleon had sent an urgent message to Desaix ('I had thought to attack Mélas. He has attacked me first. For God's sake come up if you still can.'). Desaix was presumed far away and perhaps unable to respond in time.

The Austrians were so certain of victory that in the early afternoon they took some time to regroup for a final push against the French. But Desaix had been delayed by flooded roads. He had not yet received Napoleon's call for help, but when he heard the opening cannonade, he heeded the time-honoured admonition to all commanders and 'marched to the sound of the guns'. By late afternoon his fresh forces were prepared to meet the slowly advancing Austrians. The arrival of Desaix bolstered the spirits of the hard-pressed French. Napoleon also added to that spirit as he rode among the men, calling out a reminder to the men that it was his habit to bivouac in the field. Melas had been so certain of victory that he had retired from the field, leaving the presumed mopping-up operations to subordinate officers.

Thanks to Desaix's timely arrival, it was the Austrians who were mopped up! Quick action by generals Kellermann and Marmont in support of Desaix's infantry, including effective use of artillery support, turned the battle into a rout, and Napoleon's glory was preserved. Although Austrian causalities outnumbered French by two to one, Napoleon paid a heavy price. His friend and trusted general Desaix died in the battle. When told of his death, Napoleon replied, 'Why am I not allowed to weep?'[85] He later wrote, 'I am plunged into the most profound grief for the man whom I loved and esteemed the most.'[86] His love did not, however, prevent Napoleon from ultimately trying to claim credit for the victory. His first bulletins recounting the action were accurate, giving full credit to Desaix, Kellermann and others. Later versions (including some many years later) indicated that he had sent Desaix out as a ruse and that Desaix's return had been planned all along.

Despite Napoleon's later claims to the contrary, it was truly to Desaix that he probably owed the rest of his career. A defeat here might well have broken the spell he had cast over France and led to his political downfall.

It is important to remember that, as a self-made man, Napoleon did not have the power of tradition or dynasty to preserve his power in times of adversity. As a result, he was often, one might say always, just one defeat away from potential oblivion. He understood his position well and often commented upon it. This basic lack of security would, as a matter of necessity, guide his actions throughout his career.

If Marengo helped preserve Napoleon's future, it was a precursor of the future as well. The historian Jacques Bainville called Marengo 'A Waterloo with a happy ending, with [General] Desaix as a [General] Grouchy who arrived on time.'[87] Marengo could have ended Napoleon's career; instead, it cemented his power.

Napoleon learned from his mistakes. Never again – until Waterloo – did he violate the primary battle principle of concentrating all one's forces when engaging an opponent's main force, and he was always careful to keep a powerful reserve – just in case. And from now on, he would always send out more than one reconnaissance unit.

Finally, he learned of the psychological impact of the sudden arrival of unexpected troops, both on his men and on the enemy. He would discover what it was like to be on the losing end of this impact – at Waterloo – with the last-minute arrival of the Prussians under Field Marshal Blücher.

After Marengo, Napoleon returned to Milan:

> He was received at Milan in triumph: there they called him the unparalleled man, the matchless hero, the incomparable model, with every other praise, that Italian adulation best knows how to imploy; while France, on her part, re-echoed these flatteries. The good Milanese boasted that he was come to give new liberty to his Cisalpine people. He himself spoke much of peace, of religion, of literature and of science ... To the delight of all the worthy, he re-opened the University of Pavia, that had been closed by the suspicious Germans ... To the professors ... he granted liberal stipends, so that the University flourished with fresh vigour ...[88]

While Napoleon was absent from Paris there had been reports of his defeat, even of his death. Worried discussions took place concerning who would replace the First Consul. Napoleon was all too well aware of these intrigues and returned to Paris on 2 July 1800. This, of course, put an end to the speculation regarding his fate and any replacement, and all Paris celebrated their victorious Caesar. The question of intrigues, however, would haunt the often absent Napoleon for the remainder of his career.

Marengo had been a great victory, but had not signalled the end of the campaign against Austria. It would not be until French General Moreau's decisive victory at the Battle of Hohenlinden on 3 December 1800, that the Austrians would feel compelled to sue for peace. The resulting Peace of Lunéville, signed in February 1801, completed the image mirrored by the first Italian campaign. France gained new territories and the Austrians were removed from much of Italy. The terms of peace were by no means severe; the Emperor of Austria could tell his people that he had accepted an honourable peace that would not threaten Austria's strength or influence.

There was, for now, peace on the continent.

NOTES

80 Trans. Jean Stewart and B. C. Knight. Chicago, 1958, 337.
81 Stendhal to Pauline, Milan, 29 June 1800, *To the Happy Few: Selected Letters of Stendhal*. Translated by Norman Cameron (John Lehmann, 1952; London, 1986), 38–9. Stendhal's letters make for some of his best writing.
82 *Bulletin of the Reserve Army*, 24 May 1800, in Howard, No. 627. This bulletin was signed 'Berthier', who was nominal commander in chief, but is believed to have been written by the First Consul himself.
83 Trans. Shaw, M. London, 1958, 19.
84 Howard, No. 620.
85 *Correspondance*, No. 4910, VI, 456. This account is in the official Bulletin of 15 June 1800. Also Howard, 465.
86 Ibid., No. 4909, 453. Also Howard, 463.
87 Bainville, 117.
88 Botta, *History of Italy*. Botta was a member of the Bonapartist government in Piedmont.

RELIGIOUS PEACE

The French Revolution was in very large measure an anti-clerical, even anti-religious revolution. If the members of the Second Estate, the nobility, abused the advantages of their station, no less can be said of the First Estate, the clergy. The clergy was often composed of the younger sons of nobility, who could not normally hope to inherit their fathers' title, wealth, or lands. Throughout the Middle Ages, the Church had engaged in activities that could hardly be considered to be in the interests of the common people. The sale of 'salvation' through indulgences, the Inquisition and a system of fees and other policies that were designed primarily to raise large funds to support the political ambitions and luxurious life-styles of the higher clergy had ultimately led to the Reformation. Europe had divided into Catholic and Protestant regions, but France had remained an overwhelmingly Catholic nation.

While the Catholic Church had curtailed some of its most abusive policies, it remained perhaps the single most powerful anti-egalitarian force in France. The clergy's wealth put it on a par with the nobility and led to enormous political power as well. The higher clergy – bishops, archbishops, cardinals – lived lifestyles that created resentment among not only the lay members of the Church but the lower clergy as well. The local parish priests, called *curés*, generally lived lives of relative poverty and resented the fact that so much of the money went to the higher clergy and so little to the poor.

The *curés* themselves were not exactly saintly in their lives either. Common jokes and cartoons of the period suggest a life not totally free of corruption, to say nothing of women. Nevertheless, when the Estates General came under the control of the Third Estate in 1789, it was the support of significant numbers of the *curés*, together with a few reform-minded nobles, that made it, and thus the Revolution, possible.

The Revolution unleashed an outpouring of resentment against the Church. Church property was vandalised or destroyed. Believing the statues of the Biblical kings surrounding the cathedral of Notre-Dame in Paris to be kings of France, the mobs decapitated them. Clergymen were humiliated and even frequently executed by the angry mobs. The state confiscated church lands and closed the monasteries.

Some Revolutionaries sought to harness this anti-clerical anger into more constructive areas. Talleyrand, himself once a priest, established the 'Cult of the Supreme Being'. A campaign to eliminate Catholicism, and even Christianity itself, was undertaken. This had some success in Paris and other cities, but the people in the countryside were, as they are everywhere, more conservative and more religious. In 1790 the government established 'The Civil Constitution of the Clergy', which provided for the selection of priests by election of the people and the elections of bishops by the priests. To practise religion, the priests were required to swear allegiance to this new version of the Church, and some 55 per cent did just that. These priests were given state salaries, making them, in essence, government civil servants.

In the late 1790s, the Directory opened a major campaign against those priests who had not sworn allegiance to the new order. Tens of thousands of these 'non-juring' priests were deported or, in some cases, executed. While Napoleon was in Egypt, the Directory ordered the abduction of Pope Pius VI to Valence where he died in August 1799. So the status of the Church in France was difficult to define and its future far from secure. The true Revolutionaries wanted it gone forever, while the peasants in the countryside longed for its reassuring messages, if not for its political and financial abuses. A middle ground seemed necessary if France were finally to have religious peace.

Achieving such a peace was high on Napoleon's agenda when he became First Consul. His twin goals of domestic and foreign peace would not come to pass if he could not find a way to satisfy the various factions on the question of religion. Those who would look for proof of Napoleon's desire for peace and for the welfare of the French need only look at his efforts to achieve this religious peace. His efforts also show his resolve not to allow others to dictate terms of that peace. He would negotiate with the Pope, but the ultimate solution would be on his terms.

The negotiations were long and sometimes difficult. Napoleon was determined not to return to the old system. For one thing, he knew that the people would no more stand for that then they would stand for a return of the Bourbons. Much French blood had been shed to remove the Church from its power to dominate the lives of ordinary Frenchmen and

Napoleon's claim to represent the Revolution would be destroyed forever if he gave in too much to the Church.

Napoleon also did not trust the Church. The Church at first had supported some aspects of the Revolution, but had eventually come to represent the most ardent counter-revolutionaries, especially those in the Vendée. From the beginning, the clergy supported the Bourbon cause, a fact that contributed to the hatred of the Church by the Revolutionaries. Many believed that the Church was still the champion of the Bourbon cause and could therefore not be trusted in its dealing with any other French government. Napoleon was not entirely certain that this was not the case. Perhaps more to the point, however, was the possibility that many in France might see a return of the Bourbons as the only way to return the Church to its 'legitimate' role. If Napoleon could remove this incentive for royalism, he would increase his own security to a substantial degree.

Moreover, Napoleon himself was not really a believer. He was, however, convinced that the Church could provide a sense of stability for the common people. He may not have believed, in the words of Karl Marx, that religion was the opiate of the masses, but he certainly knew that as long as there was no solution to the religious question there would be no promise of the domestic peace he – and France – so craved.

A new Pope, Pius VII, had been elected in March 1800. An Italian, Pius had seemed supportive of republicanism in the past, and Napoleon hoped to build on that. He promised the Pope that he would restore the Catholic Church as the church of France if Pius would agree to respect the 'acquisition' of church property by the state and the need to maintain state control over the clergy. The negotiations were long and success was by no means certain. Numerous drafts were prepared and discarded. Talleyrand, who was living with a beautiful woman whom he planned to marry, insisted on protection for married priests. On this point, he ultimately lost. The Pope was willing to allow the French government to keep the former church properties, but wanted restitution. Napoleon countered by offering a state salary for French clergy. Ultimately, the number of bishops was to be reduced by half, and all were to be nominated by the First Consul and invested by the Pope.

At one point, when it seemed that Pius was not going to agree to French demands, Napoleon threatened to declare a new order without the Pope's blessing. In the end, however, both sides recognised the need for mutual success, and the Concordat was signed by Pope Pius on 15 August 1801. Napoleon could not have asked for a better 32nd birthday present!

The legislative assemblies were less co-operative than the Pope. Dominated by people who remembered all too well the excesses of the Church and the hatred by the people of those excesses, they were suspicious of any return to something approaching the old order. They demanded modifications that would guard against that eventuality by reducing the power of the Pope. In the end, however, they supported Napoleon by the narrowest of margins.

Napoleon achieved much with the Concordat. He was able to pacify the opposition of the anti-clerics by pointing out that the Church was now officially under control of the government, this time with the approval, rather than the imprisonment, of the Pope. To the religious people of the countryside, he was seen as a godsend. He was praised as a true hero for opening the churches and bringing the blessings of the Holy Father back to the French people. He further cemented his image with the religious by selecting bishops who would put loyalty to France and God above loyalty to the Pope or money. They were universally acclaimed, and Napoleon's popularity soared.

The big losers in this business were, of course, the Bourbons and their royalist supporters. Their efforts to sabotage the negotiations had been rebuffed by the Pope himself. They had but two claims to the loyalty of the commoners: the tradition of the monarchy and the promise of the return to Catholicism. The first claim was tenuous at best, and Napoleon had completely deprived them of the second. If they were to remove Napoleon and seek their return to power, it would have to be through other means.

The Concordat with the Pope was signed in August 1801 and the churches were re-opened by Napoleon in April 1802. One month earlier, in March, the treaty between France and Great Britain brought the Peace of Amiens, though peace had been *de facto* for some time before that. Thus, in the short span of months between August 1801 and March 1802, Napoleon had achieved his twin goals of domestic and foreign peace. France was no longer at war with anyone inside or outside her borders. To the people of France – indeed, to the people of the world – one man alone was responsible for all this: Napoleon! The people and the legislative bodies seemed in a race with each other to heap honours upon him. Originally named Consul for ten years, a plebiscite now overwhelmingly supported his nomination as First Consul for life. This was accomplished by an Act of the Senate on 2 August 1802. Two days later, the powers of the First Consul were greatly increased, generally at the expense of the Legislative Body, the Tribunate and the Council of State. No matter, Napoleon's popularity overwhelmed any opposition, which came mainly from republicans. He was now at the zenith of his popular support; France was ready to follow him wherever he might lead, and the world watched in fascination, awe and, in Great Britain, disquiet.

Napoleon did not disappoint them. He had already showed his incredible stamina, the force of his will, the strength of his intellect and the extent of his dreams. He led a France whose borders exceeded those of Louis XIV, and Napoleon was determined to lead her to unparalleled prosperity. Even before the Concordat and the Treaty of Amiens, he had begun reforms that would become the hallmark of his early rule and the basis of much of his ultimate legacy. To understand fully Napoleon's road to glory, it is more important to study his domestic accomplishments than his military genius, for when death claimed him in 1821, his military successes had gained France little, while his domestic accomplishments have lasted to this day.

REFORMS FOR THE PEOPLE
The Economy and the Law

O
ne of the root causes of the Revolution was the disaster that passed for the economy of France. That economy reflected a society based on sharply structured inequality. Almost all the wealth and income of the nation was concentrated in the First and Second Estates (clergy and nobles). Almost all the taxes were levied on the Third Estate (everyone else). While the latter did include some people of wealth, such as moneylenders, certain professionals and a growing merchant class, the overwhelming majority of it consisted of desperately poor peasants and labourers. Even Louis XVI knew that something must be done, but he was too weak to stand up to his nobility and demand any serious reform. About 50 per cent of France's budget was dedicated to repayment of debt brought on by the wars of Louis XIV, French support for the War of American Independence and other military activities.

The finance ministers – Louis XIV's Jean-Baptiste Colbert and Louis XV's Jacques Necker – had understood the need to reform the tax structure, but were unable to enact the kind of reforms needed, because that would demand that the clergy and nobles pay closer to their fair share. The march of the women on Versailles in 1789 was not just symbolically about bread. The cost and scarcity of bread made it a very real symbol of the people's suffering and would continue to be a benchmark indicator of the state of the economy. It was financial crisis that was the main reason that Louis called a meeting of the Estates General in 1789, a meeting that led to the Revolution and the end of the monarchy.

It did not, however, lead to an end to the financial crisis. During the Revolution, the situation had continued to be chaotic, and France was deeply in debt. The Convention and the Directory had proved to be particularly inept in dealing with finances, and debt had continued to grow. Indeed, one of the reasons that Napoleon had been able to act with unusual autonomy during the first Italian campaign was that he sent a steady stream of wealth and art to Paris, which helped to balance the books of France (and of the Directors).

When Napoleon became First Consul, the debt had become intolerable, reckoned at about three times the national treasury. The economy was barely functional. Civil servants and soldiers had been paid sporadically, at best. There is a well-known story about Napoleon questioning one of his defence bureaucrats about to the numerical strength of the army. 'We do not know the strength of the army,' came the reply. 'Surely you can find out from the payroll records,' replied Napoleon. 'Sir, we do not pay the army.' 'Well, find out from the ration lists.' 'We do not feed the army.' 'Lists of clothing?' 'We do not clothe the army.' The story reflects the situation that could be found throughout France.

A great deal of money needed to be raised, and quickly, if Napoleon's successes in other areas were to be preserved. He immediately raised millions of francs from foreign and domestic bankers and a national lottery, then set about reforming the entire tax system. Part-time workers had collected taxes, a situation that led to considerable laxity in their collection. Napoleon created a special cadre of collectors, eight for each *département* (administrative region of France). These officials were required to pay as much as 5 per cent of expected revenue in advance, thus improving the cash flow. Ever mindful of the incentive system, he named the beautiful *Place des Vosges* in Paris after the first *département* to pay its full share of taxes.

Napoleon's improvements in the income tax system led to the elimination of virtually all debt and put the country on sound financial footing. Over time he also added taxes on wine, playing-cards, carriages, salt and tobacco. In 1802, when hunger caused by poor harvests again threatened the stability of the government, he immediately arranged for the government to purchase large quantities of bread and distribute it to the poor. Other government programmes, such as interest-free loans, led to the disappearance of the crisis and another reason for the common people to consider Napoleon the saviour of their nation.

Perhaps Napoleon's greatest, and longest lasting, financial achievement was the establishment of the Bank of France. This bank enabled France to eliminate high interest rates for its own loans and brought additional stability to the financial situation. Within one year, the débâcle that had been France's finances was no more. A casual observer of Napoleon, however, might not have realised the extent of his success, for to watch him in action was to watch frugality itself. He was forever attempting to cut costs and hold people accountable for every last *centime*. He eliminated paper money and established an audit system that served to squeeze every ounce of value from each expenditure.

Napoleon's frugality was the stuff of stories then and now, but his fiscal success was no minor matter. He eliminated inflation as a serious concern and never had to devalue his currency. Paper money was replaced by coinage, which served psychological as well as fiscal purposes. People had, for the first time in anyone's memory, confidence in their economy and, through it, their government.

During the Empire he would have a 20-franc gold coin minted, with his image on it. It immediately became known as a Napoleon, and no one could dispute that name's appropriateness. For the modern state to be effective, its economy must be in order. Napoleon recognised this and provided relief that not only solved the short-term problems but also established the foundation of long-term stability.

Napoleon's most famous domestic accomplishment was his legal work. France's system of laws was an unbelievable tangle. There were countless regional codes, courts, case law, almost 15,000 decrees (often contradictory) and other documents. The ancient Romans had had a far more unified system; indeed, Roman law still formed the basis of much of French law in the south, while Germanic law prevailed in the north. Napoleon once wrote, 'we are a nation with 300 books of laws yet without laws'. He wished to codify the Revolution, to secure the principles stated in the Declaration of the Rights of Man and of the Citizen. He also wanted to modernise and maintain that body of law inherited from the past that would still serve the needs of France. While the entire system of laws, both civil and criminal, needed overhaul, it was to the civil code that Napoleon turned his attention.

Napoleon was nothing if not in a perpetual rush. This was in part due to his personality and in part his understanding that the people would not show a great deal of patience. He needed to produce results swiftly or he might not get the time to produce any. He formed a committee comprised of lawyers from across France and gave them all of six months to produce a draft of France's new civil code.

It was submitted to the Council of State, who would prepare the final draft. It is true that Napoleon did not write the entire 'revision', but he did preside at almost one half of the meetings of lawyers, and he prevailed on numerous points. There was broad agreement on many areas, especially those that were a clear reflection of the republican principles of the Revolution. The law's equal treatment of all, the elimination of the last vestiges of the old feudal order, the secularisation of society and especially the marriage ceremony, were incorporated into the new code. This code reflected the needs of the middle class who had most benefited from the Revolution and who needed assurances that their gains would last. It codified their right to keep one of their most important gains, lands obtained as a result of the Revolution. Women gained property and family rights significantly beyond what they had before or immediately after the Revolution. The code provided for other things as well, including the right of men to enter any trade, craft, profession or religion they chose.

Perhaps the most interesting elements pertained to the nature of the family and its role in society. In the discussions related to this issue, we can see Napoleon's liberalism and humanity. Much is made of Napoleon's belief that a wife owed obedience to her husband. Indeed, but in that belief he simply reflected the Roman legal tradition that dominated the law in the south of France, as well as the Catholicism of most of his nation. It is also likely, based on some of his comments, that he did not take that concept very seriously.

In other areas relating to the family, however, it was Napoleon who proposed, not always successfully, more liberal provisions than those favoured by the Council of State. First and foremost of these areas was the question of divorce. The Catholic tradition of prohibiting divorce had a strong hold on many members of the Council, as it did on much of society, especially rural society. Some members of the Council also feared that liberalisation would lead to a dangerous level of social instability.

Napoleon, however, rejected those considerations in favour of the belief that the state should have no right to force people to remain married, regardless of consequences. It is one of the few areas of law where he brought his force of will fully to bear, and he was ultimately successful in getting divorce into the code. There were some restrictions, but the code brought a major new right for people, most especially women, for whom divorce was and still is sometimes a matter of personal safety.

Napoleon often had to remind the Council that the law was not just a matter of theory. Real people were involved and a few words on a piece of paper could have dramatic impact on their lives, as well as on the very nature of society. The world was now very different from what it had been, and the law needed to reflect changes and guide society into the resulting new order. It must, therefore, be a reflection of the goals set for the future – Napoleon's goals, to be sure – rather than a reflection of the never-to-be revived past.

His liberal approach to the rights and protection of women is also evident in his successful effort to see the marrying age for women raised to eighteen and to twenty for males. The more conservative Council had proposed the ages of thirteen and fifteen respectively, which reflected more the practices of the Middle Ages than of the Enlightenment.

Other family-related areas of the code promoted by Napoleon included the increasing importance of the family as a provider for its children. This included abolishing the dowry system which had often encouraged the forced marriages of young girls. He also promoted the idea that families should care equally for all children, including in the distribution of inheritances. In these areas he was unable to prevail, and they were left out of the code.

The Council struck another blow against the rights of women when they declared them to be widows if their husbands were convicted of certain crimes and under the law considered 'dead'. This intrusion in the relationship between man and wife, regardless of the desire of the wife, outraged Napoleon's sense of justice. It was nevertheless included in the code.

In early 1801 the completed code was submitted to the Tribunate for approval. Here again, Napoleon's vision proved to be more liberal than that of his peers, and the Tribunate balked at giving its approval. Not until 1804 was he able to get it passed, and even then only by having some of its most vocal critics removed.

The code was a judicial compromise between democratic ideals and the shadows of the past. Most importantly, due to Napoleon's personal and powerful interest, for the first time in French history there was a unity of law, which is absolutely critical if a country is to rise to greatness. If the new code was liberal, more protective of the rights of the people (notably women) and written in a clear and understandable style, one must give Napoleon the credit. It was through his force of will, clarity of thought and eloquence of argument that it became what it was: the most progressive system of laws in Europe.

It was, therefore, completely appropriate that in 1807 this system of laws was renamed the *Code Napoléon*. It is in many ways his most lasting legacy. It remains the basis of French law today, as well as the law of Belgium and Luxembourg and has greatly influenced the law of Western Europe, Mexico, Latin America, Japan and the American state of Louisiana. There have, of course, been changes. In France, for example, there is no longer a fine of 300 francs for having a mistress![89]

With the new system of laws came the need to provide a new legal structure. Napoleon created an entirely new legal system, based on merit rather than family connection. He created the office of *Préfet* (executive head) and assigned one to each *département*. They were to administer the law and see to it that the law was applied fairly to all citizens. This system brought much needed order and stability to the *départements*. Most of his appointments were men of revolutionary heritage and none had strong family connections to the *départements*. Napoleon's approach to the legal system was among the most liberal of the day and met with the approval of revolutionaries and even such future critics as Madame de Staël.[90] Although he had the power to do so, only on two occasions did he interfere with decisions of the *Préfets*. The most instructive of these was when he objected to the banning of a politically controversial opera; he preferred that the people should retain the freedom to hear what they wished. He also objected when a *Préfet* forced people to be vaccinated.[91]

The progressive nature of Napoleon's vision influenced his work on the criminal code as well. Against objections, he promoted the jury system. He had only modest success in maintaining this reform of the Revolution, partly because of the incompetence of some juries.

Even though he was unsuccessful in some areas, his approach to the code underlay both its letter and spirit and made it a progressive force greatly feared by the leaders of the regressive states that constituted the rest of the European continent. To the leaders of these states, still mired in their feudal-like systems, the new French law, with its guarantee of equality for all, was a very real threat to their own claims to legitimacy. It was one of the reasons why they feared and would therefore never really accept, the new French state and its progressive leader.

NOTES

89 Cronin, 200. One of the finest of Napoleon's biographers, Cronin provides an excellent discussion of the development of the legal system under Napoleon.

90 Madame de Staël was a prominent social and literary influence of the period whose *salon* was perhaps the most important in Paris. She was at first favourable towards Napoleon, but eventually became disillusioned. The feeling was mutual, and at one point Napoleon banned her from Paris.

91 Cronin, 200–201.

THE EDUCATION
OF A NATION

Les vraies conquêtes, les seules qui ne donnent aucun regret, sont celles que l'on fait sur l'ignorance. (The real conquests, the only ones that do not cause regret, are those that are won over ignorance.)[92]

All societies need an educational system; it provides skilled labour, a common cultural heritage and a love of country. A society in turmoil, one building a new order based on a revolutionary ideology, needs education even more, as the upcoming generations need to be brought in. This situation describes both the years of Revolution and the time of Bonaparte. It is, therefore, no surprise that education was a priority for leaders during both periods.

During the years immediately prior to the French Revolution, the idea of universal education was beginning to develop. Cardinal Richelieu, the power behind Louis XIII (who ruled 1610 to 1643), and later others advocated the principle that 'each one ought to have within his reach the education for which he is best fitted'.[93] However, for all the talk, it could be argued that the involvement of the French government was less than overwhelming and education was largely left to the Catholic Church. As Farrington suggests, 'The time was not then ripe, however, for accomplishing these reforms. It needed the drastic purgation of the Revolutionary period, followed by the constructive genius of Napoleon, to put them into effect.'[94]

The period of the French Revolution (1789–99) is not noted for its stability, either of policy or of government, and it may come as a surprise to the reader that this period dealt with education at all. While most literature concentrates on the activities surrounding foreign policy and internal conflicts, the leaders of the Revolution were in fact very concerned with education. In 1793, the Convention established the Committee of Public Instruction and charged it with re-ordering education in France. It is not surprising that the destructive tendencies manifest in other spheres of the Revolution were present in education as well. That which existed had to go, simply because it had existed before the Revolution.

However, it would be unfair to characterise the Revolution as merely destructive. Its leaders considered the problem of education from a variety of points of view. These included 'The duties and prerogatives of the state, the rights of parents, the potential benefits of higher education, the economic needs of the nation, the necessity for training teachers and the suitable status of the teaching profession in a republic.'[95] This list sounds very much like the debate in early 21st-century America. While education was not mentioned in the Declaration of the Rights of Man and of the Citizen, it was included in the first constitution and in the constitutions that would follow.

One of the first changes made to French society had to do with religion. Much of the Revolution can be seen as a rejection of the old order, including the prominent role played by the Church. While Revolutionaries were destroying the statues at Notre-Dame, they were also removing any vestiges of influence by the Church in the educational system. Interestingly, the great revolutionaries of France were willing to change just about everything, but they were not willing to change attitudes toward women in education. Thus Mirabeau, the Revolutionary leader, in sync with Rousseau, the philosophical 'father' of the Revolution, felt that education was for men who were to become involved in the affairs of state, while women, whose main job was to raise the family, had little need of it.[96]

During the early years of the Revolution, there was a lot of talk about education but relatively little institutional action. Many reports were issued, and some changes were made, but the internal turmoil and external conflict made domestic reform difficult. Then, with the execution of Robespierre on 28 July 1794, some level of normalcy was established and the government was able to pay more attention to educational reform. Action soon followed with the decree that teacher training was now the top educational priority. The Paris Normal School was created with a curriculum that included: 'republican morality and the public and private virtues, as well as the techniques of teaching reading, writing, arithmetic, practical geometry, French history and grammar'; and they were to use books that would be published and prescribed by the Convention.[97] This latter requirement merely reflected what was a strong French tradition, namely the centralisation of educational policy. Also instituted at this time was the establishment of a public secondary school for every 300,000 people. The curriculum for these *écoles centrales* [central schools] consisted of literature, languages, science and the arts. The decree establishing the *écoles centrales* also provided that:

> the age-range of the pupils will be from eleven or twelve to seventeen or eighteen ... every school is to have one professor for each of the following subjects: mathematics; experimental physics and chemistry; natural history; scientific method and psychology; political economy and legislation; the philosophic history of peoples; hygiene; arts and crafts; general grammar; belles lettres; ancient languages; the modern languages most appropriate to the locality of the school; painting and drawing. The teaching throughout will be in French. Every month there is to be a public lecture dealing with the latest advances in science and the useful arts. Every central school is to have attached to it a public library, a garden and a natural history collection, as well as a collection of scientific apparatus and of machines and models relating to arts and crafts. The Committee of Public Instruction is to remain responsible for the composition of text-books which are to be used in central schools and the siting of these schools is to be determined by special enactment.[98]

Here we see again the strong French commitment to centralisation. It is also of interest to note that teacher salaries were established by the national government and that the schools were to be run by a committee of teachers who were to meet every ten days (which was once per week, under the new Revolutionary calendar). Each *département* would be financially responsible for its own schools. The commitment to central financing soon weakened, however, with the responsibility for teacher salaries delegated to the town governments, to be paid by the parents.[99]

The requirement that instruction be in French may seem to be rather obvious, but it reflected a political problem of the time as well as the use of education to political and nationalistic ends. A common language is one of the most fundamental of nationalistic tools available to a country. In Revolutionary France a number of different languages and dialects were still spoken. If France were to become unified under the new Revolutionary Government, surely one measure of that unity would be a common language. Moreover, if there were to be a common language, it must fall to the schools to instruct all citizens in that language. Indeed, during the early years of the Revolution, non-French was seen as counter-revolutionary and, therefore, dangerous.[100] This extreme nationalistic attitude to the French language can still be observed in modern France.

The central schools were further strengthened, especially in regard to competition with some religion-based private schools, by a provision that required almost anyone who desired a position with the government to present evidence that he had attended 'one of the Republic's schools'.[101] This gave the state schools an enormous competitive advantage over any private efforts.

Despite all these efforts, by the end of the 18th century the position of public education in France, especially that of the central schools, was still weaker than one might have expected. There was a shortage of qualified teachers and, oddly enough, a shortage of qualified students. The schools in Paris and several other major population centres did well, but throughout the country the story was not always as positive. One problem had to do with the organisation and curriculum of the schools. There was really no continuity in the curriculum and very little in the way of required courses. Thus, a 'graduate' from a central school might or might not have met some reasonable standards, either academic or curricular. In short, the system of central schools had not lived up to its promise. It remained for Napoleon to bring some order to it.

Education was high on his list of priorities, which were in large part the priorities of the middle class. Napoleon believed in a system of merit, and for such a system to be effective there must be some form of widespread education, especially at the secondary level. Besides, the state of French education was in sad shape when he began to rule. This fact was made abundantly clear by the results of a survey of all *Préfets* in the nation conducted in March 1801, under the direction of Minister of the Interior Jean-Antoine Chaptal. There were numerous complaints regarding the lack of schools in many areas, lack of professionalism among teachers, lack of discipline and attendance by students and, in a few areas, lack of religious education.

The issues of religious and primary education were partially resolved by the Concordat between the Pope and Napoleon, which allowed some of the religious elementary schools to be re-established. These schools had provided most of the education available to girls, and their re-establishment reflected Napoleon's desire to provide education for females, though not generally the same sort of education given to boys. In 1807, he suggested that religion and assorted domestic skills necessary for the attraction of husbands should be stressed for girls.[102]

While Napoleon's comments in this note regarding women would hardly be considered progressive today, his call for them to learn arithmetic, writing and the principles of their language, as well as history, geography, physics and botany were quite progressive for the period. Napoleon has been criticised for his attitude toward women and their education, but he was merely reflecting the historical trend in France. After all, it was not until the 20th century that women in France received the right to vote, and this was almost twenty-five years later than their sisters in America.

The issue of secondary education was extremely important to Napoleon, and he would ultimately open more than 300 secondary schools. In a letter to Interior Minister Jean-Antoine Chaptal on 11 June 1801, he outlined in some detail his opinions on the structure of education for boys, dividing it into two parts: the first, for pupils under the age of twelve, the second for those over twelve. The first four classes, or grades, would teach general topics such as reading, writing, history and the use of arms. The second part would be sub-divided into pupils destined for either civil or military careers. Civil careers would stress languages, rhetoric and philosophy; military careers mathematics, physics, chemistry and military matters. Both civil and military graduates would be guaranteed employment in their chosen careers.[103]

On 1 May 1802, a law established a new system of education[104] which was to become the foundation of that which exists in France to this day.

Under this new regime, elementary schools (écoles populaires) would be the responsibility of local municipalities. Napoleon had relatively little interest in this level of education and was not firmly committed to the mass education that would result from a state-wide elementary education system. Consequently, the religious schools were to share a significant amount of the responsibility for elementary education.

Secondary education, however, was critical for the future leaders of the nation, as well as members of the bureaucracy and the military; hence, Napoleon's greater interest. France had a strong interest in the curriculum being taught, and control would be easier if she established a strong system of secondary schools under the direction of a central authority. Many of these secondary schools would be established by private initiative, including clerical, but all such schools were controlled by the state. Covering students from roughly the age of 10 to 16, they would provide instruction designed to prepare students for higher levels. Indeed, some bonus plans were established for teachers who had large number of students qualifying for advancement.[105] At the age of seventeen, students would take a test to determine their educational future. Those who passed could attend the Sorbonne in Paris or any of the provincial universities, newly re-opened by Napoleon.

The heart of the new system was the establishment of thirty *lycées*, or special secondary schools, which replaced the *écoles centrales*. Every appeal court district was to have a *lycée*, and they were to be totally supported and controlled by the state. Scholarships were provided, with about one-third going to sons of the military and government and the rest for the best pupils from the secondary schools.[106]

The *lycées* had a six-year term of study. The curriculum included languages, modern literature, science and all other studies necessary for a 'liberal' education. Students wore uniforms and received military and religious education.

Each *lycée* was to have at least eight teachers, as well as three masters (a headmaster, an academic dean and a bursar). In a move reminiscent of the modern debate on the subject, the government provided a fixed salary for teachers but additionally provided bonuses for successful teachers. Teachers were also given a pension.

Napoleon chose teachers from a list of recommendations provided by inspectors and the Institute. The inspectors were given over-all responsibility for inspecting the schools on a regular basis. Teacher training was provided by the still existing *école normale supérieure*.

The *lycées* were augmented by several hundred other secondary schools and a similar number of private secondary schools. The *lycées*, however, were the heart and soul of the system.

It is clear that the new system introduced by Napoleon had more than one purpose. It was intended, of course, to provide an educated élite that could help run the country and the military. It was also designed to provide for an increased middle class, a middle class that would be successful and hence non-revolutionary. Moreover, there was a great emphasis on patriotism in the schools, an emphasis that was to increase during the years of the empire.

The years of the Consulate produced a real renaissance in French education. Napoleon spent more on education than on almost anything else. There were more schools than ever before and more students. He used them to promote his goals of equality, and much of what he began in the Consulate has survived into the modern era. In exile on St. Helena, he wrote:

> One of my great objectives was to render education accessible to everybody. I caused every institution to be formed upon a plan which offered instruction to the public, either gratis, or at a rate so moderate, as not to be beyond the means of the peasant. The museums were thrown open to the *canaille* [rabble]. My *canaille* would have become the best educated in the world. All my exertions were directed to illuminating the mass of the nation, instead of brutifying them by ignorance and superstition.[107]

NOTES

92 *Correspondance*, 26 December 1797, No. 2392, III, 614. Letter to Camus, President of the National Institute.

93 Farrington, *French Secondary Schools*, 1910, 56.

94 Ibid., 57.

95 Vignery, *Revolution and the Schools*.

96 See Bernard, *Education* for a more detailed discussion.

97 Ibid., 154.

98 Ibid., 171.

99 See Lefebvre, *Revolution*, and Soboul, *Understanding*.

100 Ibid.

101 Bernard, 185–86.

102 *Correspondance*, 15 May 1807, No. 12585, XV, 280–84.

103 Ibid., 11 June 1801, No. 5602, VII, 210–14, partially trans. in Thompson, 78–80.

104 Lefebvre, *18 Brumaire to Tilsit*.

105 Bernard, 1969.

106 Lefebvre, *18 Brumaire to Tilsit*; *Correspondance* 22 November 1801, No. 5874, VII, 416–29. Partially trans. in *The Mind of Napoleon; a selection from his written and spoken words*, ed. and trans. J. C. Herold. New York, 1955, 116.

107 O'Meara, II, 243.

AN EMPIRE IN THE WEST
The Louisiana Purchase

When the first Europeans began to settle in North America, they did not imagine the vast extent of the lands whose edges they were just beginning to penetrate. It did not take long, however, for the exploring nations of Europe to discover, to their collective amazement, the size of the North American continent. With discovery came further exploration, claims and counter-claims of land for their countries, competition and war.

By the time the American colonies became the United States of America, the overall vastness of North America was known and large segments of it had already been staked out by the major powers of Europe. British, American, French, Russian and Spanish interests collided and/or overlapped with one another. The Americans had the advantage, of course, as they were there and quickly began what would ultimately be an inexorable march westward. It was by no means certain that the Americans would get it all for themselves and, of course, they did not (just ask the Canadians!).

Most, but not all, Americans wanted the entire continent; some were not interested in paying so much as a farthing for anything beyond the Ohio River. One man who did want the entire continent, however, would rise in influence before and after the War of American Independence. Before the constitution, before the nation, Thomas Jefferson had a vision of a United States stretching 'from sea to shining sea'. Anyone can dream, but few can bring dreams such as this to reality. Jefferson could and did. One might postulate that he was America's intellectual and visionary match to France's Napoleon. American writer and historian Stephen E. Ambrose writes of Jefferson:

> As president he said that he awaited with impatience the day when the continent would be settled by a people 'speaking the same language, governed in similar forms and by similar laws'.
>
> In an age of imperialism, he was the greatest empire builder of all. More than any other man, he made it happen. His motives were many. He sought greatness for himself and for his nation. He rejected

the thought of North America's being divided up into nation-states on the European model. He wanted the principles of the American Revolution spread over the continent, shared equally by all.[108]

The biggest single prize in the westward expansion was what was known as the Louisiana Territory. Anchored in the southern port city of New Orleans, it quickly widened as its borders went north, encompassing close to one-third of the territory of the future United States, double what it was at the time. The territory had been claimed for France under Louis XIV in 1682 by the French explorer La Salle, but in 1762 was given, along with Florida and California, to Spain.

There it stayed until October 1800. Then, by a secret treaty between France and Spain, the Louisiana Territory was returned to France. When Jefferson heard of this, he became resolved to move as quickly as possible to obtain the territory for the United States. Louisiana under the Spanish, who were weak and growing weaker, was no threat to his long-term plans. Louisiana under Napoleon, however, was quite another story. Napoleon, like Jefferson, was an expansionist, and France might well have the means to exploit this large and potentially rich territory.

New Orleans was the key to the territory, and as a first step toward ultimate control it was necessary to control, or at least have unlimited access to, that port. Consequently, Jefferson sent Robert Livingston to discuss the matter with the French, as well as the possible availability of the Floridas, modern-day Florida then being divided into East and West Florida. Livingston, who was the American minister in Paris, was to make it clear that the United States would stand for nothing less than economic access to the port of New Orleans. That was the top priority, and it was a priority that if unresolved could lead to unhappy relations between France and the United States. In the meantime, Livingston made it clear to the French that he considered the continent to be America's destiny and strongly suggested that Napoleon simply give the territory to the United States.

Napoleon had already begun to realise that the French position in America was weak. His efforts in the Caribbean had been a disaster and had brought home to him the difficulties of undertaking an endeavour so far from France. If the British fleet had severely limited the success of his Egyptian campaign, he could all too well imagine what an alliance between Great Britain and the United States could do to his effort in the Louisiana Territories.

Jefferson was smart enough to recognise that such an alliance would worry Napoleon, and he made it clear that such an alliance was a very real possibility. Even so, events played into his hands in ways he could not control. Had Napoleon's efforts in Haiti, where he had tried to maintain a French military and colonial presence, succeeded, he would probably have taken a very different approach toward the Louisiana Territory and made moves to settle and directly control it.[109] Whether or not these moves would have been successful is an arguable point, but there is little doubt that the history of this period could have been greatly altered. Napoleon's failure in the Caribbean had repercussions far beyond the tiny island sphere of its immediate activity.

So it was that American and French interests reached a happy convergence. When James Monroe, who had become Jefferson's personal representative to Napoleon, began to broach the subject of New Orleans, he was astounded to discover that Napoleon was prepared to consider selling the United States the entire territory. Monroe's portfolio did not include negotiating a deal of such magnitude, but he was quick to understand the potential and began earnest discussions.

The price settled upon was just short of a gift: a mere sixty million francs, or about fifteen million dollars, bought the destiny of a nation. Jefferson's dream suddenly having moved a giant step toward reality, he overcame the objections of some in Congress. Napoleon had objections from Talleyrand, Joseph and Lucien but paid them no heed. On 30 April 1803, the Louisiana Territory, including the city of New Orleans, was formally transferred to the United States of America.

Some in Congress immediately sought to trade Louisiana for the Floridas, which to some easterners were more appropriate areas of expansion for the nation. Jefferson would have none of it, however:

Objections are raising to the Eastward against the vast extent of our boundaries, and propositions are made to exchange Louisiana, or a part of it, for the Floridas. But, as I have said, we shall get the Floridas without, and I would not give one inch of the waters of the Mississippi to any nation, because I see in a light very important to our peace the exclusive right to it's[sic] navigation ...[110]

It would be difficult to judge which man was happier with the deal, Jefferson or Napoleon. To Jefferson, this was a vindication of his dream and his presidency; it was a legacy that might match his writing of the Declaration of Independence and his work on building the infant nation. To Napoleon, it was payment for land that he knew he could never control and a guarantee that America and Great Britain would not unite against France over the issue. More importantly, he saw the growth of the United States as an important counterbalance to the power of Great Britain; an outflanking of the Royal Navy, as it were. His well-known response to the sale foretold the future power of the United States: 'The sale ensures forever the power of the United States, and I have given England a rival who, sooner or later, will humble her pride.'

NOTES

108 Ambrose. *Undaunted Courage*, 56–57. In the author's view, there is no better written account of this aspect of America's westward expansion.

109 Dumas Malone. *Jefferson the President: First Term 1801–1805*. Boston, 1970, 251.

110 Jefferson to John Breckinridge, 12 August 1803, in *The Political Writings of Thomas Jefferson*. Ed. Merrill D. Peterson. Annapolis Junction, Maryland, 1993, 148.

Nineteenth-century
engraving of Marshal
Berthier.

Nineteenth-century
engraving of Marshal
Bessières, by Riesner.

Nineteenth-century
engraving of General Duroc,
by Ambroise Tardieu
Direxit.

Nineteenth-century engraving of
Marshal Grouchy, by Rouillard.

Nineteenth-century engraving of
General Kléber.

Nineteenth-century engraving of
Marshal Lannes.

Nineteenth-century engraving of
Marshal Masséna.

Nineteenth-century engraving of
Marshal Murat, by Gialdrau.

Nineteenth-century engraving
of Marshal Ney.

Nineteenth-century engraving by
Rouillard of Marshal Soult.

Engraving of General Rapp from his
1823 memoirs.

Nineteenth-century engraving by Vauchelet of Marshal Poniatowski.

Twelve images by Vauthier from a set of 100 Marshals and Generals of the Revolution and Empire, *c.* 1830.

Left to right, top row:
Marshal Augereau
Marshal Jeanne Bernadotte
General Count Lazare
  Carnot
General Count Armand
  Caulaincourt
Marshal Louis Davout
General Louis Desaix

Left to right bottom row:
General Count Antoine
  Drouot
Marshal Etienne Macdonald
Marshal Adolphe Mortier
Marshal Count Nicolas
  Oudinot
General Count Dominique
  Vandamme
Marshal Claude Victor

Nineteenth-century engraving
of Talleyrand.

Nineteenth-century engraving
of Barras.

Nineteenth-century engraving
of Fouché.

1814 hand-coloured engraving of
Alexander I, by Laurent.

Nineteenth-century engraving of
Barclay de Tolly.

Nineteenth-century engraving
of Bagration.

Nineteenth-century engraving
of Benningsen.

1814 engraving by Velyn of
Archduke Charles.

1814 engraving of Prince Schwarzenberg.
In this portrait he wears the order of the
Golden Fleece, the Grand Cross of the
Order of Maria Theresia, and the
Order of Leopold.

First Empire papier-mâché snuffbox
of Wellington.

Nineteenth-century print of Metternich.

French Revolutionary engraving
(*c.* 1789–92) of Louis XVI in a
locket worn by delegates to the
National Assembly.

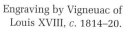

Engraving by Vigneuac of
Louis XVIII, *c.* 1814–20.

Nineteenth-century print
of Sir Sydney Smith.

THE HIGH POINT
OF A CAREER

If Napoleon was one of the great leaders in history, an argument certainly made here, then the period of the Consulate must be considered in many ways his high point. If he were a Caesar, then the Consulate was his Pax Romana even in the years when there was no actual peace. It was only during the Consulate that there were periods of actual peace, and one can only speculate on the future of France, Europe, and even the world, had peace lasted.

It was during the Consulate that French literature and drama began once again to flourish. Napoleon had always admired writers and wanted his legacy to include his remembrance as one who promoted French culture. He enjoyed reading. Even when on campaign he would take the time to attend the opera. Indeed, it was in 1800 at the opera house, La Scala, in Milan that Stendhal first actually saw his hero, First Consul Bonaparte.

Napoleon served as a patron of the arts and sciences, giving support in a variety of ways. Through his policies, the sciences were encouraged, as were advancements in art, music, literature and drama. Some consider the Consulate to have been something of a golden age of French culture, especially in literature.

There was, to be sure, more censorship than modern western democracies would deem appropriate, and for that Napoleon is often criticised. It is once again necessary to put things in their proper context: if not to justify, at least to understand. All European governments of the day exercised censorship to some extent. Direct criticism of a government was always a risky proposition and writing seen as being outside the acceptable moral code was often risky as well. The power of ideas, combined with the printing press, had challenged the Catholic Church and led to a new religious order in Europe. All governments understood – and feared – this power and were determined to take steps to control it as best they could.

Napoleon understood this as well as any ruler of the day and was quite prepared to use censorship to help maintain power. In April 1800, he gave the Ministry of the Interior responsibility for censorship of theatre and the Ministry of Police, under Fouché, responsibility for censorship of the press and all other written material, including literature.[111] In theory, no material directly opposed to the government was to be tolerated. In practice, a great deal of such material was overlooked. This was especially true of literature, which was generally seen as less threatening than the press.[112] The press was rather tightly controlled and a number of papers were shut down. Even under the much more restrictive Empire, literature was treated lightly and continued to thrive.

THE LEGION OF HONOUR

To a very large extent, it may be said that Napoleon wished to establish a meritocracy in France. His insistence on provisions for equality in the civil code and in the educational system; his promises to all factions that they would be treated equally, without regard to former rank or political beliefs; his promotion of equity and fairness in the tax system: all these are critical elements to a meritocracy. As First Consul, he had the opportunity to make countless appointments to the government, the courts, the clergy and the military. Even his sharpest critics credit him for making these appointments almost exclusively on the basis of ability rather than on the more traditional criteria. This, of course, should not be surprising, given that he can reasonably be said to have risen largely on the basis of his own talents rather than due to birthright or other factors.

It is a fact of human nature, however, that even the brightest or most highly skilled individuals do not always rise to meet their potential. Society offers a variety of powerful incentives, such as money or social status, but even these are often not enough. Reputation, a sense of honour, too, are powerful incentives.

Napoleon understood that people crave specific recognition for their accomplishments. It is for that reason that soldiers have always appreciated military medals almost as much as promotion. In war, soldiers may seek glory and honour on the battlefield. Glory and honour are sought elsewhere as well and must also be recognised. It is for that reason that virtually all societies, and many organisations, recognise the accomplishments of their citizens or members by awarding a medal, ribbon or some other item which the recipient can proudly wear or display.

Not surprisingly, therefore, Napoleon was determined to establish a method of national recognition for outstanding service to the state, whether in the military or civilian spheres. Coming as he did from a military background, it was only natural that he would establish a medal that he or others could pin directly on the person to be honoured. The military, of course, already had such honours. Napoleon sought one that would outshine all of these and be available to civilians as well. Thus was born, in 1802, the Legion of Honour (*Légion d'Honneur*).

As had been the case with many of his proposals in the development of the civil code, Napoleon was beset by arguments against his new Legion of Honour. Some, seeking to deride the very idea of such an item, called it a 'bauble'. Napoleon's response is often quoted today to justify other awards: 'It is with such baubles that men are led.'

Others objected to the same award being given to soldier and citizen, to officer and enlisted alike. To this objection Napoleon retorted that if France were to be truly egalitarian, all must be eligible for the same medal. In this he was surely right. Francklyn Paris sums it up rather nicely when he discusses Napoleon's awarding of the *Légion* to two inventors in the civilian sector:

> Oberkampf and Delessert, receiving the cross from Bonaparte – wearing the same insignia proudly displayed by the Little Corporal, the demigod of the time; the same ribbon and the same jewel worn by Ney, the 'bravest of the brave'; by Murat, the fiery and resplendent cavalryman; and lower down in the social scale, but on the same level heroically, by the drummer-boys who led the way over the bridge at Arcole – must have glowed with a pride martial in character, even though their exploits were of a peaceful nature.[113]

The *Légion* was attacked for exactly the opposite reason as well. Far from seeing it as egalitarian, some republicans feared that it was the beginning of a new nobility, a 'betrayal of the Republic by Bonaparte'.[114] Napoleon may or may not have had such developments in mind, but there can be no denying the enormous popularity that the *Légion* enjoyed with the citizens of France, then and now.

As was the case with many of Napoleon's reforms, the Legion of Honour outlasted its critics and remains one of Napoleon's most visible legacies. It is considered the ultimate honour in France and is a powerful incentive in all spheres of life. As the award is sometimes granted to those who are not French, it may be said to be a truly international award.

Incidentally, while there are traditional stories that hold to the contrary, official records indicate that no woman received the *Légion* until the 1850s. It is now available to all.

During the Empire, Napoleon combined his interest in education, especially the quality of teachers, with his concept of incentive by creating, in 1808, the Academic Palms. Designed to reward excellence in teaching, this award, like the Legion of Honour, serves yet today as an example of Napoleon's legacy. To those in academics, it is the ultimate mark of distinction within their profession, surpassed only by the *Légion* itself.

INFRASTRUCTURE: PHYSICAL AND ECONOMIC UNITY

To many politicians throughout history, the issue of infrastructure has been considered mundane at best, a drain on the treasury at worst. While all pay lip service to the need for roads, bridges, canals and even public buildings and monuments, only a few have recognised their economic and symbolic importance. Julius Caesar was one such person; his extensive public works projects gave a new sense of pride to Romans, to say nothing of quite a few good paying jobs. This did nothing to hurt his own ambitions and Caesar knew it. The Romans also had established for all time the importance of a good transportation system. It was no accident that they could boast that 'all roads lead to Rome', for they made sure that was the case. It was this system of roads that allowed such a far-flung empire to have any unity at all and made it easier for the legions to move rapidly across the empire to meet the increasing number of challenges to Rome's security.

Napoleon understood all this very well. So, many of his actions were designed to increase the unity of France; only a united France could defeat the domestic and foreign challenges with which she was beset. Laws, finances and education were important, but the keys to that unity were communication and transportation.

There was another consideration that led Napoleon in this direction. While France had very large coastlines on the Mediterranean, the Atlantic and the English Channel, she did not have the naval power to take full advantage of what should have been a major economic factor. It was therefore important that her internal transportation system be maximised to the greatest extent possible.

France is blessed with some important natural transportation corridors, and Napoleon moved to take full advantage of these. He built canals that connected Nantes and Brest, as well as the Rhône and the Rhine. This made it possible to ship goods from north to south, from the channel to the interior, all beyond the reach of the British Royal Navy, against whom he had no counter-balance. He built three great ports: Cherbourg, Brest and Antwerp.

Napoleon may not have wished to have all roads lead to Paris, but he certainly recognised the need for ease of travel throughout France and her spheres of influence. Nowhere was this a greater concern than in the Alps. Perhaps remembering his difficult trek through the Great Saint Bernard Pass, where in late May he still had had to deal with snow and ice and through which there was no road of any quality, he built not one but three roads. These roads were of the highest quality and opened transportation between France, Switzerland and Italy. Napoleon could be tight with money, but he spent an enormous amount – some 277 million francs – on a system of roads throughout France. He is not often thought of as an environmentalist or Johnny Appleseed, but he planted countless trees to protect roads throughout France from the sun. He created what today might be known as an environmental protection agency, or at least a national forest service, to protect France's natural environment, specifically forests and rivers.

While the beauty of Paris today comes in large part from the Second Empire of his nephew, Napoleon III, Napoleon Bonaparte did his share of improvements in the French capital. He was the first to pave the streets, and it was his idea to number all buildings with odd numbers on one side, even numbers on the other. While he was at it, he protected those buildings with Paris's first fire brigade. Of course, his triumphal arches and his expansion of the Louvre are among the best known of his building projects and have lasted until today.

The Consulate, then, was Napoleon at his best, especially on the domestic front. But the Consulate would end, and with it would go, in the eyes of many, the idealism with which Bonaparte was infected and with which he infected others. The question, of course, is what happened to cause this to occur. The answer is quite complex and contains elements both internal and external to the personality of Napoleon. Napoleon had sought something akin to absolute power. The power of an emperor, perhaps, but he had achieved that power while still Consul. Now he would be moved in different directions by forces largely beyond his control.

NOTES

111 *Cambridge Modern History*, 129.

112 For an excellent consideration of this overall issue, see Polowetzky, *Bond Never Broken*.

113 *Napoleon's Legion*, 30. This book is the definitive work on the subject. See also Cronin, 205–6.

114 Tulard, *Myth of the Saviour*, 123.

THE STRIKE
OF LIGHTNING

Man is by nature a violent creature. A study of history shows that we are forever seeking new ways to wreak havoc on each other by way of 'improvements' in the technology and techniques of war, torture and murder. Napoleon was destined to experience two of the three of these aspects of man's inhumanity to man.

When people or nations cannot accomplish their aims peacefully, they turn to violence. So it is with war; so also with murder. When the royalists finally realised that Napoleon was not to be the instrument of their return to power, they sought his removal. His overwhelming popularity with virtually all elements of society – including many royalists – made it clear that he could not to be removed by either electoral overthrow or *coup d'état*. They turned then to that time-tested, if reprehensible, method of more forceful and permanent removal: assassination.

In this endeavour, the British government, to its immense dishonour, was all too glad to assist. It had long given refuge to those *émigrés* and Bourbons violently opposed to Napoleon's reign. It mattered not one bit to the Bourbons and their sympathisers that Napoleon enjoyed virtually universal support in France, that he had succeeded where both the Bourbons and the Revolution had failed, that France was far better off for the advent of Bonaparte. They were Bourbons, and to rule was their right.

To the British, none of these things mattered either. Nor did it matter that they had quarrelled with Bourbon governments, that they had feared Louis XIV as much as they feared Bonaparte and might well come to fear Louis XVIII as well. That Napoleon had brought peace to Europe – a peace heartily embraced by British as well as French citizens – did not matter either. Since the fall of the Roman Empire, peace in Europe had been an exception rather than the rule. The Peace of Amiens was merely a pause in the long history of warfare between Great Britain and France, a history that would not end until the *Entente Cordiale* of the early twentieth century.

Napoleon was popular beyond anything that could be claimed by other rulers of the day. He had given the people all that they wanted and they reacted by giving him free rein over them. Not all elements of society, however, were completely satisfied with his rule. Hard-core Jacobins, those devoted keepers of the purest republican ideals of the Revolution, saw Napoleon as a betrayer of those ideals. They might applaud many of his reforms and recognise his popularity, but they could not tolerate his concentration of power into his own hands or his acceptance of the royalist elements of society, the hated *émigrés*.

It is not without irony that the other group opposed to Napoleon was precisely the group so despised by the Jacobins, namely the royalists, including many of the *émigrés* themselves. While they appreciated Napoleon's willingness to let many of them back into the country, they still longed for the power and privilege they once had. They had finally become convinced that Napoleon would never give that to them; nor would he do what they all desired more than anything else, restore the monarchy.

So it was that the two extremes of society were determined to bring about Napoleon's downfall. If they could not do it legitimately, they would turn to other means.

Napoleon most feared the Jacobins. They had a violent history and were suspected of conspiracies to kill him. The royalists, however, proved to be the real threat. In any event, Napoleon was not cowed; he was seen about Paris day and night, with only a minimum protective escort.

By the latter part of 1800, it was clear to all that Napoleon was there to stay and that the Bourbon dynasty was not going to return by virtue of any action by him. Devout royalists were determined to remove him by violence. The most famous and closest to success of their efforts was the episode of the 'infernal machine'.

Napoleon often attended the opera house; he enjoyed it and anyway Joséphine often insisted. On Christmas day of 1800, they were going to hear Haydn's oratorio *The Creation*. This work, written to an English text, had had its first perfomance in Vienna in April 1798, and Joséphine and Hortense were determined to hear it. Napoleon got into his coach and was to be followed by Joséphine and Hortense, accompanied by Napoleon's sister Caroline and General Jean Rapp, an *aide-de-camp* to Napoleon. Rapp detained Joséphine, suggesting that she should wear her shawl in Egyptian fashion. Napoleon, impatient as ever and thinking that the ladies were right behind him, ordered his coach to depart.

Georges Cadoudal, a devout royalist and trainer of terrorists, had set in motion a plot designed to end the era of Bonaparte once and for all. A cart loaded with a large wine cask was standing in the rue Sainte-Niçaise, on the route that Napoleon would take to the theatre. The cask was full of gunpowder and broken stones. Cadoudal's men had done their work well. They paid a young girl to mind the horse and positioned themselves in readiness for Napoleon's carriage. When it was in sight, they would light the fuse. The explosion would be large enough to destroy the carriage, indeed, the better part of the block.

Accounts differ as to what happened next. Either the cart was forced to move a little further away from the street, or Napoleon's carriage was going faster than expected, or the conspirators were slow to light the fuse. Whatever the case, Napoleon's carriage raced past the waiting bomb, which then exploded too late to kill him and too early to do major damage to Joséphine's carriage, which was not far behind. General Rapp relates:

> The ladies shrieked on hearing the report [explosion]; the carriage windows were broken, and Mademoiselle Beauharnais [Hortense] received a slight hurt on her hand. I alighted and crossed the *rue Niçaise*, which was strewn with the bodies of those who had been thrown down and the walls that had been shattered by the explosion. Neither the Consul nor any individual of his suite sustained any serious injury. When I entered the theatre Napoleon was seated in his box, calm and composed and looking at the audience through his opera-glass. Fouché was beside him. 'Joséphine,' said he, as soon as he observed me. She entered at that moment, and he did not finish his question. 'The rascals', said he, very coolly, 'wanted to blow me up. Bring me a book of the Oratorio.'[115]

Napoleon and his party were unharmed. The girl was one of nine killed; an additional twenty-six were wounded. More importantly, though unrealised at the time, the people were reminded that Napoleon was mortal. If the rumours of his death at Marengo had been troubling, the narrow escape from 'the infernal machine' was a real wake-up call. The success of the Revolution seemed to rest with Napoleon; there was no one else that could compare to him. The problem then, was two-fold: how to protect Napoleon from such plots and, closely related, how to ensure that his policies would prevail in the event of untimely demise. The answer to these twin problems would lead to a scandal and an Empire.

Napoleon assumed that the Jacobins were behind the plot, and many were arrested and sent into exile. Fouché tried to convince Napoleon that royalists and *émigrés* were responsible, but Napoleon refused to listen.[116] Eventually, however, the perpetrators were caught and the royalist nature of their motivations understood. The true culprits, of course, were safe in their London beds.

Almost three years later, in August 1803, Georges Cadoudal went to France himself, still determined to kill Napoleon and restore the Bourbons. This time, his plot was far more complex. He brought with him General Charles Pichegru, another devout royalist who was living in forced exile. Pichegru was convinced that he could contact presumably unhappy generals who would be very willing to remove Bonaparte and bring Louis XVIII to the throne.

It was true enough that there were some unhappy generals, though their numbers were few and their resolve weak. One possibility, and Pichegru's target, was General Jean Victor Moreau. If Moreau could convince some of his comrades to cooperate, Cadoudal's men could get close enough to Bonaparte to kill him.

Close indeed! The plot was straight from Shakespeare, from Caesar himself! When the time was right, conspirators would dress in uniforms and get close to Napoleon during a ceremony. One would pretend to give him a petition, then they would all stab him to death! *Et tu, Brute!*

All this depended on two things: Moreau's success in recruiting co-conspirators and the arrival of someone who could directly represent the Bourbon family. This last factor was the key, because without a Bourbon to take charge, there was no guarantee that there would be any move to bring them to power. One of Napoleon's brothers, or Talleyrand, or perhaps even Fouché, might take control instead. Discovery of a royalist plot could lead to a Jacobin revival. Nothing could be done, therefore, until all the players were in place.

Alas for the Bourbons, this was never to take place. On the morning of 14 February 1804, Napoleon was informed that the conspirators had been caught and arrested. Their plans had fallen apart, partly because Moreau seemed to feel he should be installed as military dictator and partly because the promised Bourbon prince had not yet arrived.

Napoleon was, naturally enough, livid at this turn of events. The conspiracy was obviously well organised and, unlike the 'infernal machine' plot, specific provisions to replace him had been made. This also removed all doubt in his mind that his real enemies were not the Jacobins but the royalists. This fact enraged Napoleon all the more. He had gone out of his way to bring them back into the mainstream of France. He had invited those who had left to return, had incorporated them in his government and restored their religion. Only on the questions of restoration of their lands and of a Bourbon king had he not given in. And this was how they repaid him? All the conspirators were caught and executed, including Cadoudal. This was not enough for Napoleon; the Bourbons must pay for this outrage directly.

It may never be known whether Louis Antoine, duc d'Enghien and a prince of the house of Bourbon, was the royalist prince who was to cooperate in the conspiracy. He was, however, living nearby in the German principality of Baden, and there was at least some evidence that he was indeed that prince. As a French citizen, he was subject to French law, and so on the night of 14 February Napoleon sent troops to abduct the young prince and bring him to trial. In captivity, d'Enghien told the soldiers that 'he had sworn implacable hatred against Bonaparte as well as against the French; he would take every occasion to make war on them'.[117] Indeed, he had already made war on France by leading troops against the Republican army in 1793. Later, despite the fact that he was a French citizen, he was in contact with British agents, a likely act of treason.

Napoleon reviewed the duke's file and discussed the matter with Talleyrand and others. He became convinced that d'Enghien was indeed involved in the plot and should, therefore, be treated as one of the conspirators. He was, accordingly, tried by a military court of seven colonels. They all voted 'guilty'. The penalty for treason was death.

Some of Napoleon's advisers were not happy at the prospect of killing the young man. They felt that mercy would better serve Napoleon's interests, that an abduction/murder would create a great deal of negative publicity. Joséphine herself asked Napoleon to spare his life. Napoleon could be a merciful man; this had been shown many times. Now, however, he felt that the time had come to make an example. If the Bourbons saw that even they were not exempt from retribution, perhaps they would cease their plotting against his life and try to wait him out. If that were the case, reasoned Napoleon, time would be on his side. Moreover, as a Corsican, the concept of revenge, of settling accounts, ran deep in his blood.

On 21 March, the duc d'Enghien was executed by firing squad. The shots of that squad reverberated throughout Europe. His execution created what was by far the greatest scandal in Napoleon's career. While most Frenchmen seemed to understand, if not support, the way he had settled this affair, foreign reaction was swift and negative. Napoleon was roundly condemned by his enemies; and many who were previously neutral condemned him as well.

Napoleon understood that this act had created controversy, but he accepted full responsibility and defended it to the last. Shortly afterwards he delivered a lengthy speech on the subject to the Council of State, a few excerpts of which are reproduced here:

> I can scarcely conceive that in so enlightened a city as Paris, in the capital of a great empire, such ridiculous rumours can be credited as those which have been circulating for the last few days. How can any one believe that a Bourbon Prince is here, that he is hiding at the German Ambassador's house and that I have not dared to have him arrested! ... We live no longer in the time of sanctuary. We are not obliged, as were the Athenians, to respect the temple of Minerva ... [we shall see] whether we owe much consideration to those, who under the cloak of diplomacy organise assassination and atrocious crimes. We shall see what is due to a family whose members have become the base tools of England. Let not France deceive herself! For here there will be neither peace nor quiet until the last Bourbon shall have been exterminated ... how, indeed, should the law of nations be claimed by those who have planned an assassination, who give orders for it and pay for it? By such a deed alone they put themselves beyond the pale of European nations. And then people talk to me of the right of sanctuary, of violation of territory! What utter nonsense! They know me very little. My veins run with blood, not water ... I ordered the prompt trial and execution of the duc d'Enghien, so that the returned émigrés might not be led into temptation ...[118]

On St. Helena, Napoleon repeatedly defended his actions in this affair. 'Was I to suffer that the comte d'Artois should send a parcel of miscreants to murder me and that a prince of his house should hover on the borders of the country I governed in order to profit by my assassination?'[119]

The duc d'Enghien had apparently sent Napoleon, through Talleyrand, a letter offering complete cooperation in return for his life. Talleyrand did not deliver the letter in time to save the duke's life. On St. Helena,

Napoleon suggested that had he seen the letter in time, he would probably have pardoned the duke.[120]

Within France, several results stemmed from the fate of d'Enghien. As stated, the royalists were silenced; they would bother him no more. Moreover, the Jacobins were silenced as well. In part, they were silenced because they saw the danger of any plots on their part. Of far greater importance, however, was their realisation that Bonaparte had finally sided with them; it was finally clear to the Jacobins that they did not need to fear a return to the Bourbons while Napoleon was in power. They could preserve much of the Revolution and prevent a Bourbon monarchy, by keeping Napoleon in power. Therefore, ironically, many Jacobins were willing to accept an emperor to forestall a king.[121]

One final point remains to be made concerning this affair. The British govenment would often deny that it supported attempts to kill Napoleon, but when Louis XVIII was restored to power, he declined to open an inquiry into the matter. Felix Markham, a British historian of considerable note, is probably right on target when he points out that: 'The complicity of the comte d'Artois and of English officials in the Cadoudal plot would have proved too embarrassing.'[122] The duc d'Enghien had led troops against the government of his own nation and sworn opposition to the current government. He had already engaged in treasonous acts and was found guilty in the 1804 plot to assassinate France's head of government. Such behaviour in any nation might well be punishable by death.[123]

NOTES

115 Rapp, 21.

116 de Melito, I, 405.

117 Cronin, 242. Cronin gives an excellent, detailed account of the two conspiracies discussed here (see 237–45).

118 de Melito, I, 617–21.

119 O'Meara, I, 293.

120 Ibid., II, 37–38.

121 Tulard, 127.

122 *Napoleon*, 99. No relation to the author.

123 For an excellent summary of the d'Enghien affair, see Proctor Patterson Jones, 'From Glory to Treachery: The Story of the duc d'Enghien', *Selected Papers of the Consortium on Revolutionary Europe 1999*.

THE FUTURE THAT COULD HAVE BEEN
The Peace of Amiens

The Peace of Lunéville, signed in February 1801 between France and Austria after Marengo and the second Italian campaign, left Great Britain isolated in her state of war against France. Prime Minister William Pitt's government had twice rallied a continental coalition against France. Twice the coalition had failed. This was too much for the English to tolerate, and Pitt was unwillingly retired from government. The new government was compelled by circumstance to seek a peace with Napoleon. They did not really want peace, for they did not trust the French, and especially Napoleon, whom they feared had great ambitions. But there were no others to join them, and they were not about to challenge France alone. Moreover, the British people were tired of war and its enormous cost. If the French wanted their natural borders and the young Bonaparte for their leader, then that was quite fine with them. They felt secure on their side of the English Channel. Their unchallenged fleet was their guarantor of freedom and security.

Security was certainly a legitimate concern. Napoleon had developed a strong relationship with Tsar Paul of Russia. While Paul failed to accept Napoleon's offer of a grand alliance, he did take other steps to distance himself from the British. Paul was strangled in his bedroom in March 1801, quite possibly at the direction of the British, and his 23-year-old son Alexander took over. Nevertheless, there was no guarantee that, despite his efforts to re-establish closer relations with the British, Tsar Alexander I would prove completely reliable in his support of British interests.

Napoleon was making moves on other fronts as well. He gained the territory of Louisiana from the Spanish, as well as the island of Elba. Other treaties began to close the door on British trade. In October 1800, France and the United States signed a treaty of friendship that included provisions for free trade on the high seas. In short, the British were being outflanked and were unable or unwilling to do much about it, at least for the time being.

Internal difficulties were also an increasing concern to the British people. Their economy had suffered as a result of the wars against

France, and the closing off of some ports of trade would do nothing but make that worse. Poverty, made worse by years of poor harvests, was entirely too prevalent and the popularity of the government was at a very low ebb. The increasing insanity of King George III did nothing to make things any better.

Reluctantly, the new British government entered into peace negotiations with France, represented by Napoleon's brother Joseph, at the town of Amiens. In reality, peace was already at hand, and the two sides had reached preliminary agreement by 1 October 1801. The Peace of Amiens, formally ratified on 25 March 1802, was a diplomatic *coup* for France and Napoleon. It effectively ended all opposition to the current situation on the continent and removed all British continental claims. Egypt, once again in British hands, was returned to Turkey, and the Order of the Knights Hospitaller of St. John of Jerusalem, otherwise known as the Knights of Malta, were to regain control of the island of Malta. France, on the other hand, kept all its natural borders as well as Holland and several territories in Italy. While the British people breathed a sigh of relief, the French were exuberant. In point of fact, France had won.

One of the more interesting 'side issues' discussed during the negotiations was the question of prisoners of war. We can get a glimpse of Napoleon's approach and of his humanity by following his actions on that issue. His attitude was reflected in a letter to France's Minister of Foreign Affairs Talleyrand dated 10 March 1800, which discusses the exchange of some specific pisoners. Napoleon goes on to say

> how unworthy of the English nation is the threat to treat French prisoners in England more harshly. Is it possible that the nation of Newton and Locke can so far forget itself? Prisoners, indeed, neither can nor should be held responsible for the conduct of their government. They depend entirely on the generosity of the capturing power. These being the principles of the French Government, it will never copy the hateful practice of reprisals.[124]

After asking his Minister of Marine the legitimate question as to why 'are the English prisoners being given a pound of beef, while the soldiers' ration is only half a pound,'[125] Napoleon then sets forth the official policy on prisoners in a decree of 14 March 1800:

The Consuls of the Republic, considering that prisoners of war are entrusted to the care and humanity of the nations into whose power the fortune of battle has placed them, decree:

Article 1. The Ministers of War and of Marine will use all means in their power to provide food and clothing for the Russian, Austrian and English prisoners. They will ensure that they are treated with every consideration compatible with public safety.

Article 2. They will also take all necessary measures to speed up the exchange of prisoners.[126]

Europe celebrated the peace, though perhaps the number who thought it would last was somewhat less than the number of celebrants. All the world became fascinated with this amazing young man who had done so much so quickly. Paris, which had always been a major destination for travellers, became even more so after Amiens. The English, especially, thronged to Paris. The French were much less likely to return the favour to London. British historian Michael Lewis discusses the large number of British visitors to Paris and then writes:

In those happy days a Frenchman was equally free to travel in Britain at all times – if he wanted to. Normally, however, he did not exercise his privilege to anything like the same extent: not because we were more than usually rude to him in wartime, but because we were apt to be rude to all foreigners always ... Besides, where to us Paris was on the road to Vienna or Rome, for the Frenchman the road to London might almost be said to stop there.[127]

Wordsworth reflects the feelings of some that all of this interest in Napoleon is misguided:

Is it a Reed that's shaken by the wind,
    Or what is it that ye go forth to see?
Lords, Lawyers, Statesmen, Squires of low degree,
    Men known, and men unknown, Sick, Lame, and Blind,
Post forward all, like Creatures of one kind,
    With first-fruit offerings crowd to bend the knee
In France, before the new-born Majesty.

Calais: August, 1802

WINDS OF WAR

The Peace of Amiens, signed in 1801, had brought to Europe a taste of peace, prosperity and friendship. Trade flourished in England, France and the rest of Europe. Tourists flocked to Paris from all over Europe. Peace brings with it untold dividends of saved lives and treasure, of scientific and cultural advancement, of the ability of people to live as people should always live: free from want and fear. Sadly, however, the history of humanity is far more the history of war than of peace. Such was to be the case in the first years of the 19th century.

Many in Great Britain had not trusted the French, even as they agreed to the peace. The vote in Parliament to ratify the treaty had been overwhelming, but it had masked the desire of many to oppose the growing power of France. As was the case throughout Europe, many British leaders wanted the restoration of the Bourbon monarchy. They had not trusted the French Revolution and were appalled at what they considered to be its excesses. Bonaparte had certainly brought stability to France, and the guillotine was no longer active, but all this meant to his opponents was that he was now free to pursue ambitious expansionist goals.

Great Britain's ambivalent attitude toward the Peace of Amiens was represented in the person of their chosen ambassador to France. Lord Whitworth had never supported the treaty and had little desire to see it last. He was none too shy about expressing these sentiments. He sent a veritable deluge of reports to his government, filled with denunciations of Bonaparte and claims that the people were unhappy with him.

While it may seem amazing that the reports of one man could be taken seriously without any corroboration, that is exactly what happened. These reports, coupled with continued fears that Napoleon would seek to expand French borders and might use the time of peace to prepare for war against them led the British government deliberately to violate the Peace of Amiens in two critical areas.

Little was said in the treaty regarding possessions on the continent of Europe. France was to return Taranto to the King of Naples, which it quickly did. The British were to evacuate Alexandria and return it to Turkey. They were also to abandon the island of Malta, which had passed to their control. The loss of these would, of course, weaken Great Britain's position in the Mediterranean, but she had accepted the terms of the treaty and was obliged to honour them. This she would not do.

The deadline for the withdrawal from Malta was September 1802. The month came and went, as did October, November and December. By the year's end, the British were still there and still in Alexandria. This situation alarmed Napoleon, who did not want war. His detractors have always suggested that he did, but any analysis of his actions, to say nothing of France's state of actual readiness for war, would lead to the opposite conclusion.

Napoleon had complied with his treaty obligations. Great Britain had not. None the less, those British who wanted war held up as examples of Napoleon's expansionist aims his actions in several areas. Modern-day detractors claim that Napoleon was simply using the time of peace to expand France's borders.[128] Even if the claim is accepted as legitimate, the fact remains that the Peace of Amiens had no provisions to forbid such actions.

Twice Napoleon had gone to Italy to remove threatening foreign influence there. The second time he captured Piedmont, he offered the return of its king, but the king refused to return. Napoleon then established a new government and made the region a part of France. In the process, he brought the people of the Piedmont the same advantages he brought to the people of France and also prevented the possible isolation of the Cisalpine Republic.

This move provided additional stability and security in the area and helped buffer France against further aggressive moves by Austria in the region. The people of the Piedmont were generally supportive of the move, and it was not prohibited, or even mentioned, in the Peace of Amiens. None the less, The British saw it as a dangerous example of Napoleon's expansionist intentions.

Their fears were further heightened by the publication of a report by Colonel Sébastiani which suggested that France could easily retake Egypt. This report was, without doubt, provocative, but could hardly be taken as a representation of Napoleon's intentions. The fact that *The Times* of London chose at this time to print large passages of Sir Robert Wilson's *History of the British Expedition to Egypt* that once again raised the false accusation that Napoleon had poisoned his own sick at Jaffa, did nothing to smooth relations between the two countries.

Personal attacks on Napoleon were hardly a sign of a desire for peace and friendship, but the attacks increased and spread to attacks on Joséphine and other family members. They were vicious in nature, and

Napoleon was understandably furious with a British government that allowed them to be published.

Finally, the British were outraged by Napoleon's intervention in what amounted to a civil war in Switzerland, a civil war that was fanned by the British government.[129] His intervention was reasonable, brought peace to the area and was accepted by all parties on the continent. To the British, however, it was unacceptable.

Malta was the primary cause of the disagreements that would lead to the rupture of the peace, but Malta was, in reality, only an excuse, a symbol.[130] The real problems for the British were Belgium and Holland. French control of these areas, especially the port of Antwerp, put them entirely too close to England for comfort and had the potential for significant restriction of British continental trade. As long as France controlled these areas, a lasting peace was unlikely.

Why, then, did Napoleon refuse to give up control of these areas, if that would have brought peace? The answer lies in the internal politics and national pride of France. Much of Belgium is French-speaking and had always been seen as a potential part of France. Moreover, the goal of gaining territory that would expand France to her so-called 'natural borders' had been a priority since the days of Louis XIV. Holland and Belgium were two of the primary gains of the wars of the French Revolution. Any leader who willingly gave them up would risk a major backlash of popular opinion in France.

One must also question whether or not surrender of these areas would, in the long run, be enough to guarantee peace. The British had long believed that their security depended on the existence of a balance of power on the continent. If France were allowed drastically to alter that balance, they could not feel secure. If the powers in Europe united against Great Britain they could ultimately trump her naval advantage and could either invade or, at the very least, destroy her trade. Therefore, like all governments, the British government followed policies that were self-interested.

Having said that, it is nevertheless unfortunate that the British chose to end the Peace of Amiens. No one would deny that Napoleon was ambitious, and he certainly wanted to – and did – extend France to her age-old dream of the natural boundaries, which included the Low Countries and the west bank of the Rhine. Still, there was good reason to believe that he was prepared to stop there and focus his ambition on the domestic issues where he was having such great success. When war was forced on Napoleon, it required him to refocus his ambition into areas of conquest. This approach would prove successful for some time, but would eventually end with his defeat and exile.

There is a great deal of irony in the other factor that perhaps made war inevitable. While it is reasonable to suggest that Great Britain was the driving force behind the various coalitions against France, the fact remains that she was unable to force any other nation to declare war on France. When these nations decided to do so it was because they could not stand – and indeed, greatly feared – the Revolutionary ideals upon which the French Republic, and then the French Empire, were based. From the beginning, they were determined to remove what they saw as a very dangerous open sore, a sore that could spread its infection to their own peoples.

This is, perhaps, the reason that they so hated Napoleon right from the very beginning. It was bad enough that he was a leader without a birthright. He was a noble, perhaps, but a *Corsican* noble, and in their gilded ranks that did not count. As the rupture of Amiens became apparent, the British press delighted in making often bitter, almost always absurd, personal attacks on Napoleon and his family. The history of the accession of kings and emperors is filled with violence, treachery, murder and politics most foul; but it was *Napoleon* who was labelled 'The Usurper'. He was to be demonised; future wars would not be against France but against 'the Ogre', and no quarter would be given. The British had made a somewhat similar attempt to demonise George Washington during the War of American Independence, but that effort was nothing compared to their effort against Napoleon.

Some British writers sought to demonise Napoleon quite literally. They divided his name – Napoleon Buonaparte – into three sets of six letters:

NAPOLE ON BUON APARTE

That this division was possible led to the rather amazing claim that this equated his name with the number 666, which some consider to be the sign of the devil. Nor was this an isolated concept. More than one political cartoon of the day involved Napoleon with old Beelzebub himself!

Indeed, the process of demonising Napoleon had begun even as Amiens was being signed in 1801. In the words of one British historian specialising in this period:

The British had always regarded Napoleon as an unscrupulous political gangster: now Whitworth's dispatches portrayed him as a deranged tyrant, of the same ilk as the late mad Tsar Paul of Russia. The more percipient began to appreciate with alarm the true nature of the new French regime, with the energies let loose by the Revolution now steered by a single untrammelled will. The ambition seemed insatiable and the hatred of Britain unrelenting. Napoleon's metamorphosis in the British mind to full-blown bogeyman, both inhuman and superhuman, was now complete and beyond debate.[131]

The irony is, of course, that by insisting on fighting Napoleon, they gave him the opportunity to conquer their territories and bring to their people the very ideas and reforms that were so feared by the old regimes. Had they left him alone, accepted him as ruler of France and one of them, it is at least possible that none of that would have happened. Napoleon was ambitious, and that characteristic would eventually get the better of him and lead to his downfall. However, for the *anciens régimes* it would be too late. They would present the illusion of remaining in power for much of the rest of the century, but their days were numbered when they first led Napoleon to cross his borders into Germany.

A lasting peace between Great Britain and France might not have been possible, but diplomatic efforts to avoid war continued. Contrary to some reports, Napoleon took no steps to prepare for war. When faced with the British desire to maintain the port in Malta, he offered other, equally strategic, options. The British insulted Napoleon by offering bribes to his negotiators.

Napoleon was not willing to accede to the British suggestion that they maintain control of Malta for a period of ten years, but he continued to try to devise a compromise that would satisfy both British demands for a longer stay in Malta and French desire that the British stay for the shortest time possible. In early May 1803 he suggested to Lord Whitworth that the British might stay for some period of time, after which control of the island might be given to Russia. This proposal was rejected and Whitworth's dispatch to Lord Hawkesbury on the subject reveals a great deal of his underlying attitude towards Napoleon, an attitude that may well have doomed all peace efforts:

To all that I have said I have only to add that it is necessary to take the violence of this man's character into the calculation. He certainly does require every degree of management in dealing with him. Were he to be driven to desperation, he might, it is true, do perhaps great mischief to this country and to himself; but it would probably not be without entailing upon us a considerable share also. My position is a very difficult and a very delicate one.[132]

Later that same day, Whitworth writes again to Hawkesbury:

I am persuaded that the First Consul is determined to avoid a rupture if possible; but he is so completely governed by his temper that there is no possibility of answering for him."[133]

In May, His Excellency, no doubt satisfied with his 'success', returned to London. Napoleon made one last effort to maintain the peace, sending him a message acquiescing with the British demand to keep Malta for ten years, provided that he could maintain Taranto for a like period. Whitworth did not give him the courtesy of a reply, but Napoleon's effort was soon rejected by the British government. On 16 May, King George held council on the subject of war or peace, and on the 18th, the Royal Navy began to seize all French ships. Contrary to law and custom, this was done without a formal declaration of war, an act that must have surely been designed to infuriate the First Consul.

Infuriate him it did. Napoleon immediately retaliated by refusing exit passports to all British citizens in France, effectively making them prisoners of war. Those *détenus* (detainees) who found themselves trapped in France by the outbreak of hostilities were mostly upper class British citizens who were in France either on business or vacation when the peace broke down. Coming from politics, law, clergy, medicine, or academia, the men among them were frequently referred to as 'traveling gentlemen', or 'TGs', and often had their families with them.[134]

Along with the 'respectable' members of British society, the *détenu* population included a less savoury group. These included a criminal element, debtors and other people whose motive for being in France was somewhat different from that of the TGs. As Lawrence points out, this presented an interesting problem for both classes of *détenu*:

This involuntary association of the honourable part of the community with individuals of a different character was disagreeable to
both parties. It was not only disgraceful to the first, but it made them
in a manner responsible for the misconduct of the others; and forced
the latter, who came abroad perhaps with the intention of reforming
among strangers, to live among their countrymen, who were
acquainted with their misdemeanours.[135]

Such, it seems, are the inconveniences of war. The British were capturing
French ships and imprisoning French merchant seamen, but were
outraged at Napoleon's action. Lord Hawkesbury wrote to Talleyrand that
while British action was consistent with 'European common law',
Napoleon's actions were 'contrary to the practice of all civilised nations'
and a 'submission to an unexampled outrage upon the universal principles and practice of that law [of civilised nations]'.[136] Neither nation's
action was completely appropriate, but neither's action was rescinded.

Although it would be some time before actual fighting began, France
and Great Britain were again at war. It is hard to imagine any advantage
from this situation for either party. Neither was prepared for war and the
citizens of both nations were quite happy with peace, as was the whole
of Europe. Even Napoleon's detractors in Europe held the British responsible. Some suggested that they should have shown as much goodwill as
France, and even Bourbon supporters understood that Napoleon was
reluctant to go to war. Charles James Fox, leader of the peace party, and
William Wilberforce, who felt that the British had violated their public
faith, echoed these sentiments at home.

Talleyrand, whose memoirs show little love for Napoleon and are in
large measure an attempt to justify his own often disreputable actions,
none the less concludes:

> The English government had made peace only out of necessity; as
> soon as the home difficulties which had caused the making of peace
> almost unavoidable were overcome, the English cabinet who had not
> yet restored Malta and wished to keep it, seized the occasion offered
> by the annexation of Piedmont to France and took up arms again.[137]

None of this is to remove all responsibility for the resumption of hostilities from Napoleon. He had failed to move trade negotiations forward, a

fact which gave the British a legitimate complaint, as the Peace of Amiens had called for the development of better trade relations. This refusal fore-shadowed what ultimately would become one of Napoleon's biggest weaknesses, namely his belief that the continent could somehow be kept from trading with Great Britain. That belief, which should have been seen as absurd, would be a major factor in his downfall.

It may also be true that Napoleon stood to gain somewhat from a war as well. Jean Tulard suggests that Napoleon needed a war to distract 'the revolutionary bourgeoisie' from his ever-increasing power; that the image of a saviour – through military glory – needed to be maintained.[138] While Tulard's suggestion that Napoleon had this in mind during the negotia-tions with the British is rejected here, it may well be that Tulard has iden-tified one possible advantage that Napoleon eventually gained. An equally strong counter-argument can be made, however, that Napoleon as the producer of peace and prosperity, supported by the army and police, hardly needed to fear general discontent with his rule.

Perhaps the historian Bainville says it best, as he describes the end of peace:

> France took up arms again without enthusiasm, with resignation, fatalistically. Bonaparte himself, with that mobility of mind which showed him affairs in their most varied aspects, would gladly have held on to this peace, the benefits of which had won him such popu-larity and gratitude; but reason told him that war was inevitable. And he was too intelligent not to see that it would be a duel to the death. He accepted it as a law of destiny, with which it was vain to parry. France accepted it likewise. Men saw that it was still the same war which had been going on since 1792. And to end it, on whom could they count if not on the First Consul?[139]

War came in May, but not hostilities. Napoleon, stymied by the Channel, could not carry the war to England; the Royal Navy would not be defeated by the French navy. Napoleon dreamed of a tunnel under the Channel, but had no 'Chunnel', no TGV in which to send his troops from Paris to London. To invade England required more than he had, so he had little choice but to wait and play the diplomatic game.

The British. too, had to wait. Mastery of the seas is not the same as mastery of the land. For that, she needed allies; none were to be had, at least for the moment. Great Britain was seen as the betrayer of the treaty; other treaties between the continental powers and France would, for a little while longer, maintain peace on the continent.

Napoleon, meanwhile, had other things on his mind.

NOTES

124 *Correspondance*, 10 March 1800, No. 4655, VI, 221, translation in Howard, No. 494.
125 Ibid., 12 March 1800, No. 4663, VI, 230 (12 March 1800).
126 Ibid., 14 March 1800, No. 4669, VI, 234, translation in Howard, No. 497.
127 *Napoleon and his British Captives*, 19.
128 See, for example, Connelly, 71.
129 Cronin, 230–31.
130 Bainville, 148.
131 Lloyd, *The French Are Coming!*
132 Lord Whitworth to Lord Hawkesbury, 4 May 1803. *England and Napoleon in 1803, Being The Despatches of Lord Whitworth and Others. Now first printed from the originals in the record office. For the Royal Historical Society*. Ed. Oscar Browning. London and New York, 1887, 220–21.
133 Ibid., 223.
134 Lewis, 20.
135 *A Picture of Verdun*, I: 20–21. Lawrence was the son of a rich planter.
136 Lord Hawkesbury to Talleyrand, 14 August 1803, *Despatches of Lord Whitworth*, 292.
137 *Memoirs of Talleyrand*, 220.
138 Tulard, 134.
139 Bainville, 152.

PART THREE

A REPUBLICAN
EMPEROR

EMPIRE

The attempts on his life had made one thing clear to Napoleon and to the nation: they were only a bullet or bomb away from chaos. Napoleon's brother Joseph could be considered a likely successor but there was no guarantee that he would be accepted by all who would make the final decision. In chaos, anything could happen. To many, the fear was that the 'anything' might be a return of the Bourbons and the end of all that France had gained during the years of the Revolution and the Consulate.

Napoleon understood this and had taken steps to solve the problem. He had been made First Consul for a term of ten years, then, after an overwhelming referendum in August 1802, for life, with the right to appoint successor. His powers were then increased to the point where he already resembled an imperial ruler.

These moves had been made with the strong approval of most of society. At first, the Republicans were suspicious. Then the near success of the royalist plots convinced them that Napoleon under any circumstance was better than no Napoleon at all. Thus, in the space of a relatively few years, the thoughts of Napoleon and others turned to the idea of an empire.

France would never stand for a king; that would bring back too many ugly memories. An emperor, on the other hand, had an entirely different connotation. It did not recall the Bourbons but rather the Roman Empire and, even closer to home, Charlemagne. The word 'empire' had already been used to describe France's hegemony over other territories, so the concept was hardly new or alarming to the people.

Moreover, Napoleon would not gain the title of emperor by birthright. He would gain it by virtue of two factors: his own talents and the will of the people. He had already shown France, and the world, what he could do. The French, at least, were pleased with what they saw and wanted more.

By 1804, public and political opinion held that Napoleon should be granted the title 'Emperor of the French'. He had no heir, a fact which no doubt consoled some of those who questioned the need of a hereditary government. But it was precisely the concept of heredity that was to be protection against plots on his life, so he was also given the right to adopt an heir if he failed to have a son of his own. The requirement that the heir be male was to the modern eye a step backward, but it was in keeping with the expectations of the time.

Many look on the establishment of the empire with amazement; the more so, given its Republican support. One must remember, however, that in accepting an empire the French did not see themselves as returning to the days of the Bourbons. On the contrary, this was a strong step to prevent just that from happening. In many ways Napoleon had proved to be a Republican, a defender of the Revolution. France must now take steps to protect the protector. The empire was, in the words of the notable French historian Jean Tulard: 'first and foremost a dictatorship of public safety, designed to preserve the achievements of the Revolution'.[140]

Napoleon consulted the various branches of government and found a deep well of support among all political wings, including those with strong Republican feelings. Ever mindful that he wanted to rule with the consent of the people, and realising that their approval of this move would disarm most of its critics, he put the question to the people, who voted overwhelmingly for it.

Napoleon and his advisers next turned to the question of the coronation. The biggest single issue was whether to ask the Pope to participate in the ceremony. Most of his advisers were against it, arguing that people would see that as a move to restore even more influence to the Catholic Church. The Concordat was still Napoleon's most controversial move, especially with the Republicans whose support for his new role he so desperately needed. Moreover, he was becoming emperor on his own merits and because of the will of the people; the participation of the Pope seemed incongruous with that all-important fact. However, Napoleon was mindful of the powerful symbolism of legitimacy that the Pope's participation would give to the man in the street, and his wishes ultimately prevailed.

The cathedral of Notre-Dame was quickly chosen as the site for the ceremony and the famous historical painter Jacques-Louis David was put in charge of designing decorations for the occasion. His painting of the event – showing an already crowned Napoleon preparing to place a crown on Joséphine's head – would, of course, come to be its defining image and one of the best known of all works of art from the period.

Empires must have a symbol, and the discussion centered on the cock, the lion, the elephant and the eagle. Each had its drawbacks; the support for the cock is reminiscent of Ben Franklin's support for the turkey as the symbol of the United States. Both the American republic and the French empire ultimately decided on the eagle.

Imperial families must also have a symbol, and for his Napoleon chose the bee. This selection reflects Napoleon's desire to provide ties between his empire and the ancient empires of Gaul. Historians of the day believed that the bee had been the symbol of King Chilpéric, who ruled the Franks in the 6th century. That claim is somewhat questionable, but the bee became the symbol none the less.

Napoleon had an excellent sense of history and understood the importance of his being seen as a part of it. While the symbols of the empire were often selected to reflect those of Rome – the Roman standards had sported eagles, for example – it was to the French emperor Charlemagne that Napoleon most wanted people to see his ties. He was able to obtain a sword claimed to be Charlemagne's, but the original crown was not to be found. Napoleon used two crowns, one designed to look like Charlemagne's and the other a gold laurel wreath of the style used by the Roman Caesars.

The Pope arrived, and all went, almost, according to plan. When the Pope realised that Napoleon and Joséphine had been married in a civil rather than a religious ceremony, he balked at his participation in the coronation. Accordingly, the two were re-married in a private religious ceremony. The Pope was happy and all went smoothly thereafter.

The reply of the average man in the street, or the average historian, if asked what they remembered most about the coronation, would probably have been the fact that Napoleon 'took the crown out of the Pope's hands and crowned himself'. This act is seen by many as impetuous, arrogant and insulting to the Pope. It is often used as an example of Napoleon's overriding ambition, or perhaps worse.

However, Napoleon had discussed this allegedly impromptu act at some length with advisers, and all agreed that it would be the appropriate thing to do. The Pope was duly informed and offered no objection. It was, then, a planned aspect of the ceremony. The question, then, is 'why?'

To understand the reason it is necessary to understand the history of the relations between the kings of Europe and the Popes. In early 8th-century France, kings were weak, and the real power resided in the 'Mayor of the Palace'. In 732, Charles ('The Hammer') Martel became Mayor of the Palace. It was he who stopped the march of Islam into central France, solidified the Christian church in his kingdom and established the tradition of a strong central government in France.

In 741, Martel's son Pepin ('The Short') became Mayor of the Palace, serving under King Childeric. He was a weak king, and in 752 the nobles chose King Pepin after he had secured the personal support of the Pope. Several years later, the Pope travelled to Paris to endorse Pepin's reign. This began a tradition of alliances between the kings of France and the Popes in Rome.

When Pepin's son Charlemagne became King of the Franks in 768, he continued that tradition. In 799, Pope Leo III was nearly killed by the citizens of Rome, but the following year Charlemagne took his army to Rome and restored him to his papal throne. The Pope, in a surprise move on Christmas Day of the year 800, crowned Charlemagne 'Emperor of the Romans' and head of a new Holy Roman Empire.

Charlemagne almost immediately recognised his mistake in allowing this to happen. In crowning him emperor, the Pope was laying claim to having the power to anoint – and perhaps remove – any secular ruler. Charlemagne made efforts to downplay this power, by banishing the Pope from the coronation of his son, for example, but the damage was done.

As a result of the Papal endorsement of Pepin and Charlemagne, the separation of Church and state was virtually non-existent in Europe. Throughout the Middle Ages and on into the reign of the Bourbons, the Church laid claim to supremacy in all matters.

That might have been acceptable to 'their most Catholic majesties', as the Bourbon kings were called, but it was not acceptable to the Republicans of the Revolution, and it was most certainly not acceptable to a self-made man like Napoleon. He was being crowned emperor as a consequence of his own talents and wanted to owe his crown to no one but the people themselves. Napoleon had no better way to set right the mistakes of Pepin and Charlemagne and to make it clear the source of his power, than to place the crown on his own head.

The Pope had objected to the imperial oath, in particular the part that committed Napoleon to 'uphold religious liberties'. He was evidently unwilling even then to accept the fact that there was more than one religion which the French citizens could follow. This was an affront to one of the most fundamental gains of the Revolution, but a compromise was reached that allowed the Pope to leave the ceremony prior to Napoleon's taking the oath.

On 2 December 1804, First Consul Bonaparte became Napoleon I, Emperor of the French. He swore an oath to rule 'only in the interests of the happiness and glory of the French people'. If the Consulate had emphasised the happiness of the French people, the Empire, though not necessarily out of design or desire, would emphasise their glory.

It would not necessarily be a change for the better.

NOTE

140. Tulard, 128.

RESUMPTION
OF HOSTILITIES

The period of the Consulate had been largely peaceful. Consequently, Napoleon had been able to concentrate on the domestic
reforms that were so necessary to the 'happiness of France' and
which are in most ways his most important concrete legacy. Even the
rupture of the Peace of Amiens did not lead to immediate hostilities. It
signalled, however, an end to the era of reform and the beginning of an
era of war. Napoleon's talent, energy and commitment were enough to
allow him to run France even while leading its armies. But without doubt
for the remainder of his career he would be most concerned with war and
the politics that surrounded it.

Napoleon did not want the state of continual war that he faced during
the Empire. These wars were the outgrowth of the Revolutionary Wars
which preceded him and the absolute refusal of the other European
monarchs to accept him as the ruler of France. This continual state of war
was due largely to the constant efforts by the British to keep the continent
at war with France. For the British alone refused formally to acknowledge
Napoleon as emperor; the other nations of Europe considered him an
upstart, but they accepted the reality of his throne.

With war declared, Napoleon concentrated his army along the coast of
the English Channel, centred on the port of Boulogne. The British
government was quite convinced that Napoleon was going to invade.
This was a reasonable belief, of course, because that is exactly what he
wanted to do. The English countryside was blanketed with broadsides
(papers handed out or posted) warning of the danger and of the dire
consequences that would follow. These broadsides had a strong effect on
public opinion and helped put the country in a psychological state of
war against France that led to increased support for the government's
policies.[141]

If it was reasonable for England to take steps that she felt were necessary for her own protection, so too was it reasonable for France to do the
same. When the Peace of Amiens was no more and war seemed
inevitable, Napoleon did what any good general or emperor would do: he
took preemptive measures to strengthen his hand before hostilities began.

Thus, when the Royal Navy seized French ships, which was a direct act of war, Napoleon made his moves. He took his army into Hanover, which was land claimed by George III, deep in German territory. This naturally upset the British, and Prussia was none too pleased either.

After being crowned Emperor of the French, Napoleon went to Italy and was crowned King of Italy in May 1805. While this signalled no real change in the political situation, the Pope and others were not happy to see this apparent increase in French claims in the area.

Meanwhile, Tsar Alexander I of Russia was becoming increasingly alarmed by Napoleon's moves. He hoped to increase Russia's influence in the Balkans and Central Europe and felt that Napoleon's actions were a threat to those goals. He was encouraged in these fears by a variety of people, not the least of which were those with pro-British interests. The British government agreed to pay large sums to finance a continental war, and out of these discussions was formed the Third Coalition of England, Russia and Austria. Austria had been twice defeated by Napoleon and forced out of Italy, an area she considered almost a birthright. Now, perhaps, she could get that back.

Austria was also unhappy with the situation in Germany. When France had moved her borders east to the Rhine, Napoleon compensated some of the local princes by giving them some of the ecclesiastical states farther east. The states of Bavaria, Baden and Württemberg were made allies of France, and Austrian influence in the area was greatly weakened. Austria was outraged by this attack on the influence of the Habsburg dynasty and sought to reverse Napoleon's actions.

Napoleon, meanwhile, was still at Boulogne, contemplating an invasion of England. While this became increasingly unlikely, his time there was not wasted. He set about reorganising his army of some 200,000 soldiers. In 1805, he renamed the Army of England the *Grande Armée* (Great Army), a name that would endure until the end of his reign. He increased its mobility and the self-sufficiency of its units and established the corps, about 25,000 men, as the basic unit. Each corps was self-contained and had all elements necessary to wage war on its own. Many of his soldiers were career soldiers. Napoleon had access to an annual draft, but he seldom relied heavily on it.

To the non-military expert, the most obvious change was Napoleon's creation of the Imperial Guard. This was his élite force, controlled directly by him, and was his ace in the hole if the outcome of a battle ever seemed in doubt. The soldiers were mostly veterans and generally taller and stronger than the average.[142]

By August, it was clear that Austria and Russia were on the move in central Europe, and Austria was on the move in Italy. Less momentous activity was under way in Hanover and Naples. Given Napoleon's past campaigns in Italy, the members of the coalition reasonably expected that Napoleon would first counter their moves there.

Napoleon, however, had other ideas. Austria was moving against Bavaria, with Russia on the way to join her. Napoleon did not want a protracted war, and here was an excellent opportunity to take on the two continental members of the Third Coalition. Even better, as the Russians were still considerably to the east of the Austrian vanguard under General Karl Mack, Napoleon had the possibility of facing each of them separately, allowing him the advantage of overwhelming numerical superiority.

In one of the most amazing secret movements of troops in history, Napoleon shifted his *Grande Armée* from the English Channel all the way into Germany. While Austria's General Mack was arriving at the town of Ülm, Napoleon, in a matter of only several weeks, was moving his entire army of 210,000 to meet him there, having stayed along the coast as long as possible, to disguise his intentions. No bulletins were issued and no press coverage of the troop movement was allowed.

By October, however, the campaign was no secret. Indeed, it was quite popular. After all, it was the Austrians who had attacked France's ally Bavaria; who should not defend an ally under attack? Napoleon's improved relations with the Church even came into play, as Madame de Rémusat noted:

> From the very beginning of the campaign pastoral letters had been read in every metropolitan church, justifying the war and encouraging the new recruits to march promptly whithersoever they should be called. The bishops now [after Ülm] began the task once more and exhausted the Scriptures for texts to prove that the Emperor was protected by the God of armies.[143]

General Mack had sought to deal a surprising and crushing blow to French interests in Germany. With some 50,000 men, he established himself at Ülm and waited for the expected arrival of the Russians. In short order, an army did, indeed, arrive. Much to Mack's dismay, however, it was not the Russian army under General Mikhail Kutusov but the *Grande Armée* under Napoleon, Emperor of the French.

Napoleon swung his forces in an encircling deployment, cutting off all hope of escape for Mack and his army. Although the Austrian Archduke Ferdinand was able to escape, Mack soon recognised the hopelessness of his situation and surrendered to the French on 20 October 1805. With hardly a shot fired or a casualty sustained, the French took almost 50,000 Austrian prisoners and all their supplies. It was an overwhelming and devastating loss to the Third Coalition, but it was only a foretaste of what was to come.

Where were the expected Russians? More than one factor may explain their absence, but one seems to have been the primary factor. It appears that in drawing up the plans for coordinated movement, no account had been taken of the difference in the calendars used by the Russians and the Austrians. While most of the world was using the Gregorian calendar adopted in the 16th century, the Russians were still using the older Julian calendar established by Julius Caesar in 46 BC. There was a ten-day difference between them. Thus, while the Russians considered themselves on time, to the Austrians they were disastrously late. On such amazing things do the fates of nations hinge.

While Napoleon was winning the land war against the Austrians, he was losing what would ultimately be a more important sea war to the British. Napoleon had pressured Spain into a Franco-Spanish alliance, and the addition of Spain's ships added instant credibility to Napoleon's naval forces. It was, however, credibility wasted. The plan was for Napoleon's fleet, blockaded in Toulon and Brest. to break out and sail for the West Indies, drawing the Royal Navy in pursuit. There, they would meet their Spanish allies and return to gain control of the English Channel and allow the French to invade.

A series of missed communications, confusion and incompetence led to a confrontation on 21 October 1805, between the Franco-Spanish fleet under Admiral Villeneuve and the Royal Navy under Admiral Lord Nelson, in his flagship, *Victory*. The result of this engagement off Cape Trafalgar was a complete disaster for the French and led to the capture or destruction of most of the French fleet.

The Battle of Trafalgar removed forever the option of a French invasion of England and determined Napoleon's strategy for the remainder of his reign. It would force him to try to defeat the British by other means, but these too would fail. It is, in fact, almost impossible to overstate the importance for Great Britain of this victory.

The British rejoiced in the victory, but they also wept. Admiral Lord Nelson, one of her great naval commanders in a history that included many great commanders, was killed at the Battle of Trafalgar. His ship had come close to the French, and a sharpshooter picked him off. Every society needs its heroes, and in Nelson the British possessed one of the first quality. Twice he had defeated Napoleon's navy and twice would prevent Napoleon from obtaining his primary goals in critical campaigns. The gigantic monument in Trafalgar Square in London befits his stature, and the square itself is today one of the most popular places for young people and people-watchers to congregate.

If Trafalgar was a disaster for the French, what was happening in central Europe was equally so for the coalition. After the success at Ülm, Napoleon moved to the Austrian capital of Vienna, where he encountered virtually no opposition.

Napoleon sent Marshal Murat and others ahead to Vienna, which was taken without a fight. To continue the campaign north, however, it would be necessary to cross the Danube by way of what was called the Tabor Bridge. Marshal Murat was in charge of gaining control of this bridge, and his methods provide one of the more interesting stories to come out of any campaign. On 12 November, backed by several battalions of grenadiers led by Marshal Oudinot, Murat and Marshal Lannes walked up to the officer in charge on the Austrian side of the river. Murat boldly announced that an armistice had been signed and that he was there to bring the news.

The Austrians were suspicious, but could hardly be blamed for being at the very least confused by the appearance of the flashy Murat. Rapp tells us of Murat's reaction when confronted by an Austrian commander:

The Marshal exclaimed 'Why do you keep your guns still pointed at us? Has there not been enough of bloodshed? Do you wish to attack us and to prolong miseries which weigh more heavily on you than on us? Come, let us have no more provocation; turn your guns.' Half-persuaded and half-convinced, the commanding officer yielded. The artillery was turned in the direction of the Austrians, and the troops laid down their arms in bundles.[144]

In the confusion, the French were able to take the bridge peacefully, prevent its attempted destruction and disarm the guns facing Oudinot's forces. The French had found a way over the Danube without firing a shot!

Napoleon occupied Vienna on 15 November 1805. Emperor Francis had moved north to join forces with Tsar Alexander, whose army had at last arrived; together they would turn to attempt to defeat a smaller army. The confrontation would come near the small town of Austerlitz.

NOTES

141 For an excellent collection of these broadsides, together with useful commentary, see Klingberg and Hustvedt, *The Warning Drum.*

142 For excellent and detailed discussions of the organisation of the *Grande Armée* and of this and all other campaigns, see Chandler, *Campaigns.*

143 *Memoirs, 1802–1808*, II, 293. Mme. Rémusat was lady–in–waiting to the Empress Joséphine.

144 Rapp, 58.

THE HEIGHT OF IMPERIAL GLORY
Austerlitz

Volumes have been written about the Battle of Austerlitz. It is seen as Napoleon's greatest victory, his finest military hour. It was a crushing defeat for the Third Coalition, a glorious victory for the French alliance; it was one of the finest battles in history. The victory was Napoleon's Trafalgar, though it would have fewer long-term implications.

The countryside around Austerlitz is typical of the region; rolling hills, plateaus, forests and fields. One of the plateaus, called Pratzen, was occupied by Napoleon's forces. By now, these numbered some 73,000 men; those of the Russians and Austrians were at least 85,000. Worse yet, there was a very real fear that Prussia, sensing victory by the coalition, would move to join it. To gain a victory against such odds would require not only brave fighting but superb tactics. Napoleon would receive the former from his men and would provide the latter himself.

He relied on deceit to obtain the advantage of surprise and to fool the enemy into weakening its centre. The deceit came when Napoleon withdrew his forces from the Pratzen Heights to the lower ground and made it appear that he was preparing to retire. He pretended to negotiate with the Russians, treating their emissary with unusual kindness and humility.

On the evening of 1 December 1805, he personally inspected his positions. It was the eve of the first anniversary of his coronation and his soldiers were determined to salute him:

> On his return through the lines of bivouac, he was recognised by the soldiers, who spontaneously lighted torches of straw: this communicated from one end of the army to the other: in a moment there was a general illumination and the air was rent with shouts of *Vive l'Empereur!* [145]

In the Thirtieth Bulletin, issued the day after the battle, Napoleon wrote his thoughts of that evening. 'This is the finest evening of my life; but I regret to think that I shall lose a good number of these brave fellows.'[146]

In his Order of the Day for 1 December, Napoleon told his troops:

Soldiers, I shall myself direct all your battalions; I shall keep at a distance from the firing, if, with your accustomed bravery, you carry confusion and disorder into the enemy's ranks; but if victory be for a moment doubtful, you shall see your Emperor expose himself to the first blows; for victory cannot hesitate on this day ...[147]

Napoleon would not have to expose himself to the first blows. At seven o'clock on the morning of the 2nd, a dense fog hid Napoleon's centre from view, a centre which he had secretly strengthened. He had weakened his right flank to entice his foes into attacking his presumed weakness. They did just that. Moving most of their troops from the Pratzen to descend on Napoleon's right, they played into Napoleon's hands by drastically weakening their own centre. However, their progress was stalled as Davout's forces arrived to strengthen the French right, even as the Russian centre was still being weakened as more troops moved to face the French right.

At just the right moment, at about nine in the morning, Napoleon's centre moved to the heights and, as the enemy position was considerably weaker than prudence should have dictated, took control of the high ground. While the Russian right flank, commanded by General Bagration, retreated, Napoleon turned on those forces attacking his left and utterly destroyed them. By late afternoon, it was all over.

The battle, often called the Battle of the Three Emperors in recognition of their presence, was an overwhelming victory for Napoleon. His enemies lost some 27,000 men (mostly Russian) killed or wounded and 180 cannon. With these losses added to the 50,000 Austrians taken prisoner at Ülm, the forces of the Third Coalition had been decimated and humiliated. The European coalition was divided and broken. There would be no further talk of Prussia joining their ranks.

If France had any disappointment, it might have been in the lack of effective pursuit of the retreating Russian army. Had this been done (and it is possible that the French troops were simply too tired and the day too far gone to allow it), the victory could have included far greater Russian casualties. The next day, Marshal Davout pursued the retreating Tsar but was tricked by the Tsar's statements, in his own hand, into believing that an armistice had been signed. The French trick at the bridge over the Danube was now used successfully against them. Had this ruse not worked, Alexander might well have become Davout's prisoner.[148]

Still, Austerlitz was 'a textbook example of how to annihilate an enemy who attacks with superior forces'.[149] Napoleon said of the battle, 'I gained a victory so decisive, as to enable me to dictate what terms I pleased.'[150] To his troops he wrote in his Proclamation of 3 December:

> Soldiers: I am satisfied with you. In the battle of Austerlitz, you have justified what I expected from your intrepidity. You have covered yourselves with eternal glory ... [upon return to France] Then you will be the objects of my most tender care. My people will receive you with rapture and joy. To say to me, 'I was in the battle of Auster-litz' will be enough to authorise the reply, 'That is a brave man.'[151]

Napoleon was more than content with his men's performance, and he did far more than use Austerlitz as an example of his own glory. To the widows of all the fallen men he granted, by imperial decree, lifetime annual pensions ranging from 6,000 francs for widows of generals to 200 francs for widows of enlisted men. He personally adopted all the fallen mens' children and found jobs for the sons and husbands for the daughters. These children were also allowed to add 'Napoleon' to their names.

While the Russians could retreat to the east, the Austrians had nowhere to go. They could no longer take the field against Napoleon; their only remaining army was south of Vienna, and even if it were to appear magically on the outskirts of Vienna, it would be of little use. The Austrian Emperor Francis had no choice but to sue for peace, and he asked for a direct meeting with Napoleon.

Napoleon was tired of fighting Austria and made it clear that this must not happen again. Talleyrand had urged him to be cautious and conciliatory, but Napoleon wanted to weaken Austria permanently. The terms of the Treaty of Pressburg, signed on 26 December 1805, were harsh. The Kingdom of Italy, of which Napoleon was king, annexed numerous Italian territories, including Venice. Napoleon's loyal allies, Württemberg and Bavaria, also received territories. Moreover, Austria was to pay a large indemnity to compensate France for the cost of the war. The Treaty of Versailles, which ended the First World War some one hundred years later, also took this approach, with disastrous results. Germany was left embittered and determined to restore her pride and power. Pressburg would bring peace, but like Germany after Versailles, Austria was bitter and open to joining future coalitions.

Napoleon placed great stock in the word given by men of honour. General Savary, who waited with French and Austrian officers while the two emperors discussed their terms, relates the final words between Napoleon and Francis:

> At any rate, the parties [the two emperors] seemed to be in an excellent humour; they laughed, which seemed to us all to be a good omen: accordingly, in an hour or two the sovereigns parted with a mutual embrace. Each of us ran to his duty; and, as I approached, I heard the Emperor Napoleon say to the Emperor of Austria, 'I agree to it; but your Majesty must promise not to make war upon me again.' 'No, I promise you I will not,' replied the Emperor of Austria; 'and I will keep my word.'[152]

Would that this had been the case! Alas, neither the Treaty of Pressburg, Francis' word, nor future ties of marriage kept Austria from turning on Napoleon.

As to Prussia, Napoleon continued to court its weak king, granting him Hanover. But Prussia was unhappy with Napoleon's moves elsewhere in Germany. In early 1806, Napoleon persuaded sixteen German princes to leave the moribund Holy Roman Empire and join the Confederation of the Rhine. While they were independent, they were under the protection of Napoleon and were expected to furnish troops for his army.

This marked the end of the Holy Roman Empire and certainly established new and, to some, troubling French influence in the German states. The Confederation only lasted some seven years, but was instrumental in bringing many of Napoleon's reforms to Germany. Ironically, these reforms, together with the obligations to Napoleon, led to increased nationalism, which ultimately turned the states of the Confederation against Napoleon in 1813.

The campaign of 1805 can tell us a great deal about how it was that Napoleon was able to rise to the heights he achieved. As a military matter, it ranks with the best campaigns in history and is by itself sufficient to place him in the first rank of the great commanders. Alexander the Great's victory at Issus was no greater than Napoleon's at Austerlitz. Napoleon's ability to analyse the military situation and take advantage of terrain, psychology and all other elements of war are never better seen than in this campaign.

It would be a mistake to see only the greatness of Napoleon's military mind at Austerlitz. The campaign of 1805 shows his ability to adapt to changing political and strategic situations as well. Trafalgar may well have been the more important military engagement of the war, but Napoleon was quick to realise its political consequences and act accordingly.

Napoleon always wanted peace; he truly fought only to achieve that aim. His position in Paris was never strong enough that he could afford continual war. War brought glory and had its advantages, but none could top the advantages of peace. He sought to conquer the British because it was clear that they would never cease trying to conquer him. And when Trafalgar removed that possibility, he quickly understood that to obtain peace he must defeat whatever coalitions arose and, more importantly, seek a political peace with Austria and, if at all possible, with Russia, the giant of the east. Only then would it be possible to tell the British that peace was to their advantage as well.

Napoleon understood all of this. His actions can be seen as steps to fulfil the needs brought on by the defeat at Trafalgar and to gain the possibilities obtained by Ülm and Austerlitz. That is why, after Davout's failure to pursue, he allowed the Russians to retreat in good order (though with the prodding of his Marshals at their rear), and that is why he released the prisoners of the Russian Imperial Guard, even though there had been no treaty between France and Russia after Austerlitz.

Napoleon did all that he could to end the continued fighting, but in the end, it would not be enough.

After Austerlitz, however, everything seemed possible.

NOTES

145 Savary. I. 2 : 132.
146 Napoleon I, *Bulletins Officiels de la Grande Armée*, 79, and *Official Narratives*, 43.
147 Ibid., 46.
148 Gallaher, J. G. *The Iron Marshal*, 112–15.
149 Ibid., 110.
150 O'Meara, I, 146.
151 *Official Narratives*, 46–47, in *Original Journals*, II.
152 Savary, I, 2, 139.

WAR AND LOVE

Another year, another deadly blow,
   Another mighty empire overthrown!
And we are left or shall be left alone,
   The last that dare to struggle with the foe.
Tis well! from this day forward we shall know
   That in ourselves our safety must be sought
                              William Wordsworth
                              November, 1806

Frederick William III, King of Prussia, was not known as a strong ruler, or a particularly bright one. Napoleon had tried to court him, giving him assurances that the French wanted only good relations. Frederick William, however, was not convinced. His erstwhile allies, Great Britain and Russia, were forming a new Fourth Coalition against Napoleon – the British had already declared war – and William hoped to use that to gain leverage against Napoleon. For their part, the other members of the coalition were naturally willing to put the Prussian army first in the field against him. The Fourth Coalition was in place by 6 October 1806.

In what was in reality foolish blustering on Frederick William's part, inspired in large part by his wife and by the other coalition members, on 7 October 1806 Frederick William demanded that Napoleon abandon the Confederation of the Rhine or risk the wrath of the Prussian army. Russia backed Prussia in this demand. The Prussian media began an anti-French campaign and the nation prepared for war. Like the First World War, it was a war desired only by the ruling classes. And like that war, it would be a disaster for the Prussians. Unlike the 20th century's first great war, however, this one would be over almost before it started.

Had Prussia joined Russia and Austria before Austerlitz, she might have changed history. Now, however, her bluster was to prove fatal, to say nothing of ineffectual. The image of the Prussian army – then and now – is one of a proud and feared fighting force. Frederick William's army was a disgrace to that image. It was a 'sad descendant of the army that had so thoroughly defeated the French at Rossbach some fifty years earlier ... overtrained in parade-ground tactics ... its armament, with few exceptions, was outdated; its soldiers were poorly fed and poorly clothed ..." [153]

The Duke of Brunswick commanded the main army. It was his 'Brunswick Manifesto' of 25 July 1792, that had threatened to destroy Paris and had thus united the French and led to their great Revolutionary victory at Valmy on 20 September of the same year. Defeated at that battle, perhaps he hoped for revenge. It was not to be.

Napoleon risked losing the benefits of Austerlitz and was not about to be intimidated by a weak king and a Tsar he had so recently defeated. Neither Napoleon nor the Prussians truly wanted war, but war it would be.

The Prussian armies were on the move, but Napoleon struck first. By moving to meet the French, rather than waiting for their Russian allies, the Prussians foolishly gave Napoleon yet another opportunity to follow his most effective strategy of separating his opponents and then defeating them each in their turn.

In two battles – Jena and Auerstädt, both on 14 October 1806 – Napoleon destroyed the Prussian army and brought Prussia to its knees. He overwhelmed a smaller Prussian force at Jena, while Davout routed a much larger force at Auerstädt. In that battle, Brunswick was fatally wounded and King Frederick William took command of the army. This did the Prussians no good, and by the end of the day they were finished as a fighting force.

Murat's pursuit completed the total French victory. Only the inexcusable failure of Marshal Bernadotte to move his troops in support of either Napoleon or Davout put a blemish on the French performance for the day. The Prussians lost some 37,000 men killed and more than 20,000 taken prisoner with virtually their entire artillery and baggage train.

In one week, Napoleon had completely defeated the descendants of Frederick the Great and destroyed, perhaps forever, the mystique of the Prussian army. On 25 October Davout led the French army into a humble Berlin.

The French were victorious but exhausted. A year of campaigns had taken its toll on their numbers, their supplies and their enthusiasm for war. Great victories are fine, but for many it was time to go home. Fresh conscripts from France and fresh supplies from Prussia helped, but Napoleon recognised that he was pushing his troops to their limit. At home, the people rejoiced in his victories at Jena and Auerstädt, but more likely from a hope for peace than for happiness at additional French glory.

The Russians, however, were still moving toward the French, and Napoleon next turned to meet that threat. Moving into Poland, the French faced the Russians under General Levin Benningsen at Eylau. Despite the reverses suffered by his Prussian allies, Benningsen was convinced that he had the upper hand. In the conclusion of his report to the Tsar of 31 January 1807, he wrote:

> I have managed to chase the enemy from the province, to cover Königsberg and to produce consternation and disorder in this portion of the French army which are already very apparent. Such are the brilliant results to which we have been led in our march toward East Prussia and the perseverance and courage with which His Imperial Majesty's troops have executed this exhausting operation. The enemy surprised in its quarters, defeated on every occasion, has withdrawn with a hurry and disorder which underline only too well the deplorable situation in which it is now.[154]

At Eylau, on 7–8 February 1807, the French and Russians fought a bloody but relatively indecisive battle. Conditions were awful and much of the battle was fought in a heavy snowstorm. The Russians, however, lost perhaps twice as many men as the French and withdrew from the field.

Eylau was one of the bloodiest battles ever experienced. In his memoirs, the Russian General Denis Davidov wrote:

> There then ensued an engagement the likes of which had never been seen before. Over 20,000 men from both armies were plunging their three-faceted blades into one another. They fell in masses. I was personal witness to this Homeric slaughter. It came to be described, justly, as the legend of our century, and I have to say in truth that over the course of the sixteen campaigns in my service record and throughout the period of all the Napoleonic campaigns, I have never seen anything to compare with it! For about half an hour you could not hear a cannon or a musket shot, only the indescribable roar of thousands of brave soldiers as they cut one another to pieces in hand to hand combat. Mounds of dead bodies were covered by new mounds; soldiers were tumbling in their hundreds on top of one another, so that this corner of the battlefield resembled a high parapet of a suddenly erected barricade.[155]

With winter well under way, the campaign paused for warmer weather. Napoleon had held the field, but at great cost. Not only had he lost many fine soldiers, but perhaps as importantly he had acquired at least some significant tarnish on his image as an invincible commander.

In June 1807, the campaign began again, and it did not take long for Napoleon to make up for the decidedly imperfect victory of Eylau. On 14 June he completely defeated the Russian army at Friedland. The Fourth Coalition was finished, and Tsar Alexander asked for peace negotiations at Tilsit.

On 7–8 July the two emperors met on a raft on the River Niemen. Prussia was, rightfully, concerned that she might get left out of the deal and sent Queen Louise to do all she could to arrange favourable terms. In this she completely failed. Alexander had been quite charmed by Napoleon and was more than willing to sacrifice Prussia to obtain peace with his new friend. Prussia lost all of Poland and several other territories; she was humiliated and could do nothing about it. Napoleon offered Hanover to Prussia, but even that was soon thereafter offered instead to the British in a failed effort to obtain peace with them.

Meanwhile, Russia and France – one should really say Alexander and Napoleon – forged a new alliance. This one had the potential to dominate Europe completely and, more importantly, bring economic and military pressure to bear on Great Britain such that she might be forced to seek peace. The peace sought by virtually all was, at least so it must have seemed, close at hand. Alas, events were to prove otherwise.

The French were victorious, but all was not entirely well. The *Grande Armée* that had been the victor at Austerlitz was no longer so *grande*, or even so French. Conscripts are seldom as effective, and certainly not as motivated, as volunteers. Victories at the beginning of a war lead to hopes for peace, hopes that are dashed as a war continues, with no end in sight.

Moreover, while the army of 1805 had been almost exclusively French, the army of 1806 and beyond was composed more and more of conscripts from other countries. Some, like the Poles, were more or less willing, as they felt that some national pride might result from successful campaigns. Others, however, were more interested in seeing the war end than of seeing additional victories and glory.

This is not to say that they were a poor fighting force; far from it, as they continued to defeat all who challenged them. The lack of national and language homogeneity, however, created problems of communication and other logistical problems that reduced their effectiveness. They would fight, and usually fight well, but after 1805 they would never be quite the same.

Still, one can easily argue that after Friedland in 1807, or at least within a year of that decisive battle, Napoleon was at the true peak of his power. In addition to his dealings with Russia and Prussia, he removed the Bourbons from control of Naples and added that area of Italy to his alliance, making his brother Joseph the king. By 1808, an uprising against the ruling Bourbons in Spain gave him the chance to add that large country to his alliance as well.

The end was as yet not in sight, but slowly, and in often quite subtle ways, the tide would begin to turn.

MARIE WALEWSKA

One of the most interesting and romantic stories concerning Napoleon is his relationship with Marie Walewska. The Poles had hoped that Napoleon would create an independent Polish state, and he had given indications towards that end. When he decided to winter in Warsaw after the battle of Eylau, the Polish nobles persuaded – some might say ordered – Countess Walewska to make herself available to Napoleon. Polish winter nights are long and cold, and the two of them quickly became not only lovers but also affectionate friends whose relationship continued even after his final fall. The emotions they shared were quite real, and Napoleon wrote to her much as he wrote to Joséphine:

> I saw no one but you, I admired no one but you, I want no one but you. Answer me at once, and assuage the impatient passion of ... N
>
> Marie, my sweet Marie, my first thought is of you, my first desire is to see you again ... I want you to accept this bouquet: I want it to be a secret link, setting up a private understanding between us in the midst of the surrounding crowd. We shall be able to share our thoughts, though all the world is looking on. When my hand presses my heart, you will know that I am thinking of no one but you; and when you press your bouquet, I shall have your answer back! Love me, my pretty one, and hold your bouquet tight![156]

In May 1810, she gave birth to Napoleon's son, Alexander Florian Joseph. As an illegitimate child, he played no direct role in French politics while

Napoleon was in power, though he did many years later under Napoleon III, when he served as the Foreign Minister of France.

While Poland never achieved the independence that it wanted, Napoleon did create the Grand Duchy of Warsaw as a component of the French Empire. He also freed the serfs and abolished slavery, bringing some measure of the reforms for which he was so well known. Grateful for that consideration and hopeful for the future, the Poles remained loyal to Napoleon until the end.

NOTES

153 Gallaher, *Iron Marshal*, 123.

154 Benningsen to the Tsar, letter in The David Markham Collection. For a translation of the entire letter, see *Napoleonic Scholarship*, I, 2, 51–52.

155 Davidov, *Service of the Tsar*, 37.

156 Thompson, No. 134.

REVOLUTIONARY EMPIRE
Imperial Reforms at Home and Abroad

As Consul, Napoleon had brought major reforms to France. As Emperor, he sought to extend many of those reforms to the rest of Europe. In so doing, he was in the most basic tradition of the French revolutionaries of the 1790s, who dreamt of a Europe-wide Revolution that would bring the principles of *Liberté*, *Égalité* and *Fraternité* to the oppressed people of those nations still mired in the feudalism of the *ancien régimes*. The leaders of French public opinion believed that if it was to be force of arms rather than the idealistic uprising of the people that brought these benefits to the beleaguered, well, that was not the fault of France. In any event, the *anciens régimes* must go.

And go they did. At his peak Napoleon ruled, to one extent or another, half of Europe. To allies such as Russia and Austria, he could have but minimal impact on their internal affairs. But to those areas in Italy, Spain and Northern Europe that he controlled more directly, he could – and did – bring major reforms.

One of the most important 'reforms' was the simple removal of some of the most incompetent leaders in European history. The deposed Bourbons of Naples, for example, were ignoring that country's heritage and its people's needs; their departure was a major step forward. The years of empire were, more than anything, years of war. This was not to Napoleon's liking; he was a master of war, but a master of reform as well. His single biggest goal for his empire was to provide all people with the liberal benefits of the Revolution and of his Consulate turned Empire. Had the Peace of Amiens lasted, had peace been the final result of Austerlitz, even of Friedland, he might well have turned his attention more fully to those reforms.

When Napoleon gained control over a territory, he took a personal interest in it. He was never content simply to allow it to continue as before, sending treasure and conscripts as their contribution to the Empire. He would write new constitutions, reorganise governments to make them more efficient, extend the rights of many citizens, including Jews, and undertake other actions to benefit the people.

EDUCATION

During the Consulate, Napoleon had moved to centralise France's educational system. As Emperor, he continued that process and worked for other educational reforms as well. He raised the issue of education in at least one meeting of the Council of State. At such a meeting in 1807 he declared:

> Of all our institutions public education is the most important. Everything depends on it, the present and the future. It is essential that the morals and political ideas of the generation which is now growing up should no longer be dependent upon the news of the day or the circumstances of the moment. Above all we must secure unity: we must be able to cast a whole generation in the same mould.[157]

Napoleon was particularly concerned with the independence of the secondary schools, wanting more direct control over their curriculum. Moreover, there were problems with the *lycées* as well. Financial constraints had limited the number that had actually opened, and competition by the private schools had limited enrolment. Napoleon's solution was to be the ultimate in centralised control of the French educational system. He established the Imperial University in 1808. The law creating this 'university' stated, in part

> the Imperial University, a body charged exclusively with instruction and public education throughout the Empire ... No school, no educational institution of any kind whatsoever, shall be permitted to be established outside the Imperial University, without the authorisation of its chief. No one may open a school or teach publicly without being a member of the Imperial University and a graduate of one of its faculties.[158]

The Imperial University was actually something of a compromise with those who wanted to eliminate private education altogether. It allowed private schools to exist, but put them under strict public control and demanded various taxes from them, designed to reduce the educational outlay of the central government. The quality of instruction in private schools was controlled, however, in part by a requirement that teachers must have degrees. Later revisions to the law reduced the number and enrollment of the private schools, especially those of the Catholic Church.

Perhaps the most important element in the development of the Imperial University was that for the first time the state took responsibility for and controlled the elementary education of its citizens.[159] Teachers were placed under stricter controls, including dress, discipline and salary.

Napoleon had long been concerned about the teaching profession. He recognised the central importance of teachers to the educational system. He had at times suggested that the teaching profession should take on some of the characteristics of an order or corporation, with very specific expectations, privileges and rewards. He had, for example, in a *Note Sur Les Lycées* (Note on the *Lycées*)[160] of 14 February 1805, suggested that teachers who were just starting in the profession might be forbidden to marry. On the other hand, he believed that by the end of his career a teacher should see himself in the highest ranks of state officials, having been placed under the protection of the Emperor himself. Teacher training was a must if the country were to be unified:

> There never will be a fixed political state of things in this country ... till we have a corps of teachers instructed on established principles. So long as the people are not taught from their earliest years ... the state cannot be properly called a nation, for it must rest on a foundation which is vague and uncertain, and it will be forever exposed to disorders and fluctuations.[161]

The purpose of education went beyond the need for an educated élite. As is the case with schools today, patriotism and loyalty to the state were a major part of the purpose of educational institutions. We would not, however, personalise loyalty today as did the law establishing the Imperial University:

> All schools of the Imperial University will take as the basis of their instruction (i) the teaching of the Catholic religion, (ii) fidelity to the Emperor, to the imperial monarchy which is entrusted with the happiness of the people, and to the Napoleonic dynasty which ensures the unity of France and all the liberal ideas proclaimed in

the constitution, (iii) obedience to the regulations of the teaching body, the object of which is to secure uniformity of instruction and to train for the State citizens who are attached to their religion, their prince, their country and their family.[162]

The system of education under the Imperial University was as follows. First was elementary education. This was Napoleon's lowest priority. Following that was the secondary education of the middle class. As before, Napoleon placed the greatest emphasis on this level of education. The *lycées* were, as during the Consulate, mainly boarding-schools supported by the state and providing a six-year course heavy on the Classics and mathematics. Along with them were the *collèges*, which were municipal or communal secondary schools, a bit lower than the *lycées*. These schools stressed French, Latin, geography, history and mathematics. There were also some independent schools known as *instituts*, which were more or less the equivalent of the *collèges*. This system was not, of course, uniquely Napoleonic; it mirrored ideas of earlier systems as well as other systems in Europe. It is also no surprise to learn that Napoleon stressed various military aspects in his schools, including uniforms, formations, music and discipline.

The real value of an institution may be in its ability to survive the ravages of time. On this basis, one must evaluate the Napoleonic educational system in mostly favourable terms. After the downfall of Napoleon, it might have been expected that his system would be abolished or greatly modified. There has certainly been some turmoil in French education over the years, especially as regards the role of the Catholic Church. During the Third Republic, the separation of Church and state was made complete and the teaching of religion was no longer part of the public school curriculum. Thus, the curriculum of the Revolution replaced the curriculum of Napoleon. The Imperial University has, of course, disappeared, but centralised control lives on in the Minister of Public Instruction. The *lycée* continues and, indeed, plays an even more important role. It is a virtually self-contained unit and graduation from a *lycée* is adequate for many careers (unlike the American high school.) As in Napoleonic times, French education is much more stratified and élitist in nature than in the American system; success and progression are based on examination results rather than on the belief in universal education.

RELIGION

I wanted to establish a universal liberty of conscience. My system was to have no predominant religion, but to allow perfect liberty of conscience and of thought, to make all men equal, whether Protestants, Catholics, Mahometans, Deists, or others; so that their religion should have no influence in getting them employments under government.

Napoleon[163]

The Catholics

The Concordat had been one of Napoleon's masterpieces, providing as it did religious tolerance and peace and good relations with the Pope. While this did Napoleon little good with the Church in Spain, it generally neutralised any possible opposition by the Church in France or elsewhere. Napoleon's ability to control the appointment of Church officials gradually increased his control over the Church and weakened the influence of the Church in society. At one point, church-goers were taught obedience to both God and the Emperor.

When Napoleon insisted that the Pope cease all trade with England, the Pope declined. Therefore, in 1808 French troops occupied the Papal States, which were then annexed to the Empire. When the Pope refused to renounce his secular power, he was forcibly removed to Savona, where he stayed until 1811. This action does not seem to have damaged Napoleon in the eyes of the great bulk of French citizens who were, after all, suspicious of the Church's motives in many areas. Still, it was one more source of complaint for those seeking reasons to oppose Napoleon. To the Spanish Church, it was an outrage.

The Jews

Napoleon's relations with the Jews in many ways represent the very best of which he was capable. The Jews, of course, had suffered the sad effects of anti-Semitism since the very beginning of their time as a people. In Europe, they had been blamed for the plague and just about every other problem encountered by Europeans in the Middle Ages and beyond. No less than Martin Luther had written strong anti-Semitic documents.

In France, such feelings ran deep, and the Church made little if any effort to counter them. The coming of the French Revolution was of only modest help, as its focus was anti-clerical rather than a promotion of religious tolerance. Jews were granted full citizenship, but little else.

The *Code Napoléon* was the first document specifically to grant religious freedom to all religions, including Judaism. This is not surprising, because as early as 1797 Napoleon was eliminating ghettos and declaring the Jews' right to live as normal citizens.[164] A year later, in Malta, he granted all Jews religious freedom as well. Later, he opened the Warsaw Ghetto, restoring freedom to Polish Jews.

Perhaps one of the most interesting 'what ifs' of history took place during the Egyptian campaign. Napoleon had expected to conquer Acre and then to move to Jerusalem. There he planned to issue a proclamation declaring Palestine an independent Jewish state. Had he done this, the history of that region would no doubt have been quite different for the next two hundred years! David Ben Gurion cited Napoleon's proclamation as part of the argument for recognising Israel that he presented to the United Nations in 1947.

In 1806, Napoleon called for a general meeting, called a Sanhedrin, of Jewish leaders to discuss various accusations made against them. The purpose of this meeting was to show 'that I am anxious to do all I can to prevent the rights restored to the Jewish people proving illusory – in a word, I want them to find in France a New Jerusalem'.[165]

Napoleon's behaviour towards the Jews was not popular with many elements of French society, including some of his closest advisers, such as Marshal Kellermann. The leaders of virtually all of the major countries of Europe protested against it, but Napoleon stood firm and France, and areas under its control, continued to grant rights to the Jews.

NOTES

157 Molé, *Life and Memoirs*, 61.
158 Bernard, 216–17.
159 Lefebvre, *Tilsit to Waterloo*, 1969.
160 *Correspondance*, 16 February 1805, No. 8328, X, 180–84.
161 Pelet, *Napoleon in Council*, 190.
162 Bernard, 218.
163 O'Meara I, 119.
164 Weider, Ben. 'Napoleon and the Jews', in *Napoleonic Scholarship*, I, 2, December 1998, 41–45. Weider has written extensively on this subject, and I have based much of my material here on his work.
165 *Correspondance*, 23 August 1806, No. 10686, XIII, 122–26; Thompson, No. 124.

A NEW DYNASTY

Napoleon was a firm believer in a meritocracy; even his creation of a new nobility can, perhaps with some difficulty, be seen as at least a nobility based on merit. With siblings, however, merit gives way to blood. To strengthen his control over his empire, Napoleon placed his brothers and sisters on various thrones. Unfortunately for him, the family blood had not bestowed merit even-handedly in the family.

Nevertheless the people now ruled by the new Bonaparte dynasty were often far better off than they had been under the Bourbons. An excellent case in point is that of the Kingdom of Naples. The Bourbons had misruled that beautiful and historic region – books were burned, serfs mistreated, wealth was incredibly concentrated even by the standards of the day – and their departure was not exactly cause for national mourning!

Joseph Bonaparte had watched Napoleon's successful efforts at reform in France and was determined to emulate his younger brother's example. He made immediate moves to remove the remaining vestiges of feudalism in Naples, taking away most of the rights enjoyed by the nobility and dividing their land among the peasants. He implemented the *Code Napoléon* and introduced tax and other economic reforms that mirrored those in France. He reduced the power and the cost of the Church and in the process balanced the budget for the first time in memory.

Joseph shared his brother's love and appreciation of history. It was Joseph who purchased the land under which Pompeii was buried and began the process of excavation that has made Pompeii one of the greatest archaeological sites in the world. He took many other steps to restore and promote history and culture, all the while encouraging the promotion of French culture as well. For his efforts, Joseph became a popular ruler and the people of his kingdom were genuinely sorry to see him go. They would never develop the same love for his successor, Marshal Joachim Murat.

When Joseph was, however reluctantly, made King of Spain, he took with him much the same reformist attitude that he had had in Naples. He reformed the government and the economy and tried to rebuild and beautify the capital, Madrid. He went out among the people, adopted their customs and tried to make himself popular. He did in Spain what he did in Naples, but it was not enough.

The reason, perhaps more than anything else, was the Catholic Church. A constitution adopted under King Joseph allowed for the free worship of any religion, as well as civil marriages and divorces and civil registration of births and deaths. This was intolerable to the Church, and it was able to use this perceived anti-Catholic bias to rally the conservative peasantry to its cause. Thus, it was not outrage at French arrogance in replacing the Bourbons that would ultimately undo Joseph's efforts. It was the effort to give the Spanish people the same enlightened freedoms that were so fundamental to the French Revolution and the newly emerging modern Europe.[166]

Napoleon made his brother Louis King of Holland. Louis was married to Joséphine's daughter, Hortense. Like his brother Joseph, Louis had not wanted the job, but Napoleon would not take no for an answer. Also like Joseph, Louis made serious efforts to reform the nation and to make it a better place for his having been king. In this, he was quite successful; he was then and still is known as 'good King Louis'.

Napoleon's relations with his youngest brother Jérôme were not always positive. Jérôme had fallen in love with and married a young woman from Baltimore named Elizabeth Patterson and in March 1805 brought her to Europe for Napoleon's approval. Napoleon, who wanted to use his family's marriages for political purposes and expected his siblings to comply, was furious. He wrote his mother an angry letter, calling Jérôme a 'prodigal son' and threatening to ruin his career if he did not do as he was told. It was his 'sacred duty to obey me' and 'to do as I command'.[167] He refused to see the young woman, or even to allow her to enter the Empire. The young couple first stayed in Lisbon, and then Jérôme went to Milan while his pregnant young wife was to wait in Holland. Even that was unacceptable to Napoleon, and she waited in England for word of her fate. Napoleon would not relent, insisted that the marriage was illegal (which it was, as Jérôme was under age) and had her sent back to America. Before she left England, she gave birth to Jérôme's son, whom she took with her to America in July. As compensation for his refusal to accept their marriage, Napoleon granted her a sizeable salary.

Jérôme, now free of his American 'entanglement', was quickly married off to Catherine, the young daughter of the King of Württemberg. He was then made King of Westphalia, a new kingdom created by Napoleon. As always, Napoleon was interested in reform, believing that this was the key to holding his empire together. His letter to Jérôme of 15 November 1807, reflects his attitude:

> The benefits of the *Code Napoléon*, public trial and the introduction of juries, will be the leading features of your government. And to tell you the truth, I count more upon their effects, for the extension and consolidation of your rule, than upon the most resounding victories. I want your subjects to enjoy a degree of liberty, equality and prosperity hitherto unknown to the German people. I want this liberal regime to produce, one way or another, changes which will be of the utmost benefit to the system of the Confederation and to the strength of your monarchy. Such a method of government will be a stronger barrier between you and Prussia than the Elbe, the fortresses and the protection of France. What people would wish to return under the arbitrary Prussian system after having tasted the blessings of a wise and liberal administration? The people of Germany, of France, of Italy and of Spain desire equality and liberal ideas. For many years I have conducted the affairs of Europe and I have reason to be convinced that the buzzing of the privileged classes is at variance with public opinion. Be a constitutional king. Even should the common sense and the intelligence of the age not require this, in your position good policy would command it. You will find yourself possessed of a force of opinion which will give you a natural ascendancy over your neighbours who are absolute monarchs.[168]

Jérôme, whatever else his faults in Napoleon's eyes, proved every bit the reformer that was desired. Like his other brothers, he reformed the tax structure, promoted religious freedom, improved trade and generally improved economic and cultural conditions. His only drawback, and in Napoleon's eyes it was a major one, was that he was fond of pomp and ceremony and was constantly spending far more than anyone, particularly Napoleon, would find appropriate. Like the English King Charles II before him, Jérôme became known as 'the merry monarch'.

Napoleon's sister Elisa was anxious to do her share as well. She and her husband Felix Bacciochi asked for and were given the principality of

Lucca in Italy. Like her brothers, she dedicated herself to instituting legal and economic reforms in her small principality of no more than 150,000 people. She paid special attention to the famous Carrara marble quarry. Famous since the time of Michelangelo, it was no longer being used to its full potential. Within a few years she had it humming again. Its most popular subject for sculpture? Marble busts of Napoleon!

Her work in Lucca was rewarded by her appointment as Grand Duchess of Tuscany. Here, she continued her crusade to promote cultural matters, including the increased attention paid to French culture. While she clashed with Napoleon from time to time, Elisa was generally a credit to the Bonaparte family.

THE FUTURE OF THE DYNASTY

When Napoleon had become First Consul, he was very young and did not need to give prompt consideration to an heir. Yet for Emperor Napoleon an heir was needed, or else his own demise might lead to the return of the Bourbons and an undoing of all that he had accomplished.

Napoleon and Joséphine did not produce any children. While the reason for this would prove to be related to a fall down some stairs experienced by Joséphine some years earlier, there was for a while some concern that the reason might be traced to certain inabilities on Napoleon's part. But when Napoleon fathered several children, most notably with Marie Walewska, the fault – if that is the right word – was clearly Joséphine's.

As would be the case with any couple, Napoleon and Joséphine had discussed the matter, and Joséphine knew that their marriage might well rest on its successful resolution. It was, therefore, cause for great celebration when Napoleon's brother Louis and his wife Hortense, Joséphine's daughter from her first marriage, gave birth in 1802 to their son, Napoleon-Charles. Napoleon and Joséphine decided to adopt the young son born of their blood, however indirectly, and make him the heir to the throne. The 1804 decree establishing the Empire designated the young man heir to the throne with the right to pass it to his male descendants.

Alas, in 1807 the little boy died, and with his death died Joséphine's chances of remaining Empress of the French.

When Napoleon returned to Fontainebleau Palace outside Paris in October 1809, he had already decided that, like it or not, he would have to divorce Joséphine. They were still in love, but he would tell her that 'France and my Destiny' forced him to do something that he would rather not.

Joséphine was not really surprised, but she played her role well enough to assure her continued fortune and gain a sympathetic place in history. She protested, she fainted, she was carried to her room. In the end, she gained possession of their home, Malmaison, and a continued role in the diplomatic life of France. The divorce was made final on 16 December 1809.

With Joséphine gone, Napoleon moved to find her replacement. His first choice was Russian Tsar Alexander's sister Anna. Already allies, however strained, the bond of marriage would tie the two ends of the continent together, cement their friendship, solidify the Continental System and literally put the 'squeeze' on the rest of Europe.

Much to Napoleon's surprise and dismay, however, Alexander was not willing to give his immediate approval. Various concerns were raised: her religion, some financial arrangements, even the question of Poland. Napoleon acquiesced in all of these, and still Alexander wavered. He told Napoleon that all family decisions were made by his mother, a woman openly hostile to Napoleon. An elder sister had been hastily married off, but Alexander's younger sister, Anne, was available. She was but fifteen and eventually Napoleon was told that he would have to wait until she was eighteen for any decision to be made.

This was a slap in the face, and it effectively ended any chance for lasting friendship or alliance between France and Russia. Napoleon valued friendship and felt his had been let down by Alexander.

Napoleon was determined to acquire one major ally by way of marriage. Of almost equal geo-political value to Russia, Austria proved to be much more interested in an alliance by blood. Austria's Emperor Francis, like Alexander, had broken his word to Napoleon by making war after promising not to after Austerlitz in 1805, but he did have certain advantages to offer. The Habsburg family was the oldest royal family in Europe; surely that would give Napoleon legitimacy with the other kings who had previously opposed Napoleon as being an illegitimate usurper to the French throne. Moreover, it was a Catholic dynasty, and Napoleon needed help in that area as well. Finally – and this was of overriding importance – the Habsburgs were notoriously prolific. A child was a virtual guarantee.

Thus, when, in February 1810, Napoleon asked Francis for permission to marry the 18-year-old Princes Marie-Louise, the Austrian Emperor was glad to agree. Napoleon was more than delighted. Finally his plans seemed to be paying off; a tie between the French Empire and the Austrian Empire, such as it was, would dominate Europe and might even force the British to seek peace on some reasonable terms.

Napoleon sent Marshal Berthier to Vienna, where the marriage would take place by proxy. Berthier was warmly received; it was clear to all that this marriage was popular on both sides. There was a round of celebrations and Berthier presented the Legion of Honour to none other than the Archduke Charles himself.

Europe seemed poised for peace. France, Austria, Prussia and Russia were now allies. There was still Spain, where Arthur Wellesley, the future Duke of Wellington, was campaigning and Napoleon's marshals had been unable to stop him. However, with all the resources of the Empire brought to bear, a military or diplomatic resolution there seemed but a question of time. Napoleon was quite willing to consider alternate solutions to the Iberian situation. Peace was at hand!

Great Britain, however, had never even officially recognised Napoleon as Emperor of the French. As long as France held Antwerp, the British gateway to Europe, she would never settle with France. Antwerp, however, was a concession that Napoleon could never make; the French people would simply not stand for it.

Peace was not at hand, and the end was drawing nearer. However, in this happy moment anyone could be forgiven for not realising these facts.

The young princess Marie-Louise arrived at Compiègne on 27 March 1810. Like all brides whose marriages to older men had been arranged without their having been consulted, Marie-Louise was unsure of how they would get along. There was a considerable difference in their level of maturity and seriousness. Napoleon did all he could to treat her well and with tender kindness, and their relationship actually flourished.

It was also consummated, and on 20 March 1811, she gave birth to their son, Napoleon-François-Joseph-Charles, known as 'The King of Rome'. Napoleon wanted a son more than anything else. Nevertheless, when told by doctors that the birth was likely to be quite difficult and that there might be a choice of saving the mother or the child, Napoleon made it clear that the mother was to be saved at all costs. So much for his lack of compassion. It was a decision that forever endeared him to Marie-Louise. Happily, both mother and son survived in fine shape.

After his victory over the Austrians at Wagram in 1809, Napoleon was no longer directly involved in any war until 1812. Spain was left to his Marshals. Napoleon returned to Paris and concentrated on governing and, most of all, on achieving peace. Tied now to the most ancient of European dynasties, he felt that even Great Britain might be willing to seek peace. He made fresh overtures, but was always rebuffed.

Napoleon's enemies, however, had continued to reject his rule. He would not be allowed to concentrate on domestic reforms or family matters. The battlefield had helped pave his road to glory. That would continue for some years after Austerlitz. Then, his road would take a different direction.

NOTES

166 Cronin, 261–63.

167 Thompson, No. 89.

168 *Correspondance* 15 November 1807, No. 13361, XVI, 196–97; Thompson, No. 153.

Engraving 'Passage du Pont du Lodi', by Nodet, *c.* 1799.

Church tower from which
Napoleon directed the
action at Lodi. Photograph
by David Markham.

1841 engraving by Huffam after Gros, showing
Napoleon at the Battle of the Pyramids.

XVII

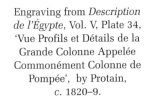

Silver 1798 medallion commemorating Napoleon's conquest of Egypt.

Engraving from *Description de l'Égypte*, Vol. V, Plate 34, 'Vue Profils et Détails de la Grande Colonne Appelée Commonément Colonne de Pompée', by Protain, *c.* 1820–9.

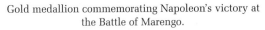

Gold medallion commemorating Napoleon's victory at the Battle of Marengo.

Column with Imperial Eagle at the battlefield of Marengo near the town of Alessandria, Italy. Photograph by David Markham.

Hand-coloured engraving of 'Infanterie de Ligne, Sergent-major plantant son Aigle sur une Redoute enlevée de vive force', by Martinet, *c.* 1816.

Caricature of Napoleon and England carving up the world, with England taking most of the world and Napoleon taking Europe.

The Plumb-pudding in danger – or – State Epicures taking un Petit Souper.
"the great Globe itself and all which it inherit" is too small to satisfy such insatiable appetites.

Engraving of the Battle of Austerlitz by Rouargue, *c.* 1840.

Letter from Russian commander Baron General Levin Benningsen to Tsar Alexander dated 31 January 1807, outlining the Russian situation one week before the Battle of Eylau.

Burl wood snuffbox with carved 'Dieppe' ivory depiction of the Battle of Wagram, after a painting by Horace Vernet, *c.* 1836–50.

Original order signed by Alexander Berthier, 6 September 1812, on the eve of the Battle of Borodino, transmitting the orders of the Emperor to Marshal Lefebvre, duc de Danzig, commander of the infantry of the Old Guard. '*The intention of the Emperor ... is that the Imperial Guard be placed by brigade, tomorrow 7th at 5 o'clock in the morning behind the left of the redoubt taken yesterday; the Young Guard up ahead, the Old Guard and the cavalry; the whole artillery of the Guard will be placed on its left.*'

Caricature 'General Frost Shaving Little Boney', signed by William Elmes, dated 1 December, 1812. Published by Tho. Tegg, No. 111 Cheapside, London.

Nineteenth century engraving 'Bataille de la Moskova, 7 Septembre 1812' by Langlois, showing the French taking a Russian redoubt.

Nineteenth-century engraving showing Napoleon's withdrawal from Russia.

German Braunschweig oil painting/lacquer snuffbox of papier-mâché with Napoleon trying to devour Leipzig, *c.* 1813–1814. The original painting is after a period caricature *The Parisian Nutcracker*. Napoleon stands on a coffin decorated with skulls and presents his sword. He is trying to crack the nut of Leipzig, but in the effort has lost some teeth which lie on the lid of the coffin. A handle to work the jaw protrudes from the back.

Engraving 'Départ de Fontainebleau, le 20 Avril, 1814', by Swebach, *c.* 1816.

1815 engraving 'Rentrée de Napoléon le Grand dans la Capitale de l'Empire Français, le 20 Mars, 1815'.

1817 engraving 'Surrender of Napoleon, Emperor of the French', by Dixon after a drawing made under the direction of a gentleman who was on the *Bellerophon* at the time.

Nineteenth-century engraving 'Napoléon à Waterloo', by Tazet after Steuben.

Lithograph
'St. Helena:
The Shade of
Napoleon
Visiting His
Tomb', by Day
and Hughe,
Lithographers
to the King,
c. 1830.
Napoleon can be
seen outlined
between the
trees.

Horn and tortoise-shell snuffbox
showing Napoleon's body being
exhumed on St. Helena, *c.*1840.

Bronze, ormolu, and marble
inkwell, with Napoleon's hat set
on sword and parchment listing
the battles of Marengo, Wagram
and Austerlitz, *c.* 1830–1860. The
hat tilts up to reveal the inkwell.

PART FOUR

STEPS TOWARDS
THE END

PRELUDE:
Napoleon's Most Intractable Foe

N apoleon's empire held out the promise of peace and prosperity throughout Europe. True, it would come at the price of homage to the Emperor of the French, but to many that was a reasonable price to pay. Great Britain, however, continued to hold out against this arrangement. When Prime Minister Pitt died in 1806 and was replaced by William Grenville, with Charles Fox as foreign minister, Napoleon hoped that peace might finally be possible.

Fox had been a supporter of peace but he was also a supporter of British interests and he did not see those interests reflected by French hegemony on the continent. Grenville had little interest in any *rapprochement* with France. As a result, there would be no peace, and Great Britain would continue to seek coalitions against the French emperor.

Napoleon was truly disappointed at this development. He knew that the French were tired of war and its attendant costs. Victories brought glory and riches, but the glory was fading and the riches were being balanced by the costs. As David Chandler has pointed out, 'But for the strains of continual wars, France would have prospered greatly.'[169] Napoleon's image as a warrior and conqueror notwithstanding, he had more reason to want peace than any other ruler in Europe.

Still, if the British wanted war, Napoleon was prepared to accommodate them. This continued conflict led, however, to three critical actions on Napoleon's part. Each seemed a reasonable thing to do; each could be rationally justified; each built on the other. Each proved to be a disastrous mistake. Napoleon is often accused of overreaching, of allowing his ego to get the better of him, of caring more for personal glory than for peace. While the first two of these charges may have some merit, Napoleon made far more fundamental mistakes. It is as a result of these mistakes, more than anything else, that the end came.

NOTE

169 *Dictionary Napoleonic Wars*, 94.

ECONOMIC WARFARE
The Continental System

The French naval defeats at Aboukir Bay and, especially, Trafalgar had removed any realistic possibility of invading England. Yet, as long as the British were willing to bankroll and promote various coalitions against Napoleon, there would be no peace in Europe. Furthermore, as long as France held the Low Countries, the British would remain committed to the defeat of Napoleon and the rolling back of at least some of France's borders. Moreover, Great Britain's policy of maintaining a balance of power on the continent was, to say the least, compromised by the existence of the French Empire.

Thus, British money, political influence and troops would continue to oppose Napoleon, and there would be no peace.

Napoleon understood this very well. He also understood that while he could defeat the British on land, this would not really change the equation. To defeat Great Britain, it would be necessary to force her to want peace more than the destruction of the French Empire. To do that, he would have to find a way to use his largely land-based military force to defeat her essentially sea-based power.

As an island nation, Great Britain was dependent upon trade for her very survival. It is for this reason, more than direct defence of the homeland, that she had historically developed such a large and effective navy. Trade with the Americas was important and trade with the Far East critical; it was this latter region that was the root cause for the Middle Eastern campaign and much of the other conflicts in the Mediterranean.

Europe, however, was of primary trading importance to Great Britain. Without Europe, her strong economy would falter and maybe even fail. That would deprive her of her most important military asset on the continent – money – and force her to demand peace on terms that would be acceptable to Napoleon.

That, at least, was the theory.

Seizing on this idea, Napoleon decided on a continental blockade of all British ships. He had already closed many of their traditionally available harbours in the Mediterranean; now he would close the rest of them. This was not a new idea; the Committee for Public Safety and later, the Directory had made efforts in that direction.

In 1806, England declared an embargo on all military-related goods sent to France. This gave Napoleon the political justification for his ideas. After his victories in 1806, he felt that he directly or indirectly controlled enough territory to achieve success. Consequently, on 21 November 1806, he issued the so-called Berlin Decrees, which announced that all commercial trade between the continent and Great Britain would from that time forward cease. Napoleon could only make this decree stick in areas he directly controlled and with those allies willing to bend to his will on the matter. This left a number of areas still open to such trade and reduced the effectiveness of the measure.

The Treaty of Tilsit in July 1807, however, brought Russia into an alliance with Napoleon and extended French control into new areas. Great Britain, meanwhile, again provided Napoleon political cover with her Orders in Council that greatly restricted trade by all nations with France. The British then demanded that the neutral state of Denmark surrender her fleet to them for 'safekeeping' until the advent of continental peace. Denmark, of course, refused this outrageous demand. In September, the Royal Navy shelled Copenhagen and seized Denmark's entire fleet. Beyond the excuse that it was in her own self interest, it is hard to justify this gross violation of international law. As Bainville suggests, perhaps 'Napoleon thought he could do as he liked because England did as she liked'.[170] The British got Denmark's navy, but Napoleon got a treaty of alliance that brought Denmark into the Continental System.

In response to the British action at Copenhagen, Napoleon issued the Decree of Fontainebleau and the Milan Decrees in late 1807, which essentially said that any ship that submitted to British inspection would be considered British and, therefore, subject to seizure as a prize of war.

While most historians concentrate on the ultimate failure of the Continental System, the fact is that for a while it met with considerable success. Neutral countries could not afford to run the risk of seizure, and France's territories and allies were initially quite effective in its implementation. Britannia was hardly brought to her knees, but she did suffer some significant economic consequences, while France's economy was helped somewhat by its increased trade within the continent.

In the long term, however, the Continental System proved a disaster. It was concern that the Iberian Peninsula was a major source of black market British goods that led Napoleon to invade Portugal in 1807. Generally considered Great Britain's oldest European ally, Portugal had ignored the Continental System and allowed all ships to use her harbours to trade in British goods. Although she tried to come to terms with Napoleon, he ultimately sent an army of occupation commanded by General Junot to secure the country. He then did little else to prepare for what must have been the obvious British reaction.

That reaction came in August 1808, when the British sent an army commanded by General Sir Arthur Wellesley to counter Junot's presence. The British were in Iberia, and Napoleon's plans were slowly but surely to disintegrate.

The Continental System developed other leaks as well. As King of Holland, Louis Bonaparte had the responsibility to govern in the interests of his people, and he was greatly influenced by the merchant class. As Napoleon's brother and having been put on the throne by him, he had the responsibility of loyalty to his brother and to the Empire. It would prove to be an impossible situation. Under heavy pressure at home, Louis chose to ignore the smuggling that was taking place.

Napoleon, however, was ignoring nothing. He complained to Louis and urged him to take strong corrective actions. He once wrote to Louis sarcastically, 'I am informed that the commerce between England and Holland was never more brisk than since the Berlin decree and the communications with England more rapid and more numerous.'[171] When it became clear that Louis would not or could not take effective actions, Napoleon forced him to abdicate his throne.

On St. Helena, Napoleon expressed his affection for Louis but suggested that he 'acted like a *préfet* rather than a king'.[172] In 1810, Holland was annexed to the Empire and newly appointed Marshal Nicolas Oudinot was sent with an army of occupation. Given the popularity of the now ex-king Louis, Oudinot was a good choice. He developed a reputation for fairness and justice beyond those of the other Marshals and he maintained the goodwill of the people of Holland.[173]

Louis the Good, meanwhile, fled to the United States, leaving behind him his wife Hortense, his sons and his country.

In 1811, Napoleon's family struck again. Marshal Joachim Murat, married to Napoleon's sister Caroline, was probably the best cavalry officer in Europe. However, as King of Naples he was a vainglorious ruler who cherished his throne above all else. He began to see himself less

French and more Italian. When the Continental System began to hurt his subjects, he too began to distance himself from Napoleon.

Napoleon was becoming exasperated with his family. None was proving worthy of the trust he had placed in them. If he had been demanding, it was still true that he had placed them on their thrones, and it was always understood that he did this because he felt their loyalty would be to him. In June 1811, he told Caulaincourt 'My family does not back me up. They are all insanely ambitious, ruinously extravagant and devoid of talent.'[174]

While the Continental System made logical sense and may well have been the only real option open to Napoleon to attempt to force peace with an unwilling Great Britain, it ultimately failed to cause enough economic damage to make a difference. Worse, it directly led to the other two mistakes that Napoleon made; two actions that contributed greatly to his downfall.

NOTES

170 Bainville, 215.

171 *Correspondance* 25 February 1807, No. 11880, XIV, 419; Bingham, II, 295–96.

172 Las Cases, III, 6, 111.

173 Eidhal, K. 'Marshal Nicolas Charles Oudinot "Le Bayard de l'armée française"', in *Napoleonic Scholarship*, I, 1, April 1997: 36.

174 Caulaincourt, *With Napoleon in Russia*, 14. Caulaincourt served as Napoleon's Master of Horse, Ambassador to Russia, and twice as Minister for Foreign Affairs. He was a trusted confidant and his memoirs are among the best available.

THE
SPANISH QUAGMIRE

In Spain by 1808, the Bourbon Charles IV was at best mentally unstable, and his queen, Maria-Luisa, and her lover, Manuel de Godoy, who served as prime minister, were running the country.

Spain was – and is – a conservative Catholic country. The peasants were not happy with the decidedly non-pious behaviour of Maria-Luisa and Godoy. Even the king's own son engaged in plots against the throne. Napoleon had already occupied Portugal to close its ports to the British and it was a simple matter to send more troops, under Marshal Murat, to Spain.

The intrigue between various members of the royal family and Godoy was absurd, and it was clear to anyone that none of them was fit to lead. The royal family was lured into becoming Napoleon's 'guests' at Bayonne, arriving there on 30 April 1808. The son renounced his claim to his father's throne, who had already abdicated in favour of Napoleon, who then offered the crown to his brothers, first to Louis and then to Jérôme. Perhaps recognising that the complexities of both politics and society in Spain would prove to be more difficult to master than Napoleon realised, both brothers in turn declined what they no doubt saw as a dubious 'honour'.

Napoleon then coerced his brother Joseph to leave Naples and become the new king of Spain. Joseph, like his brothers Louis and Jérôme, saw the pitfalls of this and tried to decline as well. Napoleon would hear none of it, however, and on 6 June 1808, Joseph became the unhappy King of Spain. Murat, whose brutal over-reaction to a riot in Madrid on 2 May 1808 gave rise to Goya's famous paintings of French repression, was then made the King of Naples on 1 August. Murat was not happy, and his appointment would later come back to haunt Napoleon.

For the Continental System to work, Spain had to be trustworthy, which is why Joseph was put on its throne. As we have noted, he made an effort to be a liberal and popular king. This was applauded by the intelligentsia, who were anxious to move Spain into the modern era. Long dominated by the Catholic Church, more known for its Inquisition than its tolerance, Spain was not a major power and its cultural accomplishments were mostly the stuff of memories.

Napoleon understood this attitude and played to it. Unfortunately, he believed that the attitude of the intelligentsia was reflected by the general populace. In this, he was completely wrong. He also felt that his Concordat with the Pope would make him at least acceptable to the Spanish Catholic Church. In this hope he was equally wrong.

The Spanish peasants were not all that fond of their Bourbon rulers. However, they did resent the way the Bourbons were being treated by Napoleon, taking it as a lack of respect for the Spanish people. Napoleon and Joseph treated them as though they were French, with French attitudes. This was a drastic misreading of the situation and would cost them dearly.

The Spanish Church, and therefore the Spanish peasants, had never accepted the French Revolution. They saw it, correctly, as essentially anti-clerical in nature and looked on with horror as the French stripped the Church of its property and power. The Concordat may have been a step in the right direction, but rather than restoring the Church's role in France, it was simply a part of a move toward religious tolerance and secular control, which would include divorce rights and civil marriages. The Spanish Church was not interested.

The French people were mostly Catholic, but many of them had come to resent the power of the Church. Only in certain areas like the Vendée did the Church still dominate the lives of the common people, and Napoleon was able to co-opt them with the Concordat and other concessions mixed with reprisals.

The Spanish peasants were far closer to the French of the Vendée than to the revolutionaries of Paris. Any promise to abolish feudalism, to bring the *Code Napoléon* or other reforms, would fall on mostly deaf ears. Napoleon thought he would be seen as the liberator of Spain. Instead, he was seen as the usurper of its crown and a threat to its Church. He did not understand that to be Spanish was to be Catholic. The Spanish had a religious nationalism unlike anything found elsewhere in Europe; to attack the Catholic Church was to attack the very essence of being Spanish.

Had Napoleon selected Murat as the new king – Murat had, after all, been serving as Napoleon's representative in Madrid and was not unpopular – perhaps it might have gone differently. Murat wanted the crown, Joseph didn't. Perhaps the people understood this and reacted accordingly.

In 1808, the British were in Portugal, the Spanish peasants were up in arms, and much of the Spanish army was actively opposing the French. Several of Napoleon's regional military governors had been assassinated. Joseph had only arrived in Madrid on 20 July, and by the 24th he had warned Napoleon 'The honest people are as little on my side as the rogues are. No, Sire, you are deceived. Your glory will be shipwrecked in Spain.'[175] Then came the setback at Bailen, where, on 22 July 1808, General Dupont's corps, 20,000-strong, was forced to surrender. King Joseph fled Madrid on the 29th and sought refuge with French troops in the north.

In August, Junot's 17,000-strong army was defeated by Wellesley at Vimiero. Although the subsequent treaty, called the Convention of Cintra, allowed Junot's army to depart without disruption – they, their baggage and their loot, were given passage to France in British ships – the situation was becoming alarming. The British were firmly in control of Portugal and the French were clearly not going to have an easy time of it in Spain. Joseph's military commander General Jean Savary's advice of a few days earlier to the king expresses well the problem they were facing:

> But what would the Emperor say? The Emperor will scold, no doubt; but words are not blows ... I am quite sure that if he were now at Madrid, he would never dream of quitting it: true it is that his presence never fails to command implicit obedience and silence all complaint. How different the case is with us! Whatever orders we may give, we find every one coming forward with excuses of fatigue or ill-health; whereas a look of the Emperor would be sufficient to rouse all those indolent men to action. No one can pretend to tread in the Emperor's footsteps: woe be to him who shall presume to imitate his example; he would be lost in the attempt.[176]

Napoleon had sent second-rate troops to Spain and they were not up to the job.

Perhaps even worse is that for the first time the French army was split into two parts widely separated from each other. Napoleon could only be in one place at a time. For now, this was not a problem because there was peace on the eastern front. But it was a situation not unnoticed by Austria and others. Austria began to enlarge her military, helped with British money. Tsar Alexander, meanwhile, was becoming less sure of his alliance with Napoleon. Napoleon's difficulties in Spain had started the vultures circling but their action was to prove premature.

After the defeat at Bailen, Napoleon decided to change the equation. He ordered an additional 100,000 of his best troops, led by several of his best Marshals, to move into Spain and defeat the insurgents. More importantly, he placed himself at their head. He arrived in November 1808 and by early December had swept the field and was at the gates of Madrid.

Then, Napoleon's normally excellent sense of diplomacy deserted him. Rather than treat the Spanish with respect and allow his brother to act as king, he completely overshadowed Joseph and issued threats to the Spanish people. Joseph, of course, was humiliated by this and tried to abdicate. Napoleon would not allow that, but the damage done to relations with the Spanish people would not be undone.[177]

The Spanish presumably defeated and the British army (which had moved into Spain from Portugal) on the run, Napoleon could understandably feel that he had achieved success. Meanwhile, the Austrians were sabre rattling in central Europe. Worse, Foreign Minister Talleyrand and Minister of Police Fouché were suspected of preparing, perhaps hopefully, for Napoleon's death. A *coup* was always a possibility and Napoleon could see that he was needed in Paris. He left his army under Joseph's command and returned to Europe.

Napoleon left a good army with a weak leader. Joseph was no Napoleon. Worse, he left a divided leadership below Joseph, Marshals whose egos and similarity of rank made any unified command difficult, if not impossible. 'He left behind a feeble king, equally as incapable of keeping, as obtaining a conquest; and marshals who, no longer restrained by the presence of an inflexible chief, for the most part delivered themselves over to their own self-love, or the indulgence of their private passions.'[178]

The 1809 occupation of the Papal States by a French army and the removal of the Pope to France made the situation even worse. It set the Church of Spain into a frenzy. From every pulpit, the French action and Napoleon were denounced.

For the next several years, the French would be in a quagmire, unable to win, too good to lose, unable to extricate themselves gracefully. Napoleon had planned to return and settle the issue. He would never get the chance.

France's Spanish campaign was a failure, but not necessarily to the benefit of the Spanish. Napoleon's comments while on St. Helena accurately reflect the outcome he sought and might have found:

> If the government I established had remained, it would have been the best thing that ever happened for Spain. I would have regenerated the Spaniards; I would have made them a great nation. Instead of a feeble, imbecile and superstitious race of Bourbons, I would have given them a new dynasty, that would have no claim on the nation, except by the good it would have rendered unto it ... I would have destroyed superstition and priestcraft and abolished the Inquisition ... The guerrillas, who fought so bravely against me, now lament their success.[179]

TREACHERY IN PARIS

When Napoleon returned from Spain to Paris in late January 1809, he found various plots in the works and discontent in the air. It soon became clear that Talleyrand and Joseph Fouché were making plans, 'just in case' and were engaged in communications with Austria and others that were not, to say the least, in Napoleon's or France's best interest. Talleyrand and Fouché disliked each other and no specific plot was discovered, but it was clear to all that they were no longer to be trusted. This was especially true of Talleyrand.

This was not the first time these two men had proved to be more interested in themselves or in what they claimed were the 'best interests' of France, rather than in the 'best interests' of the man who made them and to whom they were sworn to serve. Any reasonable person might well have expected their expulsion from the government and in the case of treason, their outright execution.

Napoleon would later live to regret it, but he only gave them a serious reprimand. He felt that he still needed the services of these two very special men. Various historians have noted that Napoleon had difficulty administering severe consequences against his defeated enemies, either foreign or domestic. In the case of Fouché and Talleyrand, leniency would prove to be a fatal flaw.

Charles Maurice de Talleyrand-Périgord had been Bishop of Autun at the time of the French Revolution. He was a man of extreme intelligence and charm, equally at home in the worlds of high society and high diplomacy. He had long since left the Church for politics and served as a diplomat in England and the United States. In 1797, Paul Barras had appointed him Minister of Foreign Affairs, a position he maintained when Napoleon became First Consul.

Talleyrand served Napoleon and France well for many years, but was always ready to switch to whichever side he saw as the ultimate winner. Napoleon was willing to remove him as Foreign Minister but never to remove him from government entirely. No matter how he behaved, Napoleon said he found it impossible not to like Talleyrand.

Joseph Fouché had been active in the French Revolution and had voted for the execution of Louis XVI. He had been quick to support Napoleon in 1799 and he soon became Minister of Police. Initially, he was fiercely loyal to Napoleon, and his vast secret police network helped protect Napoleon from various plotters. In 1810, Napoleon removed him as Minister of Police as punishment for his compromising communications with the exiled Bourbons. He was sent out of the country on diplomatic missions, but never lost touch with his informants. He supported the returned Bourbons but also kept contact with Napoleon on Elba. When Napoleon returned in 1815, Fouché was once again appointed Minister of Police but after Waterloo he worked towards Napoleon's abdication.

THE LAW OF UNINTENDED CONSEQUENCES: NATIONALISM

In Europe other events were afoot that might serve the Austrian cause. In Germany, Napoleon's reforms were having a decidedly unexpected and even more decidedly unwanted effect. While the Confederation of the Rhine was composed of a group of small states, the application of Napoleonic laws and administrative reforms began to tie them together. In many ways Napoleon could be seen as the father of modern Germany; do not, however, look for monuments dedicated to him in that regard.

Soon, forces of nationalism began to emerge, with a desire to bring all the German states together as one nation. Napoleon opposed that, because he wanted to keep any potential challenge to his hegemony from developing. This approach, however, only led nationalism and opposition to Napoleon to become one and the same. Napoleon, quite aware of these stirrings, moved to suppress them. He could do so as long as he was secure; however, when his star began to fall, it was helped on its way down by these new forces.

In Italy, monuments to Napoleon do indeed exist for his part in reunification of the nation (*Risorgimento*). As with Germany, Napoleon brought his reforms to that fragmented area and as early as the Treaty of Campo Formio in 1797 was making moves to unify some parts of the greater Italian nation.

For cultural as well as security reasons – he was, after all, Corsican and therefore of Italian heritage – Napoleon had taken a special interest in Italy. His moves towards unification at Campo Formio had been dangerous and exceeded his authority, but they had survived. When he became Emperor, he also became King of Italy and his son would become known as the King of Rome.

As had been the case with Germany, the developing feelings of nationalism led to a resentment toward French control and occupation, and there was significant unrest in the countryside. Unlike the Germans, however, the Italians stayed generally loyal to Napoleon throughout his career. After his downfall, the movement toward *Risorgimento* was given a great boost by the participation of many of his former military and government officials.

In Italy, Napoleon is today seen as something of the father of modern Italy. The splendid *Museo de la Risorgimento* in Milan pays tribute to his role, showing him in what must be described as generally heroic images.

Here, then, is another reason for Napoleon's ultimate decline. In a cruel irony, one of his best accomplishments – the spreading of reforms throughout Europe – helped lead to his downfall.

In 1808, Napoleon and Alexander met again. Austria, still smarting from her earlier defeats and loss of territory, had looked with great interest at Napoleon's ever worsening situation in Spain and the growing nationalism in Europe. With the *Grande Armée* split, with British money still pouring in, with parts of Europe becoming restless under Napoleon's rule, perhaps now was the time for Austria to regain lost territory and honour.

Napoleon, of course, was quite aware of what was happening in Austria; it was one of the two major reasons why he had returned from Spain. Austria had a serious problem, namely Russia. If Alexander could be counted on to offer strong support to the French in any conflict between France and Austria, Napoleon thought the last major continental power to oppose France could be vanquished once and for all. He had still not quite realised that there would never be a 'once and for all' as long as he was in power.

When Napoleon met Alexander, he discovered that the young Tsar's enthusiasm for his alliance with Napoleon had faded considerably. While he was certainly not turning on his friend, he was not anxious to offer any significant military support either.

Alexander was not all that strong a leader, and he was under great pressure to break agreements forged on the raft at Tilsit and turn on Napoleon. The Continental System was unpopular with his merchant class. The creation of the Duchy of Warsaw had stymied the expansionist desires of his nobles and of his own family. Worse, they saw the expansion of French reforms to the Polish serfs as a great threat to their control over their own serfs. Alexander might be enamoured of Napoleon, but the interests of the Russian aristocracy and their control of the Russian economy might be better served by the *anciens régimes* rather than the brave new world of Napoleonic Europe.

The time for a break was not yet ripe, however, and in the end, Alexander promised to fight the Austrians if they declared war on France.

Not surprisingly, Austria did indeed declare war on France in April 1809. Equally unsurprising was the reaction of the French people, even the French leaders. All knew that Napoleon wanted peace, that peace was in the best interests of France and the whole of Europe. Yet the sum total of all Napoleon's victories had been more war and the need for more victories. It was well enough to blame it on the British, on the *anciens régimes*, on whatever or whomsoever one wished. Blame aside, the people were becoming sick of war.

Slowly, almost imperceptibly, this surfeit of war moved toward recognition that the interests of France and the interests of Napoleon might not always be the same. For most, this was not dissatisfaction with Napoleon or a lack of gratitude for the benefits his star had showered on them. It was just their perception of what they saw as the new reality.

Napoleon understood this. He was torn between his desire for peace and his realisation that only the defeat, or at least the neutralisation, of the British would bring that peace. But what if they could be neither defeated nor neutralised? That was unthinkable, and so the struggle went on.

This Austrian aggression was something else again. No one could blame Napoleon for this war, but anything less than a total victory would accelerate those forces that were already foreshadowing his fall.

Within a short space of time, 20 to 22 April 1809, the French and Austrians fought three battles in Bavaria: Abensberg, Landshut and Eckmühl. Napoleon won all three, but the Austrians were able to retreat in good order, though with a loss of some 30,000 men. The road to Vienna was now open and Napoleon once again moved into the city.

In May 1809, ever anxious to take the initiative, he took control of the island of Lobau and quickly crossed to the left bank of the Danube to occupy the villages of Aspern and Essling. There, he discovered that he was outnumbered by about three to one. Even so, he would probably have won, but high water repeatedly damaged and finally broke the bridge to Lobau Island. The bridge was not of the finest quality, and the fast-moving high water pounded it with debris, much of which had been dumped into the river by the Austrians for just that purpose. In their haste, the French had not built protective barriers and by the night of 21 May the bridge was no longer usable; Napoleon was cut off from supplies and one third of his army, including Marshal Davout.

Napoleon was able to repair the bridge, but his momentum was stalled, and he eventually withdrew to the island, turning it into a fortress. Given the situation, he had actually done quite well, but there were heavy losses on both sides and, for the first time in his career, Napoleon had been forced to abandon the battlefield. Needless to say, this caused quite a stir in France and elsewhere and gave renewed hope to his enemies.

Those hopes were to be dashed. Napoleon was to have another great victory to boost his star and set him on the road to glory once again. Troops from Italy under Napoleon's stepson, Prince Eugène, arrived, as did more troops commanded by Marmont. By early July, Napoleon had almost 200,000 men available and was ready to strike the now outnumbered Austrian forces. If Napoleon had to retreat from the battlefield again, he might well be finished.

It would happen again, but not in this campaign. In the two-day Battle of Wagram, 4–5 July 1809, Napoleon defeated the Austrians, though not as decisively as he must have wished. They were finished, however, and when it became clear that no one else was going to enter the conflict on their side, on 14 October 1809 they signed the Treaty of Schönbrunn, named after the Habsburg palace in Vienna. Napoleon gained a great deal of territory and Austria was to pay a large war indemnity and, of course, rejoin the Continental System.

The Emperor Francis had broken his word, given after Austerlitz, never to fight Napoleon again, and it had cost him dearly. Yet for all his success, Napoleon could not take the comfort in Wagram that he had taken in Austerlitz or Friedland. In addition to everything else that was happening in Europe, Napoleon had made an alarming discovery. The Austrians had fought far better than he had expected; his enemies were following him into the modern methods of warfare, and all future victories would come at increasingly dearer cost. It was not a good omen.

Another bad omen had been the support, or rather the lack of support, offered by Napoleon's erstwhile ally, Russia. The Tsar had promised to fight the Austrians but ended up firing a barrage of words rather than of cannon. His support for the Continental System was also lukewarm and chilling fast. Napoleon was upset and confused; this was not to be expected of an ally. Still, he needed Russia and gave her some territorial gains for her non-participation on the battlefield.

NOTES

175 Napoleon I. *Confidential Correspondence with Joseph*, No. 412, I, 341.
176 Savary, II, 1, 279–80.
177 Dempsey, Guy. 'The Peninsular War: A Reputation Tarnished', in *Napoleon: The Final Verdict*. London, 1996, 99–100.
178 La Bédoyère, II, 524.
179 O'Meara, I, 136.

RUSSIA, 1812

We now turn to that most famous of disasters, the Russian campaign of 1812. To most casual students of Napoleon, this campaign is seen as the cause of his downfall. We have seen, however, that the Russian campaign was the almost inevitable result of the Continental System and the campaign's disastrous outcome was the almost inevitable result of the Spanish Quagmire. Only in this light can the tragedy of Russia be truly understood.[180]

Alexander and Napoleon were still allies and both wanted things to remain that way. Alexander, however, was not the absolute ruler that one might expect of a Tsar. He was greatly influenced by his mother, and his mother was totally opposed to Napoleon. Yet it was Alexander's relations with his nobles that were the most problematic. Taking a lead from Napoleon, Alexander had sought to begin some very basic reforms in Russia. But he was more Louis XVI than Napoleon I: when his nobles objected, he backed down.

There were two major problems between the two rulers. Napoleon had wanted to create a new Polish state; Alexander and his nobles were totally opposed. Indeed, they were outraged that Napoleon had created the Duchy of Warsaw and sought to have him abandon it. This Napoleon would not do; he had given his word to the Poles and he wanted a buffer between Russia and the rest of Europe. Some Poles, in the end, felt that Napoleon had betrayed his commitment to them. In fact, his support for their cause sent him to war and eventually cost him his crown.

The other major problem was the Continental System. While successful in the beginning, the blockade of British goods soon began to hurt the continent at least as much as it was hurting the British. Indeed, the cost of living in France had gone up, smuggling was rampant and France had even made some official 'exceptions' to the blockade.

This was more than Alexander and his merchant class could handle. As early as 1810, they were opening their ports to 'neutral' ships, which meant to British goods, while placing restrictions on French trade. This was in open defiance of Napoleon and by itself might well have led to war. Combined with the Polish question, it left little doubt in the matter.

Alexander prepared for war. He worked towards the conclusion of a peace with Turkey (which he achieved in May) and lured former Marshal of France and now Crown Prince of Sweden Jean-Baptiste Bernadotte to turn on the French in alliance with Russia. In return, Alexander promised help in Bernadotte's efforts to conquer Norway. Finally convinced that he was ready, Alexander delivered a set of demands to Napoleon in April 1812, the most important of which was that the French must abandon the Duchy of Warsaw. For Napoleon, this meant war.

Some have contended that Napoleon had other, somewhat more ambitious, motives for invading Russia. While in Egypt, there had been much talk of his taking his army to India, striking at the very heart of British trade in that region. Baron von Odeleben, a Saxon attached to Napoleon's staff in 1813, was certainly convinced

> many of our contemporaries treat the project of invading the East Indies, as altogether incredible and ridiculous; but, from the information I received at the French headquarters, I am confident such an intention was real. The provinces of the Russian Empire, so little favoured by nature, could not, surely, tempt the avidity of Napoleon ... Neither the conquest, then, of these provinces, nor the desire of vanquishing the Russian army ... determined the victorious chief to undertake this campaign. No – he considered the road to Moscow as but the third part of his march to India.[181]

This makes for interesting speculation, but the fact of the matter is that Napoleon had much more urgent reasons for the campaign.

Like the First World War a century later, this was a war that nobody really wanted and that some, most notably Napoleon, thought would be over quickly. Although Alexander did not really want the war, he was prepared to draw Napoleon deep into Mother Russia and employ a scorched-earth policy to prevent the French troops from living off the land.

Napoleon was an astute student of history and was therefore well aware of the fact that there was no precedent for the success of such an invasion. For all his talk of a quick victory and a quick peace, he knew well that Alexander was likely to draw him into Russia, but also realised that sooner or later – hopefully sooner – the Russians would have to stand and fight a pitched battle. Here, of course, Napoleon had history on his side; he had never lost to the Russians. The plan, then, was clear: the French would go no further than Smolensk, they would win a major battle, and the friendship with Alexander would pick up where it had been before this unfortunate 'misunderstanding'.

Historians have frequently held that the Russian campaign was the result of Napoleon's monumental ego or the result of a massive miscalculation. It was neither. It was a calculated move that made all the logical sense in the world. It was a move more by Alexander than by Napoleon. The French preparations for war were, after all, in direct response to similar moves by Russia. Napoleon made this clear to Alexander; what was made equally clear was Napoleon's desire for peace, tempered by his unwillingness to allow the destruction of the agreements forged at Tilsit. During the year prior to the conflict, Napoleon virtually pleaded for peace, but war was by then inevitable.

In any event, Napoleon saw no viable alternative. He could hardly give in to the Tsar's demands regarding the Poles, and Russia's refusal to participate fully in the Continental System would spell its doom. Nor could he sit and wait for Russia to attack him. That would give the Russians the advantage of fighting on someone else's land and of being on the offensive.

Napoleon was a master of war, and his success depended on taking the offensive. He would take that war to Russia, and let her face the consequences.

Napoleon also had what he believed would be his margin of victory. He assembled what was perhaps the largest fighting force in history to that time, an army of more than 600,000 men. While the French soldiers, who made up about half of the total, were on whom he most counted, the army truly represented his empire at its peak.[182] Twenty different nations were represented, each with its own uniform and Colours. Each also, more problematically, with its own language. French was the language of the élite and therefore of many of the officers, but not of the common soldiers.

It was an amazing and most impressive sight when, on 24 June 1812, Napoleon's army marched across the Niemen into Russia. Half a million men, a thousand cannon, soldiers and carriages as far as the eye could see. Who could blame Napoleon for believing that he would be unbeatable? Some advisers had cautioned him against the move; his ambassador to Russia, Armand de Caulaincourt, had warned as early as June 1811 that Alexander had spoken of his intention to draw Napoleon deep into Russia, concluding, 'Your Frenchman is brave, but long privations and a bad climate wear him down and discourage him. Our climate, our winter, will fight on our side.'[183] Napoleon well understood the dangers he was facing, including the possibilities of intrigue in Paris while he was gone. Even so, the general belief throughout the empire was that the campaign would be a success.

No one would have believed it if told that only a scant ten per cent of this massive army would return.

Napoleon should have given thought to another concern regarding Alexander. The Tsar knew full well the enormous army he was to face. Napoleon had effectively unified most of western Europe in a campaign against Russia that was to be fought on her soil. Only a ruler determined to fight no matter what the consequences would have taken on such a daunting task. Napoleon appears to have given no consideration to the possibility that the Tsar would refuse to fight and, if defeated in battle, would simply withdraw and live to fight again.

Another reason for concern should have been the classic nightmare of fighting a war on two fronts. Great leaders throughout history have done all they could to avoid the splitting of their forces at opposite ends of their own central territory. Yet, with the Iberian Campaign still in progress, and with success there anything but certain, Napoleon chose to open what was to be the largest offensive in his career. If anyone could achieve success under these circumstances, it was Napoleon. Indeed, by the traditional expectations of such campaigns, he had a fair likelihood of success. This campaign, however, would not be traditional.

Napoleon's army advanced, eager to fight. The Russian forces were divided into two armies, commanded by Generals Barclay de Tolly and Peter Bagration respectively. As always, Napoleon wanted to defeat first one and then the other, before they could unite.

Unlike times gone by, however, he would not get his wish. There were skirmishes, all of which were won by the French, but no decisive major battle. More than once the French came close to forcing a battle with each of the Russian armies, but confusion and hesitation lost them those opportunities. It was already becoming clear that things were not as they had been.

From the very beginning, indecision and delay were costing the French valuable time. Some of these delays were the result of poor leadership on the part of subordinates and some were the result of weather. The worst delays, however, were a function of the size of the *Grande Armée* itself. Impressive though it was, the invasion force was a logistical nightmare. Napoleon understood the problem and tried to make appropriate plans, but he and his subordinates had under-estimated the problems that would be posed by the diverse nature of their army, the great distances involved and the combination of a scorched-earth policy and the poor roads they would encounter in Russia.[184]

On 28 June 1812, Napoleon entered Vilna. Here he waited eighteen days, expecting and hoping that Alexander would appear either for battle or to sue for peace. The wait was in vain. Napoleon considered staying there for the winter, though it was only July, but an army at rest is an army that loses its will and its effectiveness. He even considered staying there longer and using the city as his base for future operations. Then he realised that it was necessary to advance and force the decisive battle that he needed. Besides, he could not afford to be absent from Paris for too long.

Eventually he decided to push on toward Vitebsk, on the northern flank of his invasion. After some heavy fighting, the French advance was delayed. This gave the Russians yet another opportunity to withdraw. Napoleon entered the city on 28 July; he had conquered more territory, but that was all.

At this point, there was a good argument for calling a halt to the operation. The French army was exhausted from the long march in extremely hot weather. The Russian winter's effect on the withdrawal from Russia is well known; less discussed is the equally disastrous effect the hot summer weather had on the *Grande Armée*. Napoleon's staff argued the point as best they. Count Daru tried his hand at convincing Napoleon to consolidate his victory, gain reinforcements and bring the campaign to a halt. In the end, however, Napoleon became convinced that he needed either to retreat or press the campaign forward. Retreat was out of the question, so on 13 August he left Vitebsk along the road to Smolensk.

Before Smolensk, he found that the two Russian armies had joined forces. On the 16th and 17th there was significant fighting in the suburbs. There was a lull on the 18th, and then Bagration's army began to withdraw, leaving Barclay's army to face Napoleon alone. Napoleon did not seize on this opportunity to catch the two armies separate from each other, however, and both armies made good their escape.

On 18 August Napoleon entered Smolensk. When making his plans in Paris, Smolensk had marked the deepest into Russia that he had planned to go. His troops had not been issued with winter clothing; there had been no thought of a winter campaign, much less a winter retreat. However, the Russians had sacked their own city and moved on. There was to be no battle of Smolensk.

Napoleon was no fool. He realised that things had not gone as he had planned and expected. His understanding of the rigours of a Russian winter was probably incomplete. Who could imagine it unless he had experienced it?

He faced a decision that had to be made, and made quickly. The town was ruined, but it was still possible that he could winter there. His supply lines were not yet over-extended and he could renew his campaign in the spring. He could recognise Poland as an independent nation, which would assure him of their loyalty and give him a new cadre of dedicated soldiers. Organising this new Polish territory would take time, but the benefits were potentially very important. It was a good option, and one that Napoleon seriously considered.

Vitebsk was another possibility. He had troops there and adequate provisions for the coming winter. He gave strong consideration to not moving forward. Either way, however, would be to admit failure. His hopes of a victory in the first twenty days of the campaign had gone, but he could still achieve victory if only the Russians would stand and fight! Moreover, delay would also give the Russians an opportunity to marshal their own forces and perhaps even cut him off from the rest of Europe. Delay until spring would also increase the possibility of intrigue in Paris. Still determined to force a decisive battle, Napoleon had to choose between two possibilities: make for the Tsar's capital, St. Petersburg, or head for Moscow, the ancient city most sacred to the Russians. In the end, it was the Russian army that made the decision for him, retiring down the road to Moscow, 280 miles away. Napoleon would set off in pursuit.

Napoleon had delayed at Vilna, at Vitebsk and at Smolensk. A fortnight's delay at El Arish had doomed the Egyptian campaign; these Russian delays took away any margin of error. Any further delay would doom the campaign. Meanwhile, the morale of the men was in decline.

Stendhal, who had been so pleased to participate in the Russian campaign, reflected the changed attitude, writing, "My own happiness at being here is not great. How a man changes! My old thirst for new sights has been entirely quenched ... In this ocean of barbarity there is not a sound that finds an echo in my soul."[185]

Meanwhile, Tsar Alexander was rallying his troops and reminding Napoleon once again of what awaited him. In a proclamation General Benningsen had posted with the Orders of the Day, the Tsar wrote:

> Russians! The enemy has left the River Dvina and has shown the intention to give battle to you. He accuses you of timidity, because he does not know or pretends not to know the politics of your system ... Desperate attempts alone are compatible with the enterprise he has put together and the dangers of his situation; but would we become imprudent and would we lose the advantages of our situation? He wants to go to Moscow, let him go there. But will he be able through the temporary possession of this town conquer the Russian Empire and subjugate a population of thirty million people? Removed from his resources by about 800 miles, HE WILL NOT, EVEN WHEN BECOMING VICTORIOUS, ESCAPE THE FATE OF THE BELLI-COSE CHARLES II. Pressed from all sides by our armies, by peasants who have sworn his destruction, who have been rendered furious by his excesses, who by reason of the difference of religion, customs and language have become his irreconcilable enemies, how will he manage his retreat? ...
>
> Too far advanced to withdraw with impunity, the enemy will soon have to face the seasons, famine and the innumerable Russian armies. Soldiers! When the moment to give battle arrives, your Emperor will give you the signal; he will be the eye-witness of your feats and will reward your valour.[186]

This proclamation, issued in August, was worthy of Napoleon himself! It is quite likely that he read a copy; in any event, it merely echoed the warning the Tsar had sent through Caulaincourt a year before. Napoleon, however, was still not listening. He had made up his mind and was determined to see it through. It all made sense, but it would not work. His failure to understand that things were no longer the way they used to be must be seen as fundamental to his downfall.

Napoleon marched toward Moscow, still seeking a major battle. He had been right about one thing, anyway: the Russians would not give up Moscow without a fight. The people of Russia would not tolerate a Tsar who did. So Alexander sent in General Kutusov to command Barclay's troops and make a stand near the town of Borodino. Napoleon had beaten Kutusov at Austerlitz, and he would do so again at Borodino.

But it would prove a hollow victory that would not matter. Indeed, it might have been better had he lost, for then his retreat would have taken place in much warmer weather.

The march to Borodino was reasonably successful. On 5 September the French fought hard and captured the Schivardino Redoubt and the surrounding area. On the 6th both sides rested and prepared themselves.

The Battle of Borodino was everything that Napoleon did not want. The Russian troops had been there long enough to chose favourable positions and dig in and fortify them. They numbered some 120,000 men and had about 600 cannon. Against them, Napoleon brought not the half million plus that he had started with, but only some 133,000 men and about the same number of cannon as the enemy. He was a long way from where he had started, and his numerical advantage had been eroded by his need to leave garrisons along the route to protect his lines of communication with Paris. Desertions accounted for the remainder, save for the few lost in the skirmishes.

Borodino was not ideal but at least it was, at last, the pitched battle Napoleon had so desperately sought. A victory here, the capture of nearby Moscow, and Alexander would finally come to terms.

Early in the morning of 7 September 1812 Napoleon issued one of his customary proclamations; one that reflected the glory of past campaigns:

> Soldiers, this is the battle you have longed for. Victory now depends on you; it must be ours. It will bring us abundance, good winter-quarters and a quick return home.
>
> Do as you did at Austerlitz, at Friedland, at Vitebsk, at Smolensk; and may your conduct today be spoken of with pride by all generations to come. May it be said of you: he was at that great battle beneath the walls of Moscow![187]

It may well be that the French were not completely sure where they were. They did not have good maps of the area. Berthier's order on 6 September to General Lefevbre, commander of the infantry of the Imperial Guard, says that they are 'en arrière de Majaisk' (behind Majaisk),[188] when in point of fact that town is 25 miles on the other side of Borodino. This may also explain why the French called this the Battle of the Moskova (River), when the actual river by the battlefield is the Kalatsha.

Napoleon had with him his best marshals and they performed well. His stepson, Prince Eugène, captured the town and Marshal Ney managed to get a foothold on a strategic area known as Three Arrows. Sensing that a major breakthrough here would lead to an overwhelming victory – a conclusion that was quite justifiable – Ney asked Napoleon to send in his reserves: the Imperial Guard.

Napoleon needed an overwhelming victory; Ney's position gave him a chance to get that victory; the 18,000 men of the Imperial Guard would probably have made it a rout. The Napoleon of old might well have done just that, but now he was more cautious. The commander of the Guard, Marshal Bessières, argued against throwing in his last reserves so far from home.

It was a logical and prudent suggestion, but it removed the possibility of an overwhelming victory and with it the last chance for a peace offering from Alexander. Napoleon was unwell and had received bad news regarding the campaign in Spain. Perhaps these were factors in his decision. It is impossible to say.

Napoleon would deny Ney's request for help once more – at Waterloo. That decision would end his career.

At Borodino, Napoleon did send Ney at least some help and soon the fighting centered on the part of the field known as the Great Redoubt, a heavily fortified stretch of high ground with more than twenty cannon dug in. Flanking efforts were ineffective and most of the action was directed in a frontal attack.

It was a blood-bath. The French were charging into grapeshot-firing cannon and thousands of Russian muskets. The dead piled up and the field ran red. A final attack led by Eugène, Ney and Murat (who was back in Napoleon's good graces and commander of the cavalry) was successful and the Great Redoubt was taken. While in range, the cannon were turned on the retreating Russians. Murat's cavalry could have chewed up them up and might even have put an end to them as a fighting force. But Napoleon refused to pursue, and the Russians got away relatively unmolested.

Napoleon had let the Russians escape at Austerlitz, and they had lived to fight another day. In three years, at Ligny, just before Waterloo, he would delay pursuit of the Prussians until it was too late. They, too, would fight another day and cost him his victory at Waterloo.

Borodino was a limited French victory but it was a victory. The Russians lost more than 44,000 men, including General Bagration, but the French losses were about 33,000, including some forty generals killed or wounded. Some 77,000 men had died in a battle that, in the final analysis, meant very little.

In the aftermath the battlefield was as dreadful as anything yet seen. The dead were piled one on another and seemed to stretch as far as the eye could see. Napoleon was reluctant to make the usual tour of the scene of his victory, but when he did he was visibly moved. At one point, a horse in his entourage stepped on a wounded soldier, who cried out in pain. Napoleon, well known for his feelings toward his soldiers, reprimanded the rider of the horse for his lack of attention. When someone pointed out that the wounded man was 'only a Russian', Napoleon snapped back 'after a victory there are no enemies, only men'.[189]

There was another grievous loss, that had even more severe long-term implications for the survivors. Thousands of horses had died on the road to Smolensk and Borodino, mostly because of lack of feed, as well from combat. Many more died at Borodino. They would be desperately needed in the retreat that was to come; instead, many more would die. In the end, Napoleon lost perhaps as many as 200,000 horses. These would be dearly missed in the campaigns of 1813–14, where they could have made some of Napoleon's victories more complete and, just possibly, turned the tide in his favour.

The road to Moscow was now open and Napoleon entered the city on 15 September 1812. He had expected a deputation of city nobles. He found instead an almost deserted city, with only a few thousand inhabitants, including a large number of recently released criminals. Napoleon moved into the Kremlin. That night, the Russians put the torch to their own city. The French could do little to fight the fires – the Russians had left behind no fire-fighting equipment – but they did manage to save about 20 percent of the city.

Popular belief has long had it that Napoleon burned the city. This would have made no sense. The season was getting late and he might well choose to winter there. To do that, he would need the very houses that burned to the ground. Even so, there were plenty of stores, and wintering in Moscow remained a strong possibility.

Napoleon sent messages to Alexander in his capital of St. Petersburg, a two-week round trip for the couriers. He received no reply. He tried again, but the courier was sent back far short of his destination. The same thing happened to a courier sent to Kutusov. Winter was approaching and decisions had to be made.

The question at Moscow was the same as at Smolensk: stay or move. In the case of Moscow, there was only one direction to move, and that was back. Despite the fire, there were plenty of provisions for the troops and plenty of shelter. The city was defensible, and the spring would bring with it new opportunities. True, there was the problem of the increasingly vulnerable supply lines and the fact that being out of Paris so long had political risks. It was also true that Prussia and even Austria might see his delay as a sign of weakness and turn on him, cutting him off from France. Even so, staying was probably the best available option. Count Daru, his trusted adviser, argued for that option:

> Remain here ... make one vast entrenched camp of Moscow and pass the winter in it. He would answer for it that there would be no want of bread and salt: the rest foraging on a large scale would supply. Such of the horses as they could not procure food for might be salted down. As to lodgings, if there were not houses enough, the cellars might make up the deficiency. Here we might stay till the return of spring, when our reinforcements and all Lithuania in arms should come to relieve, to join us and to complete the conquest.[190]

For some time, it seemed as though this was the option to be taken. Napoleon ordered entertainment to be provided. Stendhal seemed convinced of it, though concerned for the quality of the entertainment when he wrote, 'It looks as though I'll spend the winter here; I hope there'll be some concerts. There will certainly be theatrical performances at the Court, but what kind of actors will be in them?'[191]

Napoleon, however, with the support of his advisers, opted to return to Smolensk. This would shorten his lines of communication and allow him to add to his army those soldiers and supplies that had been left to guard those lines. Still, Napoleon delayed. Only the loss of some of Murat's cavalry in a skirmish outside Moscow moved him to action. On 19

October, thirty-five days after it had entered the city, Napoleon's army began its long march home.

He had planned to return by a southern, much warmer, route, which would have provided more food. It was already cold; winter had come early. But his way was blocked by the Russians. He defeated them in a skirmish, but feared that they would regroup and continue to block his withdrawal. Reluctantly, Napoleon moved farther north; from Borodino on, he would be on the same road by which he came; a road that was devoid of all forms of nourishment – but not of Cossacks.

Ironically, had Napoleon sent out proper reconnaissance, he would have discovered that the Russians had withdrawn and the southern route was open after all. Much of what was to follow need not have happened.

In leaving Moscow, the issue of what to do with the wounded was raised. Many, including Rapp, felt that they would be better off being left in Moscow; the Russians were not Turks and they would be cared for in accordance with western standards. Napoleon, however, feared for their safety and insisted that they be brought along, telling Rapp, 'I would not leave a man there; I would give all the treasures of Russia not to leave a single man behind. We must take horses, wagons, carriages – anything to carry them on.'[192]

The French soldiers had been happy and optimistic when they left Moscow. They had looted the city and their baggage-train was stuffed with the plunder they had acquired. But this slowed them down and when the horses began to die, most of the loot was left behind. When they realised that they were retracing their exact steps, which meant passing the unburied dead of both sides at Borodino, their mood sank.

By early November, winter had struck with a vengeance. The horrors of the retreat are well documented and need not be repeated at length here. Men froze to death as they marched; the dead were stripped of all they possessed; horses were eaten and their carcasses used as shelter. For most, there was little discipline, only the will to survive. Napoleon marched with his soldiers; Ney provided a heroic rear-guard, proving himself 'the bravest of the brave', as he would be known ever after.

Still, some kept their spirits up. Sent ahead to Smolensk to organise supplies, Stendhal wrote to the Countess Daru on 16 October, 'Apart from one person, our conversations are the most tedious in the world ... Apart from this, everything goes well; we have not seen a woman since the postmistresses of Poland, but by way of compensation we are great connoisseurs of fires.'[193] The rejoining of rear-guard forces led by Oudinot and Victor provided a lift to spirits, as well as to the fighting capacity of the army.

Smolensk was not what had been expected. The few stores remaining there had been devoured by the advance troops; there would be no respite there, no winter quarters. Those who still remained must move farther west.

By now, Napoleon had heard of even worse news than that coming from Spain. General Malet, confined to an asylum in France, had escaped and managed to head a plot to seize power. He and his accomplices convinced several key officials that Napoleon was dead in Russia and very nearly gained control of the government. Their plot was halted and they were executed.

The plot was bad enough. Even worse was this startling and depressing fact: when people thought Napoleon was dead, not one person moved to proclaim the King of Rome as Napoleon II, with the Empress Marie-Louise as Regent. All that Napoleon had done to assure a smooth succession, a continuation of his reforms, his dynasty, had evidently come to naught.

Clearly, he was needed in Paris.

There was one last obstacle to be overcome: the Beresina River. Winter had been cruel to the withdrawing army and was to play one last trick on them. It had actually been mild in this part of Russia and the river was not fully frozen. There would be no easy crossing on the ice, and the bridges had been destroyed. Napoleon had reasonably expected that the river would be frozen and had thus abandoned his pontoon bridge-building equipment two days earlier.

His engineers were able to build two bridges, one for the men and one for the horse transport. With Ney holding off the pursuing Russians, much of the army was able to cross the bridges, which were then destroyed. David Chandler estimates that in the three-day crossing some 20–30,000 combatants and perhaps 30,000 non-combatants became casualties.[194] All the same, the effort was a major success, one of the best in military history, and Napoleon gets much of the credit for his coolness under such potentially disastrous conditions. Indeed, throughout the withdrawal from Moscow, he showed more composure than he had on the way there.

223

None the less, without the relatively fresh forces of Oudinot and Victor, the courageous efforts of the bridge-builders and Ney's rearguard actions, all might well have been lost.

With the army relatively safe on friendlier territory, Napoleon left for Paris on 5 December 1812. He was needed there far more than with the troops; it was time to start what must be a very quick recovery. By the 18th he was in Paris, but the nightmare was just beginning.

On the 16th, the 29th Bulletin of the *Grande Armée*, dated 3 December, had been published in Paris. It was notable for its blunt honesty:

Until 6 November the weather was fine, and the movement of the army was executed with the greatest success. The cold weather began on the 7th; from that moment, every night we lost several hundred horses, which died at the bivouac. Arriving at Smolensk, we had already lost many cavalry and artillery horses ... The cold, which began on the 7th, suddenly increased; and on the 14th, 15th and 16th the thermometer was sixteen and eighteen degrees below the freezing point ... The roads were covered with ice; the cavalry, artillery and baggage horses, perished every night, not only by hundreds, but by thousands, particularly the German and French horses. In a few days, more than 30,000 horses perished; our cavalry were on foot; our artillery and our baggage were without conveyance. It was necessary to abandon and destroy a good part of our cannon, ammunition and provisions.

This army, so fine on the 6th, was very different on the 14th, almost without cavalry, without artillery and without transports. Without cavalry, we could not reconnoitre a quarter of a league's distance; without artillery, we could not risk a battle and firmly await it: it was requisite to march in order not to be constrained to a battle, which the want of ammunition prevented us from desiring ... This difficulty, joined to a cold which suddenly came on, rendered our situation miserable. Those men whom nature had not sufficiently steeled to be above all the changes of fate and fortune, lost their gaiety, their good humour and dreamed but of misfortunes and catastrophes ... The health of His Majesty was never better.[195]

This last remark was probably meant to be more than a general reassurance to the French people or even to Marie-Louise. The Malet conspiracy had shown all too clearly how fragile was his hold on power; with this he was making sure that people understood that he was alive and was coming home.

How, then, to assess the campaign of 1812, beyond the obvious fact that it was an unmitigated disaster? Disaster, yes, but was it avoidable? Critics point to Napoleon's unbending will, over-extended ambition and loss of contact with reality. The first two of these can be dismissed out of hand. Russia had betrayed him. Had he allowed that to happen unchallenged, the Continental System which, though flawed, was beginning to show at least signs of success, would be finished and with it his hopes of forcing the British to the peace table. Moreover, his acquiescence with Russia would have signalled his weakness and without doubt led to actions by Prussia and perhaps even Austria; the outgrowth of that might be yet another coalition against him. His defeat, of course, had much the same effect.

Those who doubt this analysis need only look at the campaigns of 1813–14 in the next chapter.

Napoleon understood this well. Later in life, he was willing to admit that his moves in Spain had been a mistake but he would never agree to that description being appplied to 1812.

Perhaps Napoleon can be rightfully accused of having lost touch with reality. Not the reality of the political situation, but the twin realities of the new attitude of the Tsar and the problems of the Russian winter. To the end, Napoleon could not understand that not one – or ten – victories in the campaign would have forced Alexander to the peace table. Alexander had told him as much, through Caulaincourt and through his proclamation, but Napoleon did not hear.

As to the winter, Napoleon had never expected to go to Moscow, perhaps not even to Smolensk. He was drawn in, little by little. But it had never been too late. Before Moscow he had delayed unnecessarily. But the delay at Moscow was the fatal delay. Had he declared victory and left, or even wintered in Moscow, all might have been well. Leaving four, even three weeks earlier could have allowed him to miss the worst of the deprivations his army ultimately faced during their withdrawal. Wintering in Moscow might have cost him his horses (because of lack of feed), but fresh horses and reinforcements could have arrived in the spring and then the campaign could have been taken to the Tsar.

But he did none of these things, and he and his men paid a terrible price for his indecision and delay.

NOTES

180 We will not discuss the military operations in great detail. There are many books on the subject. One of the most detailed from a military operations point of view is George Nafziger's *Napoleon's Invasion of Russia*, Novato, CA., 1988. One should also read Chandler, *Campaigns*, 739–861 for an excellent recounting and analysis of the campaign.

181 Odeleben, *Circumstantial Narrative*, I, 13. This is one of the rarest and most important of the memoirs of the period.

182 Chandler, *Campaigns*, 756. Accounts vary as to the exact numbers, but there is no better source for military detail than this monumental work by one of the greatest of all Napoleonic historians.

183 Caulaincourt, *With Napoleon in Russia*, 6.

184 See Chandler, *Campaigns*, 556–61 for a detailed discussion of the logistical difficulties.

185 Letter to Félix Faure, Smolensk, 24 August 1812, *To the Happy Few: Selected Letters of Stendhal*, trans. Norman Cameron (John Lehmann, 1952; London, 1986), 139.

186 Durdent, R. J. *Campagne de Moscow en 1812*. The month of August is the only date given in the proclamation.

187 *Correspondance*, 7 September 1812, No. 19182, XXIV, 240; Caulaincourt, *With Napoleon in Russia*, 96n.

188 Original Order in The David Markham Collection.

189 Ségur, *Expedition to Russia*, I, 344.

190 Ibid., II, 81–82.

191 Letter to Félix Faure, Moscow, 2 October 1812, *The Private Diaries of Stendhal*. Ed. and trans. Robert Sage. New York, 1954, 484. Stendhal began to keep diaries in 1801, and continued his effort throughout his Napoleonic career. They provide, of course, some of the best insights into his life, and the priorities he established while at various stages of his career. Unfortunately, there are almost no entries for the period of his Moscow experience. It is presumed that they were lost during the difficult withdrawal from Russia.

192 Rapp, 223.

193 *To the Happy Few*, 148.

194 Chandler, *Campaigns*, 846. For an excellent eye-witness account of the crossing, see Segur, II, 269–303.

195 *Correspondance*, 3 December 1812, No. 19365, XXIV, 377–82.

PART FIVE

THE
FINAL COLLAPSE

MIRAGE OF RECOVERY
1813–1814

As the year 1813 opened, Napoleon was back in Paris, where he quickly consolidated his domestic power. For now, at least, there would be no more talk of his replacement. He began immediately to raise a new army and replace the lost cannon and other equipment. But he could not replace the trained horses that he had lost in Russia.

The Tsar was now free to follow the policies he wanted. The Continental System was probably doomed, but short of further action against Russia, there was nothing to be done about it.

Alexander, however, had other ideas. Emboldened by his success, he began to see himself as something of a mystical liberator of Europe, or at least of Germany and Prussia. His army did not halt at his borders, but continued in pursuit of the withdrawing French, moving into the Grand Duchy of Warsaw. Some of the Prussian soldiers were already changing sides, and by March Prussia had declared war on France. Napoleon's worst fears were being realised: a new coalition was being formed.

Still, there was little doubt in Napoleon's mind that he could deal with the Russians and the Prussians, even with his newly recruited army. He had, after all, a blood alliance, through his marriage to Marie-Louise, with the other great European continental power, Austria. With Austrian troops, he would be in fine shape. Even without their help, as long as they did not turn against him, he felt secure.

Napoleon did what he could to keep Emperor Francis I on his side. He reminded him of traditional Austrian fears of Russian expansion. He appointed Marie-Louise as Regent when he was on campaign and formally, with great ceremony, named his son his heir. To make war on Napoleon would be to make war on his own daughter and grandson! What father could possibly do that?

Meanwhile, Napoleon needed to deal directly with the Prussian/Russian threat. In May, having rejoined his troops, he defeated the invaders at the Battle of Lützen. Shortly afterwards, he routed them at Bautzen and regained control of all the territory west of the Oder. Given more cavalry, each of these victories would have been far more decisive and at the very least would have sent a message to the Austrians.

Francis, much like Alexander before him, had promised troops but failed to deliver them. Instead, he offered to mediate between Napoleon and his two adversaries. Napoleon had just won two important victories, but he agreed to talk to Foreign Minister Count Clemens Metternich.

An armistice was called, and Napoleon was glad of the opportunity to enlarge and train his young army. However, it soon became clear that Metternich was not acting as a helpful ally or even as a peace-seeking neutral. The terms he offered were so outrageous that no one could possibly have expected Napoleon to accept them, especially after having won two battles. Metternich, i.e., Prussia and Russia, wanted Napoleon to give up most of the gains achieved since he became First Consul.

Napoleon tried to strike a bargain but he was unwilling to give in to all their demands. For Metternich, there would be no bargaining; it was take it or leave it. If Napoleon took it, he would retain an ally and possibly achieve peace, at least for a time. But he saw the cost as too high. His dreams of carrying his reforms throughout Europe and of overthrowing the old order in favour of a new enlightenment would be dashed by this so-called peace.

Even his position at home would be weakened. True, he would have brought peace, but many would wonder why he was prepared to surrender so much after twice defeating the enemy. Many, too, would wonder why so many husbands and sons had died in Russia and elsewhere, if the end result was to give back so much of what they had earlier won with their blood.

No, it would not be possible to accept these terms. All parties knew it; the entire process had been a sham. Each had gained some time to solidify his position. The others had the nerve to accuse Napoleon of being the aggressor. As the British had done before, they wished to demonise him, to personalise the war as being against him, not France, and thus separate him from his own country. Here is where the myth of Napoleon's monumental ego forcing Europe into war really takes hold. It was nonsense, but planting it met with some success.

The armistice had been good for all sides, but much better for the allies. Prussia and Russia had gained Austria, whose move away from Napoleon was now complete. Napoleon's effort to use marriage to secure his relations with Austria had failed. Joséphine had been sacrificed to no avail.

Great Britain was marshalling her financial resources; the end was near. On 12 August 1813, three days before Napoleon's forty-fourth birthday, Austria declared war on France. The armies that now marched against Napoleon were not the armies of old. They no longer feared the invincible Napoleon; they even scorned him. Worse, they had learned from the master, they had abandoned the old ways of fighting and would now turn Napoleon's mastery of the art of war against him.

There would be various peace offerings, the last being a return to the borders of 1792 – as if all that happened since then had not happened at all. However, there would be no real guarantees of French security. The offers were not really meant to be serious; the real goal was to crush Napoleon. If he unexpectedly accepted them, additional demands would be made. Always there was the fallback position that the British must be consulted. The meaning of this was plain: there would be no peace as long as France retained Belgium. Thus, there would be no peace. As Tsar Alexander's *aide-de-camp* put it:

> The negotiations ... failed of success, for this plain reason, that neither side brought anything like sincerity to the discussion. Alexander warmly insisted on the necessity of continuing the contest and exerted himself to infuse the same spirit into his allies, some of whom were satisfied with seeing the French driven out of Germany ...[196]

The plan was simple. If, as Wellington once said, Napoleon's hat on the battlefield was worth fifty thousand men, the allies would try to avoid him as much as possible and defeat his far less worthy marshals.

It worked. Napoleon defeated the allies in Silesia and Dresden, but the tide then turned. Vandamme was captured, and Napoleon's Marshals Macdonald, Oudinot and Ney were defeated in separate battles. One by one former allies became foes – Bavaria, some states in the Confederation of the Rhine – and Napoleon was becoming isolated, even from his marshals. Tired of war, they had seen the writing on the wall and didn't like the way it read.

On 16–18 October Napoleon, trapped near Leipzig, fought a force three times his size. In the middle of the battle, the Saxon army switched sides and fired on the French. When the traitor Bernadotte attacked with 60,000 Swedes, Napoleon himself led the counter-attack, putting the Swedes and Saxons to flight.

Running out of munitions, sorely missing his cavalry, rebuffed in a last effort to accommodate Austria, Napoleon attempted to retreat. All but one bridge had been destroyed and chaos was the order of the day, but the French army was getting across in good order.

Then, another disaster struck. For some reason, French sappers blew up the remaining bridge before some 20,000 soldiers were across. Some made it, others, including Prince Poniatowski, who had just been made a marshal, were drowned. About 15,000 were taken prisoner; added to the 73,000 killed or wounded: 'the Battle of Nations', as it was to be called, was a disaster from which the French could not realistically hope to recover.

Any who doubt that it was British insistence on war that led to Napoleon's downfall need only read the Earl of Aberdeen's dispatch to Viscount Castlereagh after the battle, which reads in part:

> That ray of hope for the salvation of the civilised world, which has so steadily beamed from our own happy shores, is now rapidly diffused over the whole Continent. If anything can add to our feelings of exultation, as Englishmen, at this prospect, it is the reflection that this event will be mainly attributable to the unshaken constancy and perseverance of Great Britain.[197]

Even Napoleon's strongest supporters and admirers were beginning to lose heart.

> The reverses of the 19th produced in general a very unusual depression among the most zealous admirers of Napoleon. Without predicting the end of his brilliant career, or breaking out into invectives, it was looked upon as possible that, at the return of the army, the nation herself would be disaffected towards her chief.[198]

It was to be all downhill from now on. Napoleon still had a good army and he still had an empire. But more rapidly than could ever have been imagined, that empire vanished. The entire Confederation of the Rhine had gone and with it went Holland. Even Marshal Murat, King of Naples, married to Napoleon's sister Caroline, falling under her traitorous spell, conspired with Metternich for guarantees of his own throne at the expense of his support for that of Napoleon.

Murat felt that he was justified in this move, because he feared that Napoleon had

> expressed a resolution to dethrone him and incorporate Naples with the kingdom of Italy ... The king [Murat], when informed of Napoleon's resolution, boldly avowed in his presence, that he would defend his throne by means of arms; and he ever afterward felt that there was no security for his kingdom, whilst the French maintained dominion in Italy.[199]

Napoleon was now forced to fight on French soil. He had been quite effective in Germany, losing only to overwhelming numbers and treachery. In 1814 in the Campaign of France, he would be brilliant.

Having returned to Paris, he arranged for its defence, burned state papers that he did not want read by the allies and re-affirmed Marie-Louise as his Regent. He knew that he had little hope of success and authorised renewed peace negotiations without conditions.

When he discovered that the two armies marching on Paris had split, he seized the opportunity for the one great victory that could turn the tide. He quickly destroyed a Russian corps attached to Blücher's Prussian army; from his celebration, one might have believed it to be Austerlitz! This victory was followed by several more, and suddenly it was the allies who were stunned into seeking an armistice.

All came to naught, however. Napoleon could not be everywhere at once, and while he was winning a series of victories, his marshals were being defeated. They had become disheartened; their willingness to follow the Emperor was coming to an end. Napoleon had been brilliant, but perhaps in the final analysis he had 'reckoned too much upon the faults of his enemies, as well as on the consequences of his accustomed wiles and, in fine, on the resources of his genius'.[200]

Napoleon, too, had become disheartened. He stayed in the front lines, oblivious to danger. Perhaps he wanted to die, to leave the throne to his son that way, before his final defeat made that less likely. It is hard to be sure, but in any event he lived.

In Paris, treachery was once more afoot. Not surprisingly, it was led by Talleyrand. While there was still some thought of having Marie-Louise serve as Regent and giving the crown to Napoleon II, the real intent was to restore the Bourbons. In the words of Count Lavallette:

While the Emperor, opposed by all the armies of Europe, was struggling like a lion, running from one to another, thwarting all the manoeuvres of the enemy by the rapidity of his movements, deceiving them in all their calculations and exhausting them with fatigue, other foes, much more dangerous than they, were in Paris entering into a secret league with foreigners, to hasten his fall.[201]

And the allies were approaching Paris.

NOTES

196 Mikhailofsky–Danilefsky, *Campaign in France*, 2.
197 'Leipzig, 22 October 1813', in Odeleben, II, 445.
198 Ibid., II, 47–48.
199 Macirone, *Interesting Facts*, 21.
200 Odeleben, I, 136.

201 Lavalette, *Memoirs*, I, 81. He was Napoleon's aide-de-camp during the Italian campaign, and became Postmaster General of the Empire, with many secret police duties. He was condemned to death in 1815, but escaped.

26

TREACHERY
AND DEFEAT

In March 1814, Napoleon was faced with a difficult choice. He and his army were 100 miles east of Paris and the allies were marching on the city. It was quite possible for him to move about the countryside without serious challenge, inflicting damage to the allies' rear, their lines of communication and units not attached to their main force. He could have consolidated his forces, added new soldiers from various fortresses, declared a *levée en masse* (a declaration based on the principle that all citizens must be available for service in times of emergency) and attacked retreating allied forces near Saint-Dizier.[202] Marshals Marmont and Mortier were not far away, and if they joined him he would have a formidable fighting force.

There was talk of abandoning Paris as the Russians had abandoned Moscow; let the allies have it, for all the good it would do them. Like Hannibal before him, perhaps Napoleon could range the countryside, rallying support, bringing back the spirit of the Revolution when it became clear that the allies wanted to restore the hated Bourbons.

A guerrilla war, with its accompanying damage to the French countryside, however, would be a great risk both in terms of military feasibility and political acceptability. It might well play into the hands of those who claimed that Napoleon was allowing his own ego to supplant the interests of France.

Regardless of those arguments, the fact was that Marmont was being pushed towards Paris and would not be able to join Napoleon. Moreover, it was also clear that his marshals insisted that what remained of the army be brought to the defence of Paris. Consequently, Napoleon began a race against the allies for his capital city.[203]

This offered him another option for snatching victory from the jaws of defeat. If Marmont was in Paris, together with the National Guard and other military units, perhaps Napoleon could close on their rear, sandwiching the allies between the defenders of Paris and his own forces. As he later told Montholon, '... they [the allies] would never have given battle on the left bank of the Seine with Paris in their rear'.[204]

The approach of the allied army to Paris was, however, having a demoralising effect on the citizens of that city. In addition to the political intrigue that was eroding support for Napoleon, there was the very real fear that the allies would bombard the city. The Parisians were well aware of what happened to people whose city was captured by an enemy army and they wanted no part of the rape and pillage that would almost certainly follow. They were constantly inundated with reports that the Prussians or, worse, the Russian Cossacks, were determined either to burn Paris to the ground in revenge for Moscow, or embark on an orgy of looting and violence. The English press published reports of such threats and the Paris newspapers carried the same stories. If these stories in the French papers were intended to encourage the citizens to fight even harder, they had quite the opposite effect.

Morale in Paris, and Napoleon's chances of success, took another turn for the worse when Marshal Augereau was defeated at Lyon on 23 March. Although he could have continued the fight, he chose instead to betray Napoleon and join the Bourbon cause. It was a crushing blow.

Napoleon had left instructions that the Empress Marie-Louise and their son, the King of Rome, were to leave the city if it were under immediate military threat. The presence of French troops and Napoleon's own approaching army notwithstanding, his brother King Joseph and the Regency Council, who together governed in the Emperor's absence, decided that it was time for her to withdraw from Paris.

Napoleon's supporters opposed this idea, feeling that she could help inspire the troops to defend their city and save it for the Emperor's return. Those who were conspiring to return the Bourbons were, of course, quite pleased to see the major challenge to their plans leave the centre of the political action that would soon follow.

Had Marie-Louise, daughter of Austrian Emperor Francis I, Regent of France, mother of the King of Rome, the declared heir to the French throne, stayed in Paris, two important things might have happened. First, she might have been able to give inspiration to those people defending the city, to rally the troops and, just as importantly, the citizens to a patriotic stand against the forces of tyranny that were approaching their gates.

Even more importantly, she might have served as a rallying point for those who, while willing to accept the fall of Napoleon, were not interested in the restoration of the Bourbons. There had been no Bourbon on the throne of France for more than twenty years, and there was certainly no outcry for their return beyond that of the usual crowd of royalists who had never accepted the verdict of history.

Some writers have heaped abuse on Marie-Louise as not having been worthy of Napoleon. This could have been her finest hour, and she tried to make it so. She objected to the departure, stating her desire to do all that she could to help defend the city. Nevertheless, the imperial party left Paris, while Joseph stayed to direct its defence.

During the campaign of 1814, Marie-Louise and Napoleon kept up an active correspondence. Napoleon was quite in love with his young wife and had a great deal of trust in her. It is also true that by now his primary concern was probably not in keeping the throne for himself, but in assuring it for his son. Marie-Louise kept him informed of the various political happenings in Paris. Napoleon was very aware that moves were being made to seek peace at whatever cost, including that of his own throne.

He had also learned that he could no longer trust even his family. Joseph was in charge of defending Paris but was also involved in the politics of the situation. Napoleon repeatedly warned Marie-Louise not to trust Joseph:

> My dearest Louise, I have received your last letter ... I am sorry you showed the King [Joseph] your father's letter and your reply. You trust this prince too much ... Everyone has betrayed me. Will it be my fate to be betrayed also by the King? I should not be surprised if such were to be the case, nor would it break my fortitude ... Keep him at a distance ... I tell you again, keep the King out of your confidence and away from your person ... All this depresses me rather; I need to be comforted by the members of my family [his siblings], but as a rule I get nothing but vexation from that quarter. On your part, however, it would be both unexpected and unbearable. Goodby, my dearest. All my love.[205]

Another little-discussed topic of events of this period is the correspondence between Marie-Louise and her father, Emperor Francis I of Austria. He, of course, had what should have been a vested interest in seeing that any peace accord with France protected the position of his daughter.

Seizing upon that idea and anxious to do what she could to help her husband, Marie-Louise wrote pleading for peace. In one of his replies to her, Francis wrote:

My dear Louise ... If I have not written to you for some considerable time, it is because of political considerations, as I have explained in a recent letter to your Husband. No one is more alive to the present situation than I, and I take a most sincere interest in all that pertains to you and yours. That, after all, is only natural, and for that very reason I cannot but wish that your Husband would bring the war to a speedy conclusion. Any peace which, by bringing France within limits fixed with due regard to the strength of the other powers will secure for her that peace at sea of which she has so long been deprived, is honourable, practical and acceptable. Peace at sea can be achieved only on the terms already offered, and without such a peace no happiness is possible either for Europe or, most particularly, for France ... With the restoration of trade, with a government based on a lasting peace, your Husband will receive the blessings of the fairest state in Europe. His memory will be cherished by his subjects, his dynasty firmly secured. Those who are giving him different advice are his greatest enemies; no one desires his good more sincerely than I do ... Were I his only adversary, we could arrange matters more easily between ourselves, but a separate peace with Austria ... would merely do him a great deal of harm ... if the Emperor wishes for peace, he must do what is necessary to obtain it ... Your affectionate father Francis.[206]

Marie-Louise replied that Napoleon could only accept a peace that did not bring dishonour to France and to himself, but it did not matter. Francis, like all the other allies, would not be content as long as Napoleon was on the throne. Nothing had changed since 1804 or, one should probably say, since 1800.

When the Empress and the King of Rome left Paris on 29 March 1814, the citizens of Paris believed that all was lost. Hortense wrote that the National Guard was 'completely discouraged' and that the citizens were 'indignant at this family that seemed to be abandoning them in the hour of adversity'.[207] As Napoleon and Marie-Louise had feared, her presence was necessary to give the defenders of Paris hope.

Making sacrifices had never been in the nature of the citizens of Paris, and with the allies at the gates they were not interested in starting now. 'Instead of volunteering to build redoubts, they moved any valuable furniture to the country. Instead of chipping in with money, they buried their napoleons in their gardens.'[208] Napoleon heard of this and was both outraged and saddened. His sadness with the unfortunate turn of events is reflected in the Sixteenth Bulletin of 5 April 1814: 'The occupation of the capital by the enemy is a misfortune which deeply afflicts the heart of His Majesty ...'[209]

Joseph and most of the government left Paris on 30 March, just hours before Napoleon's arrival. Napoleon had left orders that there was to be no one available to negotiate with the allies if they entered the city. Talleyrand, however, was up to his old tricks. He had decided that the best future for France – and, especially, for him – lay with the restoration of the Bourbons. Ordered to leave Paris, he made a show of trying to leave but, amazingly, had 'lost' his passport. His diplomatic status would have been enough to get him out but this ploy enabled him to stay. He conspired with the allies for Napoleon's abdication and replacement by the Bourbons. When Tsar Alexander entered Paris, he stayed at Talleyrand's home; at that moment, any hope for Napoleon was essentially gone.

Even so, the Tsar was not especially interested in putting the Bourbons back on the throne. He understood that this would scarcely reflect the popular will of the people. The daughter of his ally, Francis, was available; she and her young son could be easily manipulated into policies that would restore Europe to the borders of 1792. Talleyrand had his work cut out, but he was up to the task.

Napoleon arrived several hours too late on 30 March. The French troops were evacuating; soon the allies would be in Paris. Angry but still hopeful, he retired to Fontainebleau to await further developments. Caulaincourt describes his reaction:

'What cowardice!' was his first remark. 'Surrender! Joseph has ruined everything. Four hours too late! ... If I had come four hours sooner, all would have been saved,' he added in sorrowful tones.[210]

Under Talleyrand's influence, the legislative body established a provisional government, led, of course, by Talleyrand himself. While Napoleon prepared for further military and diplomatic action at Fontainebleau, Talleyrand deprived him of his political support and prepared the way for the return of the monarchy that so many had died to remove.

Napoleon still had tens of thousands of soldiers in the area; resistance was still possible. Perhaps of greater importance, his forces could be used to increase his bargaining power for retention of his throne or of its succession to his son. Tsar Alexander saw things that way. He had initially agreed, with pressure from Talleyrand, to support restoration of the Bourbons but he was beginning to waver.

On 3 April, led by Marshal Ney, a group of the remaining marshals that included Macdonald, Berthier, Oudinot and Lefebvre, informed Napoleon that they, and their men, were no longer willing to fight. He must abdicate in favour of his son and be prepared to retire from the scene. This meeting became known as 'the revolt of the marshals'. Napoleon could have fought on, but his ambition for his throne was less than his ambition for his son's succession and the maintenance of all the positive changes he had brought to France. The following day, 4 April, he abdicated in favour of his son and Marie-Louise as Regent.

Caulaincourt and several marshals took this abdication to Tsar Alexander. He had been willing to return the Bourbons, but here was a way to assure peace, satisfy many of those in France who still supported Napoleon and put the daughter of the Emperor of Austria on the throne. If he did not accept this abdication, the war might continue. This looked like a winning proposition and he prepared to accept it.

Talleyrand, however, had another ace up his sleeve. He was in contact with Marshal Marmont, trying to persuade him to abandon Napoleon. Any hope of a military or diplomatic victory for Napoleon was dashed when Marmont marched his Sixth Corps, with its 11,000 troops, into the arms of waiting Austrian soldiers. Marmont, who fancied that he was saving France, was instead delivering its fate to the Bourbons. Talleyrand clearly was the more clever, and Napoleon was finished. For their part, the soldiers of the Sixth were furious when they realised that they had been duped and they made every effort to extricate themselves from their situation, but to no avail.

Marmont's action remains to this day a prime example of treachery in French history.

The desertion of Marmont's corps convinced the Tsar that there was no need to be anxious about Napoleon's remaining power or influence. He wanted to do the right thing for France. Talleyrand now spoke for France and he called for the Bourbons. Napoleon's conditional abdication was rejected. He could abdicate unconditionally, or fight; either way, it was over.

Feelings of gloom pervaded Fontainebleau. The revolt of the marshals was bad enough; even worse was what followed. Read the words of Louis Marchand, Napoleon's faithful friend and valet:

The time for defections had arrived: Prince Berthier had left the Emperor, assuring him of his return. This old friend never appeared again. During the day, the Emperor called for his first valet Constant: he had left, never to return either. His Mameluke Roustam had left for Paris and was not seen again. His surgeon M. Yvan had also abandoned him. Those he had the most right to count on, having heaped kindness on them at the peak of his power, were deserting him in adversity.[211]

On 5 April the so-called Provisional Government of France voted to call Louis Stanislas Xavier to assume the throne of France as Louis XVIII.

This turn of events was dismal for Napoleon. Marmont's defection strengthened the unwillingness of the marshals to continue to rally the troops. An attack on Paris was even worse to them than the return of the Bourbons. Napoleon had been rebuffed in his efforts to abdicate in favour of his son (which had been a real possibility until the treason of Marmont). This, said the marshals, left only one choice. He must give up the throne without conditions.

Some have said that Napoleon was driven by his ambition alone and that he placed his own good above that of all others, including France. If this were so, he could have continued fighting, for the army loved him more than they obeyed the marshals. He might not have been able to save the throne for himself, but he might have saved it for his son.

Napoleon was not prepared to ask further sacrifice from his soldiers or from the people of France. Faced with the loss of all he had sought; faced even with the knowledge that so much of what he had done to reform France would be undone by the Bourbons, he was unwilling to fight on. On 11 April 1814, Napoleon abdicated unconditionally, saying, '... there is no sacrifice, not even that of life, which I am not ready to make for the interests of France'.[212]

Napoleon knew that he still had the army, but he also knew that the French people had given up. He could no longer count on their unqualified support, especially in Paris. The reasons for this loss of the support of the French people were always understood and feared by Napoleon. As his secretary Fleury de Chaboulon wrote:

As long as good fortune waited upon Napoleon, his most ambitious attempts commanded the applauses of the nation. We boasted of his profound political wisdom, we extolled his genius, we worshipped his courage. When his fortunes changed, then his political wisdom was called treachery, his genius, ambition and his courage, foolhardiness and infatuation.[213]

When Count Dumas returned to Paris just after the abdication, he 'found all my companions already detached from the imperial system ... it seemed as if the government that had just ceased was nothing more than an historical recollection.'[214]

Even so, one should not assume that further action by Napoleon would have been futile or even necessarily in the worst interests of France. Caulaincourt writes:

> The Emperor's personal position could not be worse than it was; and there was doubtless some glory to be had from fighting to the death in defence of a crown that had been won by such splendid feats of arms. His Majesty still had resources enough to carry on irregular warfare and, as he quite reasonably said, the enemy's presence in France and the course of the war itself would have bettered his situation from day to day. France might have been ravaged; she might have suffered the effects of a prolonged occupation, of a war that would have embroiled many of her best citizens. But she might also have been tempered anew by that harsh schooling. Her energies restored, she might not perhaps have witnessed in her capital the signing away of half her territory, of a navy equal to Britain's and of arsenals better stocked than the rest of Europe's put together.
>
> None of these considerations was overlooked by the Emperor. Unquestionably, then, it was his wish to spare France the miseries of civil war. Mere personal advantage would have led him to prefer such a war, which promised many a chance of success to a genius of his stamp and which, in return for such risks of death as he had always taken lightly, afforded no prospect more disagreeable than that which he was being compelled to face.[215]

Tsar Alexander had suggested, and the other allies had agreed, that Napoleon should be sent to the island of Elba. Alexander saw this as quite fair to Napoleon, as it had a nice climate and they spoke his native Italian there. It was, in fact, an honourable exile, though other deposed monarchs had been allowed to retire in comfort to England or elsewhere. But not, it seemed, the Ogre of Corsica.

One burning question had been at the top of Napoleon's concerns, once he realised that there would be no succession for his son. He wanted to be reunited with his wife and son. If at all possible, he would have liked the two of them to join him on Elba. Realising that she might not be all that fond of such isolation, he tried to get the allies to grant her Tuscany, which was only a short boat trip from Elba. The allies, however, wanted no part of such a potent threesome being reunited. Instead, they gave her the Duchy of Parma, which was landlocked.

This worried and saddened Napoleon. If they were trying to keep him from his wife and son, how could they be trusted when they seemed to be offering him an honourable and humane exile? Even before he left for Elba, he had reasons to suspect treachery.

Napoleon wanted Marie-Louise to join him but was unwilling to ask her directly. She, for her part, wanted to rejoin her husband but did not have the strength of character to overcome the opposition of those under whose control she was inexorably sinking. In their exchange of letters, Marie-Louise shows that she was more and more inclined to join Napoleon. Metternich, however, began to apply pressure. In the end, she agreed to go to see her father, thus postponing her trip to rejoin Napoleon.

On 12 April, Napoleon's world appeared to be falling completely apart. He received the Treaty of Fontainebleau. To his dismay, he found that rather than Tuscany, Marie-Louise was to get Parma, Piacenza and Guastalla; she was to become the Duchess of Parma. There were no provisions for her ever rejoining Napoleon, or even provisions for periodic visitations. It was all too clear that the allies would not tolerate their reunion.

Determined to foil their plans, he sent instructions for her to come to him immediately. Sadly, it was not to be. She had already left for Vienna. The duplicity of Talleyrand and the wily manoeuvrings of Metternich had deprived him of the one thing he had left for which to live. His hopes were dashed when he received a sad note from his wife, written on 11 April, only a few miles from where he waited:

I am sending you a few lines by a Polish officer who has just brought me your note to Angerville; you will know by now that they have made me leave Orléans and that orders have been given to prevent me from joining you, and even to resort to force if necessary. Be on your guard, my Darling, we are being duped, I am in deadly anxiety on your behalf, but I shall take a firm line with my father, I shall tell him that I absolutely insist on joining you and that I shall not let myself be talked into doing anything else. We have brought away as much of the treasure as we could, I will get it through to you by every possible means, but I think it much more likely that I shall bring it to you myself.

Your son is fast asleep at the moment, I myself am not at all well. I shall be quite firm about not going further than Rambouillet, you can rely entirely on my love and my courage when the times comes. I love you and send you a fond kiss.

Your Darling Louise[216]

Napoleon was crushed. The next day he sent a letter to his wife, designed to remove any feelings of guilt she might have about events. It is a poignant letter, but it would never reach her:

My dearest Louise, I have received your letter. I approve of your going to Rambouillet, where your father will be joining you. This is the only consolation left to me in the midst of our misfortunes. For the past week I have been eagerly looking forward to the moment of your meeting. Your father has been led astray and has behaved badly towards us, but he will be a good, kind father to you and your son ... Good-bye, my sweet Louise. I love you more than anything else in the world. My misfortunes only affect me in so far as they grieve you. As long as you live, you will be lavishing your affection on the most devoted of husbands. Give my son a kiss. Good-bye, my Louise. All my love.[217]

Napoleon then summoned Caulaincourt. It was three in the morning of 3 April. Napoleon voiced his fears of what would happen to him: indignities, assassination, prison; anything was possible. He then had Caulaincourt bring a folder in which he kept all his letters from Marie-Louise. He embraced his old friend and then asked that the letters be given to her.

Soon I shall exist no longer. Take the Empress my letter then. Keep her letters, with the portfolio they are in, to give to my son when he is grown ... Tell the Empress I die in the conviction that she gave me all the happiness within her power and that she never gave me the least cause for disquiet ... Listen to me – the time runs out ... You are to tell Joséphine that she has been much in my thoughts.[218]

Napoleon had taken some poison that he always carried with him. It was beginning to have its effect and he held tight to Caulaincourt to make sure no help was summoned. Caulaincourt finally broke free and called for help, including the Emperor's doctor Yvan (who in fact had not yet deserted). Napoleon, vomiting and in great pain, asked the doctor to give him more poison to finish the job. The doctor refused.

Napoleon wanted to die, but what the dangers of war had not accomplished would not be done by poison so old as to have lost its full potency. He recovered and wrote a letter to Joséphine:

My head and spirit are freed from an enormous weight. My fall is great, but at least it is useful, as men say. In my retreat, I shall substitute the pen for the sword. The history of my reign will be curious. The world has yet seen me only in profile; I shall show myself in full ...

Adieu, my dear Joséphine. Be resigned, as I am and ever remember him who never forgets and never will forget you. Farewell, Joséphine.[219]

A few days later, a letter arrived from Marie-Louise, sparking new hope that they might yet be reunited. His hopes raised, his will to live returned and he began to plan for the trip to Elba.

NOTES

202 Houssaye, *Campaign of 1814*, 333–37.
203 Chandler, *Campaigns*, 1000.
204 Montholon, *Memoirs*, II, 265.
205 Napoleon I, 12 March 1814, *My Dearest Louise*, No. 110, 118–19.
206 Ibid., 6 March 1814, No. 108, 114–17.
207 Hortense, II, 78.
208 Cronin, 361.
209 Posted at Rennes on 5 April 1814. Found in *Official Narratives*, 431, in *Original Journals*, II.
210 Caulaincourt, *No Peace*, 29.
211 Marchand, *In Napoleon's Shadow*, 44.
212 *Correspondance*, 11 April 1814, No. 21558, XXVII, 421. Trans. in Baron Fain, *The Manuscript*, 250–51.
213 Chaboulon, *Memoirs*, I, 3–4.
214 Dumas, *Memoirs*, II, 480.
215 Caulaincourt, *No Peace*, 202–3.
216 *My Dearest Louise*, 11 April 1814, Nos. 167, 169.
217 Ibid., 13 April 1814, Nos. 168, 176.
218 Caulaincourt, *No Peace*, 255–58.
219 Napoleon I, *Confidential correspondence with Joséphine*, 335–36.

ELBA

Tis done – but yesterday a King!
   And arm'd with Kings to strive
And now thou art a nameless thing
   So abject – yet alive!
Is this the man of thousand thrones
   Who strew'd our Earth with hostile bones,
And can he thus survive?
    Since he, miscall'd the Morning Star
Nor man nor fiend hath fall'n so far

            Byron, *Ode to Napoleon*

The terms of the treaty that resulted from Napoleon's abdication included a provision for him and his family to keep their titles and granted him a pension of two million francs per year. Napoleon was given the Island of Elba 'in full sovereignty and property', with a guard of 400 soldiers.[220] The treaty did not require him to remain on Elba nor did it forbid him from ever returning to France.

Napoleon had been concerned with his safety during his trip to Elba. The British government, to its credit, offered to provide escort, together with commissioners representing the other allies, and a naval escort. Satisfied, Napoleon prepared to leave. It would take a week for the allied commissioners to be ready. To kill time, Napoleon read books and papers about the island. If he was to be their Emperor, his subjects must feel that he knew whereof he governed.

On 30 April, in a scene that ranks among the most poignant in history, Napoleon said good-bye to the soldiers of his Old Guard. He had already selected his personal guard from among them. Originally fixed at only four hundred, the number of volunteers was such that he was eventually allowed to take a contingent of 1,000 hand-picked men. There were many more, of course, and they waited his farewell in the stone court of Fontainebleau Palace near Paris.

It was an emotional *adieu*:

Soldiers of my Old Guard, I bid you farewell. During twenty years you have been my constant companions in the path of honour and glory. In our late disasters, as well as in the days of our prosperity, you invariably proved yourselves models of courage and fidelity. With such men as you our cause could not have been lost; but the war could not be ended: it would have been civil war, and that would only have brought France more misfortune. I have sacrificed our interests to those of the *patrie* [homeland] I am leaving. You, my friends, continue to serve France. Her happiness was my one thought; and it will always be the object of my wishes. Do not deplore my fate; if I consent to live, it is so that I can again serve your glory. I want to write about the great things we have done together! Goodbye, my children! I should like to press you all to my heart; at least I shall kiss your flag ...

Napoleon kissed the flag ... his emotion and those of the assembled soldiers, were obvious, and sobs were heard among the ranks of these old veterans who had shared so much with their General and Emperor. Tears were also to be seen among the allied commissioners and others there to observe and then to conduct the Emperor to his new home.

Farewell a second time, my old companions. Let this last kiss be impressed on your hearts.[221]

With that, he entered his carriage and rode away.

The trip was not uneventful. There were those who blamed him for the fall of France; propaganda had done its job and those from whom sacrifice is asked may legitimately be unhappy when that sacrifice seems to have been made in vain. There were incidents: knives brandished, stones thrown, insults hurled and a hanging in effigy. At one point he donned a disguise for what he perceived to be his own safety.

On 28 April, 1814, Napoleon set sail in the British ship, *Undaunted*, arriving two days later at his domain of Elba. The British had delivered him safely; they also provided Colonel Sir Neil Campbell as their commissioner. He was there to keep an eye on Napoleon and to provide some measure of protection from hostile action against the once and future emperor.

Another sadness would soon come to him. On 29 May, his beloved Joséphine died of pneumonia at their home in Malmaison. They had remained in love to the end. She had stayed unmarried and kept their home as if he would someday return. Her children Hortense and Eugène were with her when she died. Napoleon was in mourning for two days. Not for the first time, he must have wondered at the wisdom of giving up that love for what had proved to be an illusory political benefit.

He spent much of his time on Elba in a serious effort to improve conditions there. It was a very small island whose population numbered only a few thousand. He revised the laws, improved the collection of taxes and initiated a number of physical improvements. He extended the meagre road system and improved the defences sufficently to fend off all but the most massive attack on his fortified island empire. Providing for the cultural life of his subjects, he even started a theatre.

Napoleon's mother came to join him in his exile. This did wonders for his spirits, and the two spent a great deal of time together. His sister Pauline, loyal to the end, also came to stay with her brother. It was Pauline who provided most of the gaiety on the island, organising balls and other social events. But the steady round of parties proved but a sad reflection of past glory. Elba was not Paris.

Two of his mistresses managed to visit him for a time, most notably the Countess Walewska. She wanted to stay but he was afraid of the scandal. She loved him as much as had Joséphine or Marie-Louise, but he sent her and their young son away.

Political leaders and other important people would visit him and he discussed politics with them at great length.[222] Napoleon was especially cordial to British visitors and went out of his way to see that the British representative Colonel Campbell felt welcome in his court.[223] In December he had two lengthy conversations with Lord Ebrington, a nephew of Lord Grenville, his most adamant opponent in the British government. Ebrington wrote that Napoleon answered any questions 'without the slightest hesitation and with a quickness of comprehension and clearness of expression beyond what I ever saw in any other man'.[224]

Slowly but surely, Napoleon began to realise that Marie-Louise and their son were never going to join him on Elba. In fact, her father had forced her to return to Vienna, to Schönbrunn Palace. Her father had assigned her as *aide-de-camp*, one General Count Neipperg. A dashing man with smooth manners, he was under orders to keep Marie-Louise from any further interest in going to Elba.

In fact, he was essentially under orders to seduce the young woman, to steal her from her husband. On a trip to 'take the waters' at Aix, and later on a trip to Switzerland, he did just that. From now on, there was no further talk of her joining her husband, who never heard from her again. When Napoleon died years later, Marie-Louise married her lover, the father of her two youngest children, and they ruled in Parma.

Napoleon's son was raised as an Austrian prince and died of tuberculosis in 1832 at the age of twenty-one.

Napoleon became bored. A man of his immense energy must always have something to do; a man of his vast intellect must always have something *meaningful* to do. His life on Elba met neither of these requirements.

Had Marie-Louise been given Tuscany, and had the allies been cooperative, he might have lived the life of any number of princes, spending part of his time in Tuscany and part of his time in Elba with her. This had been his plan, and the idea had made exile seem bearable, even for a man of youth and energy like Napoleon.

He had told Joséphine, Caulaincourt, his Old Guard and others that he would write his memoirs. While on Elba, he wrote not so much as a page. Had he stayed there, he might well have done so. Events, however, were conspiring against his staying on Elba. One way or another, it seemed his destiny was elsewhere.

Talleyrand, who owed Napoleon so much, had not been content simply to remove him from France. He feared his return, perhaps realising that if that happened his own life would be in great peril. Talleyrand had great influence over the new King, Louis XVIII. Considering that the king owed his throne to Talleyrand, this was not altogether surprising.

Talleyrand had Louis XVIII send countless spies to Elba. Meanwhile, the French press printed stories about Napoleon that were reminiscent of those propagated by the British press in earlier years. Character assassination was back in style. Worse, there were plots being formulated to assassinate Napoleon or at the very least remove him from Elba.

After Napoleon's downfall, the allies convened a meeting in Vienna to decide how to divide up post-Napoleonic Europe. Hosted by Francis I, it was an expensive affair with a constant round of parties mixed in with the business at hand. Ominously for Napoleon, Talleyrand represented France at the bargaining table. While there, he never missed an opportunity to promote his belief that Napoleon needed to be removed to a safer place, far from Europe. Several possibilities were mentioned, including a small island off the coast of Africa called St. Helena.

Napoleon was made aware of these plans and was quite concerned. He took measures to protect himself from assassination and redoubled his efforts to defend his island. His personal guard was small, but he would not be taken without a fight.

Without an army, however, he would be vulnerable to whatever action the allies chose to take.

The treaty to which all the allies had agreed promised Napoleon an annual pension of two million francs and an annual pension of three hundred thousand francs each to his mother and his sister Pauline. These amounts would have been enough to sustain Napoleon's life-style, as well as, more importantly, his military forces, whose expenses gave Napoleon serious fear of running out of money.

In a move of absolute stupidity, or perhaps as a calculated effort inspired by Talleyrand, Louis XVIII never paid Napoleon or any of the other Bonapartes the pensions promised by international treaty. If it was a move simply not thought out, it was stupid because the lack of funds helped persuade Napoleon to return to France and thereby threaten Louis' throne.

If it was a calculated effort, it was designed to remove Napoleon's ability to pay his small army. Most would then have to leave his service, opening the island to easy conquest. Either way, it pushed Napoleon to take bold measures that he might otherwise have foregone.

France's allies were alarmed at this bald refusal by the King of France to honour the very treaty that had established his kingdom. Neil Campbell, who kept up a steady stream of reports on Napoleon's activities, wrote that not to pay the pensions was to risk Napoleon's return to either France or Italy. In one dispatch written to Lord Castlereagh on 6 December 1814, he wrote: 'I beg leave to repeat my opinion that, if the means of subsistence which he was led to expect on coming to Elba are given to him, he will remain here in perfect tranquillity, unless some great opening should present itself in Italy or France.'[225]

Italy was a possibility because Napoleon and Murat had re-established good relations, giving Napoleon a potential base of operations. With Marie-Louise in Parma and Napoleon presumably popular with many of the Italian people, he could establish himself there and dare anyone to come and get him. It would be just possible that the rest of Europe, tired of war and faced not with Napoleon's small force on Elba but a much larger force in Italy, would not interfere with him.

While Italy was a possibility, Napoleon's heart was in France. He was convinced that the French people would soon tire of Louis XVIII and that their resentment over the loss of virtually all the French conquests since the days of the Revolution would lead to even greater discontent.

Napoleon was right. Louis XVIII was not, in fact, without compassion and he was, even in Napoleon's estimation, well meaning. With his ascendancy to the throne, however, came hordes of noble *émigrés*. These hard-core royalists hated the Revolution and hated Napoleon. They were determined to turn back the clock, return France to its pre-Revolutionary condition and reclaim their titles and privileges.

Louis tried to re-assure the people of France. He restored civil liberties somewhat from their war-status restrictions. He granted a Constitutional Charter, which was designed to convince the people that there would be no return to the pre-Revolutionary days. He swore that the days of absolutism were over, but the behaviour of the aristocracy around him told another story.

French peasants and middle class citizens were watching and did not like what they saw. Peace was wonderful but they did not want it at this price. They were fearful that the land that had been confiscated and sold to them would be given back to the *émigrés* and that the system of privilege would return.

To some, Napoleon became the hero of the Revolution. They adopted the violet as their symbol. It was against the law to have images of Napoleon displayed in one's home, but many citizens found ingenious ways to get round that restriction. False-bottomed snuffboxes and art with hidden images of Napoleon were to be found everywhere.

Some units of the *Grande Armée* had been disbanded, but the soldiers did not assimilate well into society. France's economy had little room for them, and they were disgruntled at the loss of glory their defeat had brought. For them, most of all, the loss of the Emperor had been a very personal loss. Napoleon had never lost the love of his soldiers; even the conscripts of 1813 and 1814 were devoted to him. They never forgot that he was one of them.

Napoleon knew all this of course. Visitors were continually bringing stories of the fears of the people and of his resurgent popularity. Soon, he began to believe that the people would welcome his return to power.

Given his own insecurity on Elba, this temptation grew alluring. It only needed a spark to set it aflame.

That spark came on 15 February 1815, when Napoleon was visited by Fleury de Chamboulon, who had been one of Napoleon's sub-prefects. He brought with him a message from Hugh Maret, Napoleon's former Foreign Minister. According to Maret, whose opinion Napoleon had always valued, the people were 'clamouring for Napoleon's return'.[226]

Napoleon was not surprised. He had often predicted such dissatisfaction and with it the resulting desire for his return. Later on St. Helena he told Las Cases that he had anticipated this upon his departure from Fontainebleau. He explained: 'If the Bourbons, said I, intend to commence a fifth dynasty, I have nothing more to do here; I have acted my part. But if they should obstinately attempt to recontinue the third, I shall soon appear again ...'[227]

He had told Caulaincourt at the time of his abdication: 'If the Bourbons are wise, they will change only the sheets on my bed; they will give employment to the men whom I have trained. Their followers are nothing but passions and grudges with clothes on. With men such as those, they can do nothing unless it is reactionary, and they will ruin themselves.'[228]

From Napoleon's point of view, things had come to a head. He was running out of money and would soon be easy prey for betrayal by Talleyrand, or murder by someone seeking a place in history. He had given up all hope of seeing Marie-Louise again, at least as long as he remained in his current status. The thought of Italy was intriguing, but his real claim to legitimacy lay in France. There also he would find his army.

The decision was made: the eagle would fly to France.

Only Napoleon's closest associates were told of his plans. General Bertrand was pleased with the opportunity to return to France. General Drouot, on the other hand, tried to talk him out of what he saw as a monumental misadventure. He sensibly pointed out that challenging the military might of France and possibly of the Allies, with some 1,100 troops involved a certain amount of risk![229] Napoleon's mother gave him encouragement with the words 'Go my son, go and fulfill your destiny ... I see with sorrow that you cannot remain here.'[230]

Napoleon showed all of his old abilities. He studied maps of France; he organised the preparations down to the last detail. His retirement had not deprived him of his enormous abilities, and he brought them to bear on this one last effort.

As luck would have it, Neil Campbell was leaving for a ten-day trip to Italy. This gave Napoleon a window of opportunity. As he had so many times before, he saw an opportunity and seized upon it.

There is a theory that the English deliberately gave Napoleon this opportunity, because they were dissatisfied with the actions of the Bourbons. This is a fascinating possibility, and by no means beyond the realm of reason, but documentary evidence to support it has as of yet not been found.

NOTES

220 For a complete translation of the treaty, see Fain, *Manuscript*, 271–82.

221 *Correspondance*, 20 April 1814, No. 21561, XXVII, 422–23.

222 A set of Napoleon's letters and orders, which reflect his activities on Elba, can be found in *Le Registre de L'Ile D'Elbe: Lettres et Ordres Inédits de Napoléon Ier (28 mai 1814–22 fèvrier 1815)*. Paris, 1897.

223 This was not entirely for social reasons, because Napoleon felt the need to keep a strong and ready link to the Allies, should there be a threat to his personal safety. For a good discussion on this, see Houssaye, *The Return of Napoleon*, 11–13.

224 Ebrington, *Two Conversations*, 19–20. This is a typed copy of his original 1814 manuscript, published as a pamphlet in 1823, which describes his two conversations with Napoleon while on Elba. These conversations were noted in Pasquier's memoirs.

225 Campbell, *Napoleon at Fontainebleau and Elba*, 343. This is the best primary source for Napoleon's activities on Elba, and among many other things, relates countless fascinating conversations between Campbell and Napoleon.

226 Cronin, 385–86.

227 Las Cases, II, 3, 30–31.

228 Caulaincourt, *No Peace*, 192.

229 Thiers, Adolphe. *History of the Consulate*, V, 423–24.

230 Ibid., 423. This reminds one of Alexander the Great's father Philip who told his son 'Look thee out a kingdom equal to and worthy of thyself, for Macedonia is too little for thee.'

ONE HUNDRED DAYS
The Eagle Returns

On Sunday, 25 February 1815, Napoleon set sail for France in the *Inconstant*, accompanied by the *Saint Esprit* and the *Caroline*. Together, these ships carried 1,100 men, 40 horses and four cannon. He left a letter for General Lapi in which he informed the general of his departure, indicated his satisfaction with the residents of Elba and entrusted the care of his mother and sister to them.

As he went aboard *Inconstant*, he exclaimed to those around him, using the words of Caesar, 'The die is now cast.' The Mediterranean was Napoleon's Rubicon! Prior to his departure, Napoleon prepared an eloquent bulletin for his soldiers still in France:

> Soldiers! In my exile I heard your voice! I have arrived, despite all obstacles and perils! Your general, called to the throne by the people's choice and raised upon your shields, has been returned to you; come and join him ...
>
> We must forget that we have been masters of other nations; but we must not suffer any to meddle in our affairs ...
>
> Soldiers! Come and rejoin the flag of your leader. He exists only because of you; his rights are but those of the people and your own; his interest, honour and glory are no other than your interest, honour and glory. Victory shall arrive on the run: the eagle along with the national colours, will fly from steeple to steeple up to the towers of Notre-Dame: then shall you be able to show your scars with honour; then shall you be able to boast of your exploits; you shall be the liberators of the motherland.
>
> In your old age, surrounded and admired by your fellow citizens, you will be listened to with respect as you recount your great deeds; you shall be able to say with pride: 'I too was part of this Great Army which twice entered Vienna, entered Rome, Berlin, Madrid, Moscow, cleansed Paris of the blot which treason and the presence of the enemy left upon it.' [231]

His similar bulletin to the French people reminded them that they had been defeated because of the defections of Marshal Augereau in Lyon and

Marshal Marmont in Paris, thus snatching defeat from what he claimed would have been a sure victory![232]

Finally, he prepared a bulletin for the soldiers he was most likely to face upon landing and marching toward Paris, which read in part, 'Soldiers, the drum beats the general, and we march: run to arms, come and join us, join your Emperor and our eagles ...'[233]

Napoleon had always been a masterful politician, and these bulletins are a case in point. He had three audiences in these messages: the army, the people and the allies. He needed all three on his side if he was to have any chance of success.

His first audience was the army. Napoleon could not succeed if he encountered any real resistance. Indeed, he predicted the necessity and the result: 'I shall arrive in Paris without firing a shot.'[234] To avoid a confrontation, he appealed to the army to join him in overthrowing the treachery of others and restoring their glory. He includes references to his 'willingness' to respond to their 'calls' that he return.

To the people of France the message was pretty much the same. The France to which he was returning, however, was not the France he had left in 1814. However much they might hate the Bourbons and however much they might welcome him, the people would not be interested in new military adventures. To them, conquest and empire were things of the past. He needed to convince them that he understood this. If he succeeded, the people might be willing to support him in a new role of constitutional emperor. His appeals to glory and revenge, therefore, were tempered with a recognition that times had changed and control over other nations was no longer on the agenda.

This latter point was especially important for his third audience, which was the Congress of Vienna. As it turned out, Napoleon misjudged their readiness to rally against him. Even so, he understood that they would need some sort of reassurance that he no longer harboured a desire to engage in imperial conquests. Accordingly, these bulletins deliberately stressed his domestic goals and specifically renounced a return to empire. *We must forget that we have been the masters of other nations.*

Napoleon landed in France at Golfe-Juan on 1 March 1815, at 4 o'clock in the afternoon. The Emperor had returned; the great adventure had begun. It was the stuff of legend, but it had not started in a very legendary fashion. Earlier in the day, Captain Lamouret, sent by Napoleon to ascertain the situation there, demanded the surrender of the garrison at

Antibes. Instead, he and his twenty grenadiers were taken prisoner. Napoleon decided to leave them behind; he understood that the first shot fired would break the spell of his arrival and lead to disaster. He instructed General Cambronne, 'You are not to fire a single shot. Remember that I wish to win back my crown without shedding one drop of blood.'[235]

There had been another ominous development as well. Upon arriving in France, Napoleon relates:

> Very soon a great crowd of people came around us, surprised by our appearance and astonished at our small force. Among them was a maire [mayor] who seeing how few we were, said to me: 'We were just beginning to be quiet and happy; now you are going to stir us all up again.'[236]

This was not the kind of thing Napoleon wanted to hear and it reduced his optimism for the success of his venture.

Napoleon took the mountain road to Grenoble rather than pass close to the large garrisons at Toulon and Marseilles. He might have won them over but the danger would have been great. Provence was a royalist stronghold and it would have been risky to take this more direct route to Paris. He no doubt remembered the unfriendly reception he had received travelling through Provence on his way to Elba.

This meant leaving his cannon, carriage and sixteen supply wagons behind and marching along narrow mountain roads, often in single file. Even today, the road is narrow and travel by car on the *Route Napoléon* is painfully slow.

At Grasse, as elsewhere along the route, Napoleon was given a mixed reception. Most citizens were confused by this unexpected turn of events and in any case were unwilling to gamble on either the Bourbon king or the returning Emperor. In Stendhal's words, 'The people allowed them to pass without giving the least sign of approval or of disapproval.'[237]

The route was mountainous, climbing to 2,500 feet, descending into a valley, climbing again to 3,000 feet, all on the first day. Nevertheless they made very good time. At some points, the soldiers had to scramble along ice-bound ravines, with Napoleon following breathlessly.

Along the way Napoleon talked with peasants, soldiers and towns-people. Most of them were surprised to see their Emperor at all, let alone on foot in the snow. Some were less than excited, some attempted to encourage him, others offered him their hospitality. On 2 March at the village of Escragnolles, Napoleon met the Abbé Chiris, the parish priest, who offered him two eggs.[238]

At Castellane (3 March), the surprised villagers provided food and drink for Napoleon and his men. Napoleon sent messages to his supporters in Grenoble, it being critical that he capture that city without difficulty. He also sent messages to Marshal Masséna asking for his support.

By 5 March Napoleon had entered the town of Sisteron. It had been an uneventful day for him, but not for Louis XVIII, who that day learned of his return. After consulting with Minister of War Soult, it was decided to make the major stand against Napoleon at the city of Lyon. At this juncture, Napoleon's adventure did not seem a major threat.

As Napoleon and his entourage drew closer to Grenoble, roads began to improve. As a fighting force they were still modest, but Napoleon had his troops in fine marching order and their emotional appeal was enormous. Officials at Bras d'Or told Napoleon that the people would be pleased to see him on the throne, provided that conscription was not renewed. Napoleon's reply: 'A great many foolish things have been done, but I have come to put everything right. My people will be happy.'[239] Soon the reaction of the people along the way turned from curious to encouraging; eventually, crowds of peasants were standing by the road side, cheering.

The first part of his journey had been easy, as there had been no organised resistance. The first real test of his chances for success came at Laffrey, a short distance from Grenoble, whose commanding General Jean-Gabriel Marchand had sent Major de Lessart and a battalion of the 5th Regiment of the Line to put an end to Napoleon's adventure.

Napoleon had realised that this would happen and, showing his command of all elements of the situation, sent some Polish Lancers ahead to feel out the situation and try to convince the soldiers of the 5th not to fire on Napoleon. They reported that the general feeling was that there was little fear that they would take hostile action against Napoleon.

De Lessart, however, was determined to do his duty, setting the scene for an emotional and historic confrontation. Napoleon and his soldiers came into view, their band playing the *Marseillaise*. His soldiers carried their arms at rest; they were not approaching as to battle, but in peace.

As Napoleon approached, Captain Randon ordered the soldiers of the 5th to open fire. Nothing happened. Then Napoleon spoke to the soldiers.

Accounts differ as to his exact words but the local commemorative plaque reads: 'SOLDIERS! I am your Emperor. Do you not recognise me? If there is one among you who would kill his general, HERE I AM!'[240]

The answer was a resounding: *'Vive l'Empereur!'* The confrontation was over. Indeed, it seems that the soldiers had not even loaded their muskets. It was a good day for Napoleon, because later Colonel Charles de La Bédoyère surrendered the 7th Regiment of the line, with its 1,800 men.

The commanding officer at Grenoble refused to open the gates, but the people and soldiers, shouting 'Vive l'Empereur!', tore them down and escorted Napoleon to the *Hôtel des Trois Dauphins*. The pieces of the gate were placed under his window, with shouts of 'For want of the keys of the good town of Grenoble, here are the gates for you.'[241] General Marchand, meanwhile, had fled the city.

By now Napoleon had some 4,000 seasoned infantry, twenty cannon, a regiment of hussars and more men arriving all the time. The citizens were warming to his return; in some areas a revolutionary fervour had arisen that had not been seen since the days of France's great revolution. Thus it is no surprise that he recalled, 'On my march from Cannes to Grenoble I was an adventurer; in Grenoble I once more became a sovereign.'[242]

While in Grenoble, Napoleon had meetings with a number of public officials, making it clear that he no longer wanted to expand an empire. He acknowledged his past mistakes and swore to be a constitutional monarch: 'I have been too fond of war; I will make war no more: I will leave my neighbours at rest: we must forget that we have been masters of the world ... I wish to be less its [France's] sovereign than the first and best of its citizens.'[243] He presented himself as the spirit of 1789, returned to do battle with the spirit of feudalism, to relieve them of the oppressive policies of the Bourbons and especially of the *émigrés*. He would never again seek to conquer others and only desired that foreigners would treat France in the same manner.[244]

On 8 March, Napoleon and his growing army left Grenoble for Lyon. The comte d'Artois, aided by Marshal Macdonald, was determined to defend Lyon and end the threat from the Ogre of Corsica. The soldiers, however, refused to pledge allegiance to the king, and it was clear that they were not about to fight their emperor. The sullen refusal of the soldiers to cry *Vive le Roi!* told the comte d'Artois all he needed to know, and he left Macdonald to do the best he could. It was not enough. Macdonald must have known that nothing was going to stop Napoleon when, as he inspected the preparations for the defence of Lyon, he discovered that nothing had been done. One of his staff officers arrived with news:

'A reconnoitring party has just returned.'
'What had it seen?'
'Napoleon's advance-guard.'
'Far away?'
'Just coming into the suburb of Guillotière.'
'What happened?'
'The two parties drank together.'

Macdonald made one last effort:

As I reached the bridge-gates, cries of 'Long live the Emperor!' burst from the other side of the river. On the quays the crowd took up the shout and echoed it in a deafening manner.

I instantly put into execution the design I had formed of making some show of resistance. I intended to gain the head of the bridge with my staff, stop the first who appeared, seize their weapons and fire. The bridge was blocked by troops in columns.

'Come along, gentlemen!' I cried, 'we must get down.'

We jumped off our horses and hurried along on foot as rapidly as we could, but scarcely had we reached a quarter of the distance when the 4th Hussars, Napoleon's scouts, appeared at the other end of the bridge. At this sight officers and soldiers mingled their cheers with the shouts of the populace; shakos were waved on bayonets in token of delight; the feeble barricades were thrown down; everyone pressed forward to welcome the new arrivals to the town.

From that moment all was lost.[245]

Unable to stop Napoleon, and fearful of his own troops, Macdonald beat a hasty retreat.

While in Lyon, Napoleon began to act like a ruling monarch. He dissolved the two Chambers, the legislative bodies controlled by the king, and called for new laws to be passed that would make his reign more constitutional in nature.[246] He wrote to Marie-Louise, asking her to be in Paris on 20 March, their son's birthday. He re-established the imperial magistracy and demanded that all recently returned *émigrés* leave the country. Remembering 1814, he ordered the arrest of Talleyrand, Marmont, Augereau and others.

As he had throughout his march toward Paris, Napoleon emphasised his new approach to governing: 'I was hurried on by the course of events, into a wrong path. But, taught by experience, I have abjured that love of glory ... I have renounced forever that grand enterprise; we have enough of glory, we want repose.'[247]

Marshal Michel Ney, the bravest of the brave, Prince of the Moskowa, had declared for the monarchy earlier than many of those who ultimately left Napoleon, and he had led the so-called revolt of the marshals in 1814. After the return of the Bourbons, he had retired in great comfort and could not have been particularly pleased to hear of Napoleon's latest gamble.

Determined to show his loyalty to Louis XVIII and to keep France at peace, Ney began to organise a force to oppose Napoleon's march to Paris. He even pledged to bring Napoleon back in an iron cage, a pledge which amused more than impressed Louis XVIII.

But Ney was moved by Napoleon's proclamations and admittedly torn in his loyalties, but he doubted whether his old master would have forgiven him for the marshals' revolt at Fontainebleau.

Napoleon was well aware of preparations being made to halt his advance, including those by Ney. Based on what had happened so far and the growing strength of his fighting force, he did not really fear defeat. But it was important to him that he arrive in Paris without having fired a shot. Any other scenario would bring into question his claim to have returned at the demand of the people and with the support of the army.

As Napoleon advanced through the Franche-Comté and Burgundy, the support of the people was more open. These areas had prospered under the Empire. Prosperity brings support; this was friendly territory. The enthusiasm of the people was great, and crowds greeted him wherever he went. At Mâcon, at Châlon, at Villefranche, Napoleon was greeted by crowds chanting, '*A bas les nobles! à bas les prêtres! à bas les Bourbons!*' (Down with the nobles! Down with the priests! Down with the Bourbons!) A commemorative plaque tells us that some 60,000 people cheered him at Villefranche.[248]

Ney's preparations were slowed by poor organisation on the part of the government. Meanwhile, Bonapartist pressures were mounting. Napoleon had Bertrand write orders to Ney and other forces that were preparing to oppose him. To Ney he promised 'I shall receive you as after the battle of the Moskowa.'[249]

As they had at Grenoble and Lyon, some of Napoleon's soldiers went forward and intermingled with some of Ney's. In conversations with his officers Ney found that the cause of the Bourbons was not quite the effective rallying-point that he had expected. He swore that he would fire the first shot, but this pledge seemed to have little effect on his soldiers. Meanwhile, they kept hearing news, propagated by Napoleon, of the great desire of France and Europe to see the Empire restored.

By 14 March, Ney had decided to join in Napoleon's gambit. A proclamation to his troops read, in part:

> The cause of the Bourbons is lost for ever ... Liberty is at length triumphant; and Napoleon, our august Emperor, is about to confirm it for ever ... Soldiers! I have often led you to victory; I am now going to conduct you to that immortal phalanx, which the Emperor Napoleon is conducting to Paris. ... Long live the Emperor![250]

On 17 March Napoleon arrived at Auxerre, where he was greeted by the *Préfet*. He spent the day discussing his plans with a wide assortment of people and later met Ney. The scene must have been dramatic: Ney, overcome with guilt and apprehension, Napoleon relieved that this final major obstacle was removed and he once again had the services of 'the bravest of the brave'.

With Ney in hand, the remainder of the march to Paris was anticlimactic. Paris was alive with Bonapartist fervour. One banner proclaimed these words supposedly from Napoleon to the king: 'My good brother: there is no need to send any more troops; I already have enough!'[251]

The hopelessness of the king's situation was summed up by General Thiébault's observation that 'I was the only person holding out for the King either around or in Paris.'[252] Perhaps there is no better illustration of the rapid growth of Napoleon's support than the following sequence of Paris broadsheet headlines periodically passed out on the streets to keep the citizens informed of his three-week march to Paris:

The Tiger has broken out of his den!
The Ogre was three days at sea.
The Wretch has landed at Fréjus.
The Brigand has arrived at Antibes.
The Invader has reached Grenoble.
The General has entered Lyons.
Napoleon slept last night at Fontainebleau.
The Emperor proceeds to the Tuileries today.
His Imperial Majesty will address his loyal subjects tomorrow![253]

While further royalist resistance was possible – and feared – Louis XVIII fled on the night of the 19th. He had given a very effective speech to the Senate, declaring that he would die upon his throne, but within four days, he had left for Belgium. As Macdonald says in his defence, 'It must be said in fairness that he could not count upon any resistance being made to Napoleon.'[254] General Rapp expresses it with rather more bitterness:

> But all these worthies, so ardent for the treasury, for decorations and commands, soon showed the amount of their courage. Napoleon appeared, they were eclipsed. They had flocked to Louis XVIII, the dispenser of favours; but they had not a trigger to pull for Louis XVIII in misfortune.[255]

Next day, street vendors celebrated the return by selling medals showing a bust of the Emperor and the date. To add insult to injury, the Paris Mint, which had so recently produced medals celebrating the reign of Louis XVIII, began to plan for a new series celebrating the return of the Emperor.

By the evening of 20 March, Napoleon had re-entered Paris. Tens of thousands cheered his return. The palace had been made ready and his step-daughter Hortense was there to greet him. He had made an amazing journey.

Napoleon's return had brought excitement and hope to many, apprehension and fear to others. It was immediately seized as a great romance, another chapter in the continuing saga of the great man. General Thiébault, who had remained with the Bourbons but joined Napoleon upon his return wrote:

Never did Napoleon exercise a greater moral influence than at that moment. If the return from Waterloo was to complete the melancholy work of the return from Moscow, the impression made by this return from Elba was worthy of that produced by the return from Egypt.[256]

The first phase of the One Hundred Days had drawn to a close. The romance was at an end; it was time to deal with reality.

THE NEW IMPERIAL ORDER

Napoleon was faced with two major problems, both of which had to be solved almost immediately if he were to have any chance of success. Possession of Paris was a good start, but he had to re-organise the government in a way that the politically powerful people around him would support. Without that, he might find himself powerless, or at least obliged to rule by the force of the army. That would be impossible, and his effort would have failed.

He also had to deal with those nations who had deposed him and whose goodwill he now needed to court. His only real hope for success lay in the possibility that at least most of the nations of Europe would be willing to leave him alone for the time being and wait to see if his words of peace had any meaning.

Louis XVIII had brought back the rule of the Bourbons but he had not brought back the notion of absolute monarchy. He had been willing, perhaps reluctantly, to have a legislative body. But that body's power had been restricted and the size of the electorate greatly reduced from that of the Consulate and Empire.

If Napoleon was to obtain the support of the people, he needed to be seen as a protector of the liberal ideas of the Revolution, but also of those ideas more associated with British notions of liberty. To achieve this, he employed a masterful political stroke.

Benjamin Constant was the intellectual leader of the liberals of Paris. He had been dismayed at Napoleon's return and had written articles comparing Napoleon to Attila and Genghis Khan. Presuming that this would make him *persona non grata* in Napoleon's Paris, he then fled to Nantes.

Napoleon the intellectual respected men who stood by the conviction of their ideas, even to the point of opposing his own. He had shown that throughout his reign, most notably in the development of the *Code Napoléon*. Napoleon the politician needed the support of someone recognised as a symbol of liberalism to all of France.

Napoleon asked Constant to join him in Paris and to write a new constitution based on his, Constant's, liberal ideas. Constant was at first suspicious, but when he realised that Napoleon was serious he was more than pleased. Intellectuals seldom have the power to put their ideas into operation; this was an opportunity almost too good to be true.

Constant's constitution provided a two-chamber legislative body that would meet in public, a greatly expanded electorate, jury trials and the abolishment of censorship. It was a government worthy of the Revolution, of Napoleon and of the Council of State, and a plebiscite of the people put it into effect on 22 April 1815.

There certainly was more domestic work to be done, but Napoleon's main concern now lay elsewhere. His reception in Paris had been tumultuous but did not necessarily reflect the opinions of all the French. He remembered the comment of a mayor when he first landed, 'We were just beginning to be quiet and happy; now you are going to stir us all up again.'

Throughout his return to Paris, Napoleon had stressed his desire for peace. He wrote to all the other nations, promising to respect the treaty that had brought peace in 1814 and to keep France within the 1792 boundaries, thus surrendering any claim to Belgium or Holland. His days of war and empire were over; he just wanted to be the enlightened ruler of France.

Peace was necessary if Napoleon was to remain in power. The one thing that would lose him the support of his nation was a return to war. He knew it and did everything in his power to secure that peace, but success would depend less on his abilities of persuasion than on the whims and fears of the other nations.

When Napoleon decided to leave Elba, he had had to make a very difficult decision as to timing. The Congress of Vienna had brought together sovereigns and their representatives, making concerted action far easier than if they were in their respective capitals. Knowing this, Napoleon had wanted to postpone his departure from Elba for France until the Congress had ended.

That would have posed further problems; for all he knew, the Congress might continue for a another year. More ominously, the Congress might decide to have him removed to a remote island or to a prison. Thus, to wait ran a very real risk of ending all possibility of his return.

In addition, he knew that all had not been sweetness and harmony at the Congress. Russia and Prussia were often in sharp disagreement with Austria and Great Britain over Poland and a variety of other issues. Perhaps this disagreement might work to his advantage.

But in the event, the decision to return while the Congress of Vienna was still assembled would prove to be fatal for Napoleon and a disaster for France.

Under Louis XVIII, France had entered into an alliance with Austria and Great Britain. This secret treaty had been uncovered by the ever-faithful Caulaincourt. Napoleon, reasonably enough, wanted to use that alliance to help maintain the peace. In Austria, he had his father-in-law, his wife and his son. Surely that would be enough to give him breathing-space.

He had always had supporters in England and his new moderate to liberal constitution might give them heart. Their biggest concern, Antwerp, was satisfied. Perhaps they, too, would honour the alliance and give Napoleon a chance to prove his peaceful intentions.

It was not to be. There would be no peace with Napoleonic France. Not surprisingly, the primary focus for this turn of events was none other than Talleyrand. As he had in 1814, he convinced the allies that Napoleon could not be trusted, that they must declare him an international outlaw and march against him until he could be removed, this time for good.

Any hope for peace with Austria was dashed when Murat, wanting to seize what he saw as a golden opportunity to gain control of the whole of Italy and create a drain on Austrian forces that might otherwise fight Napoleon, declared war on the Austrians and marched against them on 15 March. He was defeated at the battle of Tolentino on 2 May and fled to France, seeking the protection of Napoleon.

Napoleon knew nothing of Murat's intention to make war on Austria and he was furious when it happened. Here he was, trying to convince the world that he meant peace, and there was his brother-in-law making war on his father-in-law! From the standpoint of Austria and the other allies, it was proof enough that Napoleon could not be trusted. Napoleon, who could have used Murat to good advantage at Waterloo, refused to see the man who second only to Talleyrand had upset his plans. He complained that Murat had betrayed him in 1814 and had done so again in 1815.

Under the prodding of Talleyrand, the allies issued a proclamation declaring Napoleon to be an international outlaw:

The Powers declare that by breaking the convention which had established him on the island of Elba, Napoleon Bonaparte has destroyed the sole legal title to which his existence was attached, that by reappearing in France he has placed himself outside the pale of civil and social relations, and that, as the enemy and disturber of the peace of the world, he has delivered himself to public justice.[257]

NOTES

231 *Correspondance*, 1 March 1815, No. 21682, XXVIII, 3–5; Marchand, 159–60.

232 Ibid., 1 March 1815, No. 21681, XXVIII, 1–3; Fleury, I, 177–80.

233 Ibid., 1 March 1815, No. 21683, XXVIII, 5–7; Fleury, I, 181–82. 'The general' was the name of a drumbeat call to arms.

234 Houssaye, *Return*, 45.

235 Ibid., 49.

236 Gourgaud, *Talks of Napoleon*, 175.

237 *Life of Napoleon*, 172.

238 Tulard and Garros, *Itinéraire*, 462. This unique book details Napoleon's daily activities throughout his career.

239 Ibid., 63. See also his proclamation to the Hautes and Basse Alpes '... the cause of the Nation will triumph again!' *Correspondance*, 6 March 1815, No. 21684, XXVIII, 7.

240 The plaque reads 'SOLDATS. Je suis votre Empereur. Ne me reconnaissez–vous pas? S'il en est un parmi vous qui veuille tuer son général, ME VOILA!!! 7 Mars 1815' (my translation).

241 Fleury, I, 195–96.

242 Gourgaud, 175.

243 Fleury, I, 198–99.

244 Thiers, V, 434–35.

245 Macdonald, *Recollections*, II, 260–62.

246 Decree of 13 March 1815. *Correspondance*, No. 21686, XXVIII, 8–9.

247 Fleury, I, 231

248 When travelling in search of Napoleonic sites, plaques, and monuments, it is important to have a guide. That is, the *Guide Napoléonien* (Paris, 1981) or its more recent replacement *Répertoire mondial des souvenirs napoléoniens* (Paris, 1993), both written by Alain Chappet, Roger Martin, Alain Pigeard, and André Robe. These books detail every Napoleonic site of any kind anywhere in the world, and are an invaluable resource for the Napoleonic traveller.

249 *Correspondance*, March 1815 (no day given), No. 21689, XXVIII, 10–11.

250 Fleury, I, 259–60n.

251 Chandler, *Waterloo*, 19.

252 Thiébault, *Memoirs*, II, 417.

253 Macdonald, II, 257.

254 Ibid., II, 280.

255 Rapp, 339.

256 Thiébault, II, 419.

257 Young, *Napoleon in Exile*, I, 20.

THE ROAD
TO DESTINY

And art thou he of Lodi's Bridge,
    Marengo's plain and Wagram's ridge,
    Or is thy soul like mountain-tide
That, swelled by winter storm and shower,
    Rolls down in turbulence of power
A torrent, fierce and wide?
    Reft of these aids, a rill obscure
Shrinking unnoticed, mean and poor,
    Whose channel shows displayed
The wreaks of its impetuous course,
    But not one symptom of the force
By which these wrecks were made
        Sir Walter Scott, *1815 The Field of Waterloo; A poem*

PREPARATIONS

If it was to be war, Napoleon needed to move swiftly. The British and Prussian armies were relatively close at hand, in Belgium. The Russians and the Austrians did not pose an immediate threat thanks to the poor state of their organisation and their distance from France. Napoleon organised the government and mobilised the country. He was able to field 300,000 soldiers, not counting the National Guard.

There were hindrances, however. The legislature was dominated by people who were not really all that happy with Napoleon. The new constitution gave them more power than had confronted him in the past and they slowed down the process.

Other problems developed as well. Napoleon's chief of staff had always been his old friend Marshal Louis-Alexandre Berthier. He was unexcelled at this job. He had remained with the Bourbons, but there was hope, even expectation, that he might rejoin his old comrade-in-arms. True, he had escorted Louis XVIII to safety, but the example of Marshal Ney gave Napoleon hope about Berthier.

When the news came that on 1 June Berthier had fallen to his death from a window in his home at Bamberg, hope faded to gloom. Napoleon was saddened by his death; sad also that all hope of engaging his great talents was gone. To this day, historians suspect that he may well have been pushed to his death by royalists fearful of his return to the service of his Emperor. Fate seldom hinges on one man alone, but Berthier's loss under any circumstances was a blow to Napoleon's chances of success.

The reason is simple. Berthier had been the chief of staff *par excellence*. He understood his Emperor well and was able to make clear the sometimes confusing orders issued by Napoleon. Some of the mix-ups and confusion of the Waterloo campaign would almost certainly have been avoided if Berthier had been in charge.

Berthier's replacement was Marshal Soult, an excellent commander but one who had never been chief of staff. In his final fight for survival, Napoleon needed his best officers in the field, but he kept Soult at his headquarters. Worse still, he left Marshal Davout as Minister of War in Paris. Of all of his remaining marshals, Davout was the best soldier and his absence would be deeply felt at Waterloo. Davout understood this and wanted to be one of Napoleon's field commanders, but Napoleon insisted. He needed a good Minister of War, but there were other, better choices, and Napoleon should have recognised this.

Thus, Napoleon's best remaining warriors, Soult and Davout, were relegated to posts for which they were unsuited and were replaced by men equally unsuited to lead Napoleon's army in the field.

Marshal Michel Ney was a top-flight cavalry commander and absolutely fearless in combat. His return to Napoleon had been an important positive development beyond the resulting lack of opposition from Golfe-Juan to Paris. His appointment as commander of one of Napoleon's wings at Waterloo was good from a political standpoint, in that he then served as an example to others who had switched to the Bourbons, perhaps encouraging them to return to the service of the Emperor. His military abilities, however, did not extend to the level of strategic understanding needed by a wing commander. Still, one must be fair to Ney in this matter. He only received his appointment on 15 June when the campaign was well under way and he had no time to review his command structure or consult with either his staff or Napoleon.

Napoleon's other wing commander was Marshal Emmanuel Grouchy. He too was an excellent cavalry commander and initially had been assigned that role. But shortly thereafter he was given command of Napoleon's right wing, which called for understanding and initiative beyond his capabilities. As commander of the cavalry Grouchy would have been an asset; as it turned out, he may have been the cause of Napoleon's defeat at Waterloo.

One last person must be mentioned in this litany of mistaken appointments. Joachim Murat had been nothing but trouble for Napoleon and had returned to France in disgrace. It is quite understandable that Napoleon decided to have nothing to do with him, and in something approaching normal conditions this would have not been a major problem.

Napoleon, however, was not experiencing anything like normal conditions. He was short of soldiers and, worse, short of top commanders. Whatever his faults, Murat was – and still is – conceded to be one of the greatest cavalry commanders of his day, perhaps of any day. Like Ney, he was not lacking in courage. Moreover, he might well have been something of an inspiration to his soldiers. Napoleon should have swallowed his pride, subdued his anger and taken Murat to Waterloo.

During the One Hundred Days, Napoleon is said to have been ill, lethargic, unsure of himself and even confused. Nowhere can this be seen more clearly than in his selection of people to run his government and his army. His usually excellent judgement of character, his ability to match the man to the job and his willingness to take decisive action, all left him at this most critical moment. If we wish to determine the reason for the failure of Napoleon's return, at least as far as the Battle of Waterloo is concerned, we need look only as far as the appointments we have discussed.

General Thiébault saw Napoleon shortly before he left to join his troops marching towards Belgium. His description of Napoleon is worth reading in full:

I never took my eyes from Napoleon, and the more I studied him the less could I succeed in seeing him as he had been in the days of his strength and his greatness. Never has the impression which the sight of him made upon me at the moment when destiny was about to pronounce between the world and him, ceased to be present to me; his look, once so formidable and piercing, had lost its strength and even its steadiness; his face, which I had often seen, now beaming with kindness, now moulded in bronze, had lost all expression and all its forcible character; his mouth, compressed, contained none of its ancient witchery; his very head no longer had the pose which used to characterise the conqueror of the world; and his gait was as perplexed as his demeanour and gestures were undecided. Everything about him seemed to have lost its nature and to be broken up; the ordinary pallor of his skin was replaced by a strongly pronounced greenish tinge which struck me. A prey to the darkest forebodings, I left the palace where I was never to see him again and returned to my house full of wishes which I did not believe.[258]

Napoleon was continuing to try to obtain peace. He wrote to his wife, to Francis I of Austria and to the Prince Regent of Great Britain. For his efforts, he received not so much as a single response. The allies, it seemed, were steadfast in their determination to crush him.

Given that, it was imperative that Napoleon take the first action. He could not afford to wait until a combined force of perhaps 600,000 troops moved in from two directions across the borders of France. No, he must use his old tactic of divide and conquer. The British and Prussians were in Belgium; Napoleon would march to meet them, hoping to keep them apart and to defeat each in turn. It was his only chance. It was a good choice and it nearly worked.

On 12 June, Napoleon's army of about 125,000 men marched toward Charleroi. He joined them on the 13th. On the morning of the 15th, they routed the Prussian force at Charleroi, who had no idea the French were coming. As he had in 1805 when he marched to Ülm, Napoleon had managed to maintain a very high level of security.

Wellington was at a ball in Brussels when he was given the astounding news of Napoleon's action so close to his army. He and the Prussians decided to make their stand at Quatre Bras and Ligny, respectively.

Things were starting reasonably well for the French, but already there was an evil omen in the air. General Louis Bourmont, a corps commander under General Gérard, abandoned his troops and deserted to the allies. Once again the spectre of treachery was seen. It cast a pall over the soldiers, including Napoleon.

Wellington had some 96,000 men under his command and Blücher had about 117,000. Napoleon needed speed, secrecy and a perfect execution of his plans. He accomplished only the first two of those requirements. Almost from the beginning there were delays and confusion. Even so, by the evening of the 15th, Napoleon was in a good position. He had seized Charleroi and had kept the two allied armies apart. The normal course of action would be to turn on first one and then the other, allowing him to have at least some level of numerical superiority.

On 16 June, Napoleon's army would do what it almost never did. It would split into two wings and fight two separate battles: Ney against Wellington at Quatre Bras; Napoleon and Grouchy against Blücher at Ligny.

Both Ney and Napoleon were slow to engage. Ney should have moved right away to secure the cross-roads at Quatre Bras; had he done so, Wellington would have been kept at bay and the road to Brussels would have been clear. Ney continued to delay, fearful that he was facing a larger force than was the case. By the time he began to move forward, his fears had come to pass, as Wellington had brought up reinforcements.

Ney finally moved into action and fought bravely as he led several cavalry charges against Wellington's squares. Wellington held firm, and Ney failed to capture Quatre Bras and drive Wellington out of the area.

Grouchy and Napoleon were also later than expected in beginning their major offensive. The plan had been to crush the Prussians so that Napoleon could then turn on Wellington and the English army. They were somewhat surprised that Blücher offered battle that day, but when it finally became clear that he was prepared to fight, the French advanced.

At one point in the battle, Napoleon was disturbed by some laughter from one of his aides. Napoleon turned sharply, saying 'Be a little more serious, sir, when faced with all these brave men killing each other.'[259]

The battle at Ligny went quite well. Blücher was being pushed back; it was time to follow the plan and begin an attack upon the Prussians' rear.

It is risky to claim for any one event the causation of all that followed. The campaign of 1815 has several such events beginning at Ligny and Quatre Bras and ending in the last moments of Waterloo itself. So too, it is hard to fix blame on any one individual. There can be little doubt, however, that what transpired next was the strangest event of the campaign. It represented all that was wrong with Napoleon's staff selections and will ever be in the final ranks of those events considered the cause of the campaign's ultimate failure.

Jean-Baptiste Drouet, comte d'Erlon, was in command of a corps under Marshal Ney. His corps was placed on Napoleon's left and Ney's right flank. He was ordered, at the critical moment, to come across from Napoleon's left and fall on Blücher's rear. This move, if properly executed, would assure the total destruction of the Prussian army as a fighting force.

As the battle began to go well for the French, Napoleon himself sent orders to d'Erlon, telling him to move to cut off the Prussians' line of retreat. This d'Erlon began to do, but got the route wrong and actually ended up moving behind *French* lines. Naturally enough, this caused confusion and delay, costing Napoleon valuable time and momentum.

The mistake was corrected and the battle continued, Napoleon assuming that he could finally count on d'Erlon's soldiers to fall on the Prussians. Suddenly, to his surprise and horror, he instead saw d'Erlon's corps marching *away* from the Prussians! At the very moment they were needed the most, they were leaving?

The reason was all too simple, and perhaps predictable. Ney, still certain that he was facing far more British than he could handle, sent an order to d'Erlon to come to his aid and fall on the right flank of the *British*! Ney had never been informed of Napoleon's orders to d'Erlon who, for his part, must now have been completely confused. Perhaps the inclination should have been to obey an Emperor rather than a Marshal, even though Marshal Ney was his direct superior, but for all he knew the plans had changed and he was needed at Quatre Bras.

Disastrously for the French, he spent the day marching first towards one battle and then towards the other, never participating in either. His effect at Ligny could and would have been decisive. The Prussians would have been routed. It is too easy to pin the blame on d'Erlon, though he surely shares some part of it. He did, after all, follow orders, though perhaps he should have given priority to those of his Emperor rather than those of his Marshal. Regardless, good staff work would have never allowed it to happen, but Napoleon was not served with good staff work.

Two more events deserve mention before we leave the successful but not decisive actions at Quatre Bras and Ligny. At one point, Blücher himself was overrun by the French. They failed to realise that he was there, however, and he made good his escape. It was his force of will that made much of the difference at Waterloo; without it the result would almost certainly have been far different.

The other item has to do with the pursuit, or rather lack of pursuit, given by Grouchy. At the end of the day, the French settled in, declining to give chase to the retreating Prussians. Napoleon issued no orders, and Grouchy took no initiative. Had some effort been made, the Prussian losses might have increased.

The real problem came next day. Napoleon was slow to act; he was not well, but he should have realised that swift action was necessary. If Ligny and, especially, Quatre Bras had not gone as well as they could have, all the more reason to move quickly before the allies could take any action of their own. A fast move against Wellington might still lead to a great victory.

No such action ensued. When Wellington heard of Blücher's defeat and withdrawal, he realised that Napoleon would soon be joining Ney. Unhappy with his position, he ordered a withdrawal. By the time Napoleon finally arrived, Wellington was long gone.

Most especially, the Prussians must not be allowed to regroup. Another Prussian force under Count Friedrich von Bülow was not far away and Blücher's troops must be prevented from uniting with them. Grouchy would be sent with 33,000 men, but would leave not early in the morning, but at about noon. Napoleon's delays had been dangerous to his cause, but Grouchy destroyed any chance of success. He had not even adequately prepared his men for what he knew would be their ultimate task; they were not in marching order when the order to march finally came. This delay in departure was costly, but its cost was greatly increased by Grouchy's leisurely pace of pursuit.

The Prussians initially withdrew towards Liège and their lines of communication to Prussia. Blücher had been slightly injured, and the Prussians felt that Wellington had broken his promise to come to their assistance. They would regroup to fight another day. Blücher recovered quickly, however, and insisted that they withdraw in the direction of Wavre. This would give them at least some chance of re-uniting with Bülow and going to Wellington's assistance.

Napoleon, meanwhile, rejoined Ney and together they followed Wellington towards Brussels. Ney had not pursued Wellington. Had he done so, he could have inflicted significant damage on the retreating army. As Napoleon arrived, a heavy rain had started to fall. There would be no hot pursuit of the British, and Wellington would have ample time to prepare for their arrival. By early evening, the French had arrived in the fields near the small town of Waterloo. There, they spent the night and prepared for the actions of the next day.

NOTES

258 Thiébault, II, 421–22.
259 Marchand, 243.

WATERLOO
AND ABDICATION

When Napoleon arrived at Waterloo on 17 June, he should have, by all reason, already lost the battle. His staff appointments had caused disastrous confusion and disorder. The performance of his wing commanders had been lacking. Napoleon himself was responsible for several delays that cost him some additional chance of victory.

He should have already lost, but events were to show that he could still win. His soldiers were somewhat heartened by their success at Ligny. The Prussians were out of sight and surely Grouchy would keep them so. Wellington was retreating; Napoleon's real fear was that he might not turn and fight, but slip away in the dead of night to regroup elsewhere.

Napoleon had faltered but had achieved just enough success to make victory still possible.

Much has been written about this most famous of battles; this account will not go into the great level of detail necessary for those who would understand all aspects of victory and loss. Still, there is something to be gained from at least a brief consideration, especially if we seek better to understand the nature of the man, Napoleon, and the reasons for his ultimate failure.

Napoleon was in generally good spirits on the morning of the battle, 18 June 1815. Wellington had stayed to fight. True, he had taken the high ground at Mont St-Jean, but Napoleon would drive him from it and march to Brussels. There was, however, already one major problem. It had rained all the previous day and much of the night. Throughout the night, Napoleon had been given reports on the condition of the field by Marchand and Drouot, his commander of the Imperial Guard.

The rain had delayed their arrival; the condition of the roads had exhausted the French troops and kept the supply wagons from getting food to them. The rain would allow Blücher's arrival, just in time. To many, the rain would seem to be the main cause of Napoleon's defeat.

By morning, the rain had stopped but the field was a morass, giving a decided advantage to the defenders of the high ground. Again, the question of delay. To move forward was to risk fighting without cannon that might become mired in the mud. To delay? One word: Blücher!

At breakfast, all was well. Napoleon's brother Jérôme warned of the possibility of Blücher marching from Wavre, but Napoleon dismissed this out of hand. After some discussion, he decided to let the ground dry more and delayed his move until eleven in the morning. It was a reasonable decision, but there was no good decision to be made.

The battle opened at about half-past eleven with the standard barrage from many of Napoleon's 246 cannon. They sounded fearsome, but most of Wellington's men were behind a ridge and the barrage was not all that effective. Ninety minutes later, Napoleon sent in d'Erlon's corps. These troops were Napoleon's freshest, having spent more time marching than fighting!

Napoleon also sent Jérôme against the walled farm of Hougoumont. Intended as a diversion, it would become a major battle and last much of the day. Jérôme fought bravely, but far more men were lost than had been expected and he made more effort than had been called for in his orders.

Hougoumont, despite the valiant effort by Jérôme and his soldiers, would never fall. The primary explanation probably is that very little in the way of cannon-fire was brought to bear. This defies reason because, even though thick woods surrounded much of the farm, a few holes knocked in the walls and it would probably have been all over.

D'Erlon was shocked to face first massive fire from Wellington's troops and then the attack of the Scots Greys cavalry. Stunned, his men retreated back across the valley, pursued by the Greys. Napoleon countered with his Cuirassiers and Lancers, and the Scots Greys were destroyed as a fighting force. This was small consolation; his attack had failed and he had lost several thousand men in the process.

By early afternoon, the first elements of the Prussian army had arrived. Napoleon was amazed to learn that Ligny had not eliminated them and that Grouchy had not defeated them. He desperately needed Grouchy's 33,000 men, but they would never arrive. They neither stopped, nor even hampered Blücher. Napoleon had split off one-third of his army and had nothing to show for it.

It is legitimately debatable whether Grouchy could have arrived in time. Evidence seems to indicate that he heard the cannonade in the morning and then was urged by his subordinates to 'march to the sound of the guns', that age-old admonition to all soldiers of all armies to go to where the fighting is and they can make a difference. He refused to do so, feeling that his responsibility was to keep his sword in the back of the

Prussians. Had he attempted it, he would probably have arrived in time even if it had taken him six or seven hours. His cavalry might have arrived even sooner. Grouchy need not even have arrived at Waterloo itself. If he threatened the Prussians before their arrival at the battle, the effect would be the same.

To be fair, Grouchy would have had to worry about the Prussians to his north. He chose worry and caution over daring and even logic, and continued his march to Wavre. There he did indeed engage the Prussians, but it was only one division; three more were arriving at Waterloo. By failing to march to the sound of the guns at Waterloo, Grouchy earned forever – rightfully or wrongfully – the blame for Napoleon's loss.

Napoleon was now fighting a two-front battle, with only two-thirds of his army.

If there is one symbol of the futility of Waterloo, it occurred in the afternoon. Michel Ney led a succession of cavalry charges against the British troops. Hatless, sword in hand, shouting orders, time and time again he charged their positions. Sustaining great loss, he would overtake the cannon, only to find the British in square, a four-sided formation presenting rows of muskets and bayonets. Cavalry against square is a difficult proposition at best; recall the Mamelukes in Egypt.

The way to overcome this is to send in infantry support. Squares are sitting ducks against infantry; a combined attack might well have driven Wellington's forces from the field. But there would be no infantry. At one point Ney had more than 9,000 cavalry charging almost uselessly against the squares, but not a single infantry battalion in support. Brave, heroic, dashing the attack certainly was. It was also one of the biggest military blunders in history.

Nor would Ney's cavalry bother to spike the guns while they were under French control, even though they carried the necessary equipment and such action was part of their training. When the British infantry formed squares, the artillerymen took refuge in their centre, taking with them their ramrods and other materials to prevent the guns being turned on themselves. It is possible to drive a lead spike, narrow at one end to allow entry, much wider at the other, into the small firing hole of a cannon. With a few hard blows the lead spike is tightly wedged and unlikely to be removed during the remainder of the battle.

An army so deprived of even a significant portion of its guns in this manner is greatly weakened, but no one thought to spike so much as a single gun. It is entirely possible that the act of spiking the guns might in and of itself have turned the tide for the French; their losses would have been far fewer, and the British might well have felt compelled to withdraw.

Ney did manage to capture the walled farm called La Haie Sainte, which gave the French a good position from which to make a final assault on Wellington's forces. Here again, Napoleon's failure to engage adequate artillery against the vulnerable walls of a fixed target caused unnecessary delay and increased casualties.

Initially led by Napoleon and then by Ney, five battalions of the Guard marched up the hill towards the awaiting British. The battle was fierce, and the French were gaining ground, inflicting very heavy losses.

Suddenly, fresh Prussian troops appeared on Napoleon's right flank. To the French, who had been told that the troops in the distance were those of Grouchy, this was a massive psychological blow. Just as the French were realising who these troops were, Wellington released his Hussars and other cavalry. A few of the Guard faltered. It was enough. Quickly the word was passed that the invincible Imperial Guard had been repulsed. Cries of *La Garde recule!* (the Guard retreats) were heard throughout the ranks. True or not (Napoleon's Bulletin of 21 June said that the cries were heard and the rout was on, while Marshal Ney claimed there were no such cries and the retreat was confused but not a total rout[260]), the will of the army to fight evaporated, and in a mass of chaos and confusion the French fled the field. Blücher was right when he told his army: 'Destiny was still undecided, when you appeared issuing from the forest which concealed you ... Nothing could stop you in the career of victory ... your progress caused in them disorder, dispersion and, at last, a complete rout.'[261]

Napoleon left under protection of the Guard and eventually had to abandon his carriage and continue on horseback. Blücher was determined to make the victory a rout, and his pursuing cavalry killed many retreating French soldiers and threw the rest into disorder, confusion and panic. There would be no hope of rallying the troops. Napoleon returned to Paris, hoping to rally the government and the people to his cause. He still had substantial numbers of troops available to him, including Grouchy's relatively rested men. Perhaps there was still hope.

When Wellington and Blücher met, Blücher is said to have said 'Quelle d'affaire!' Later, Wellington would refer to Waterloo as a 'near run thing'.

ABDICATION AND ...?

Fit retribution! Gaul may champ the bit
    And foam in fetters; but is Earth more free?
Did nations combat to make *One* submit;
    Or league to teach all kings true sovereignty?
What! shall reviving Thraldom again be
    The patched-up idol of enlightened days?
Shall we, who struck the Lion down, shall we
    Pay the Wolf homage? Proffering lowly gaze
And servile knees to thrones? No; *prove* before ye praise!
                    Byron, Canto III of *Childe Harold*

When Napoleon returned to Paris, news of his overwhelming defeat had
already arrived. He had hoped to rally his government, consolidate his
soldiers and at the very least lead the defence of Paris. This was not to be;
the long knives were out, and Napoleon was finished. Had he hastened
more quickly to Paris and then directly to the assembly, he might have
held sway. He also had the right to dissolve the assembly, but he believed
until it was too late that they would support him.

It quickly became clear that he was not going to retain power.
However, there was much sentiment for maintaining his dynasty and he
was urged to abdicate in favour of his son (who was, of course, still in
Vienna). This he agreed to do with the declaration:

People of France! In undertaking to defend national independence, I
was counting on the unity of all efforts, all wills and the help of all
national authorities. I had reason to hope for success, and I had
challenged the declarations of all the powers united against me.
Circumstances appear to have changed. I offer myself in sacrifice to
the hatred of France's enemies. May their declarations be sincere,
and may they want only my person. My political life is at an end,
and I proclaim my son Emperor of the French, under the name of
Napoleon II. The ministers shall form a provisional government
council, and on behalf of my son I urge them to organise without
delay a regency by means of law. Unite for public salvation and to
remain an independent nation.

Signed: Napoleon, 22 June[262]

The provisional government consisted of some of Napoleon's supporters, such as Caulaincourt and General Carnot, but also had such as Fouché, who was determined to bring back Louis XVIII. The two chambers passed resolutions in support of Napoleon II, but they were worded in such a way that all they really did was declare the throne to be vacant. This was the work of Fouché who, in the words of Caulaincourt '... was regent *de facto*. He was the central point of every intrigue; and by a thousand hidden springs he controlled the deliberations of the assembly.'[263]

The assembly also had Fouché send letters demanding that the allies accept peace with France, accept their choice of their new government and allow Napoleon to leave the country peaceably. Regarding the Bourbons, the letter stated in part, 'The first and most solid pledge, that the allies can give the French nation of their intention to respect its independence, is to renounce without reserve all design of subjecting it anew to the government of the Bourbon family.'[264]

These demands were rejected, of course, and since the throne was open, Wellington decided to choose who would rule. Louis XVIII would, in fact, be returned to the throne.

Napoleon had moved to Malmaison. There had been delays in providing his safe conduct passes and escort; delays perhaps designed to foil his attempt to leave the country for a destination of his own choice. However, Napoleon created just as much delay, as he seemed unable to make up his mind where he wanted to go. He often talked of retiring to America, where many of his supporters urged him to go. There were ships available but time was of the essence. Still he procrastinated. He stayed five days at Malmaison. Marie Walewska and their son came to visit him and offered to join him in exile. It was a tearful meeting. Napoleon would not allow her to follow him into exile. They parted and would never see each other again.

On 29 June, he said goodbye to his mother and Hortense and went to Rochefort, on the coast. His delay had been costly; the British ship *Bellerophon* was now guarding the harbour.

On 8 July Napoleon boarded the French frigate *Saal*. He was still awaiting safe conduct passes for passage to America but it soon became clear they woud not be forthcoming. The allies did not want him at large in America. Several plans were prepared for him to escape by way of either neutral ships, a number of which had offered their services, or aboard a French frigate. It would still be possible to try to sneak out, hidden in a neutral ship, but Napoleon found that idea too undignified, not to say risky. Also considered too risky was the possibility of over-whelming the *Bellerophon*, which they outnumbered two to one, and making good his escape in a French warship.

Marchand suggests that Napoleon chose the wrong ship, though he could hardly have known it. There were two French ships available. Had he boarded the *Méduse*, he would have found a captain determined to take him to America.[265] If this is true, his fate had hinged on the smallest and most arbitrary of decisions. British Captain Maitland of the *Bellerophon* himself later acknowledged that he would have been unlikely to prevent a coordinated escape attempt by the French ships.

In the end, Napoleon decided to retire to England. The British had allowed other deposed monarchs do that, and perhaps he would be given the same opportunity. He sent word of his desire; Captain Frederick Lewis Maitland would only promise to accord him all honours and escort him to England, where his fate would be decided by others.

That was good enough for Napoleon, who had more faith in the British than he could justify. He wrote a letter to the Prince Regent:

> Your Royal Highness, faced with the factions that divide my country and the enmity of the greatest powers in Europe, I have ended my political career; I come like Themistocles to sit by the hearth of the British people. I place myself under the protection of their laws, which I request from Your Royal Highness, as the most powerful, the steadiest, and the most generous of my enemies.[266]

Napoleon's return for the Hundred Days is sometimes criticised. There can be no argument that France suffered for his defeat at Waterloo, even beyond the men who were killed. The allies claimed they were fighting Napoleon, not France, but they took vengeance on France far more than on Napoleon. France's borders were further restricted, this time to their pre-Revolutionary status. All the territorial gains from the Revolution on, including Belgium, Holland and the left bank of the Rhine were lost. Many of the art treasures taken from other nations that France had been allowed to keep in 1814 she was forced to return in 1815. A large war indemnity was demanded.

A number of Napoleon's supporters were condemned to death. The most notable among them was Marshal Michel Ney. He was a true

French hero but the king was determined to have his revenge. Despite the objection of Wellington, but with the support of a number of his peers, now anxious to prove their allegiance to the restored Louis XVIII, 'the bravest of the brave' was executed in Paris by a firing squad. It was a sad day for France.

It was not the case that Napoleon had returned merely to satisfy his ego. He had been betrayed by the allies and by Louis XVIII who had ignored their own treaty with him and his safety was in serious doubt. France was not happy with Louis XVIII. Napoleon's popularity was immense, and he thought he would rule France peacefully. Had he been allowed to do so, France would have benefited from his enlightened rule.

The allies never gave him the chance to be a man of his word. Accordingly, it is to them that much of any criticism that is to be made of the Hundred Days must be directed.

NOTES

260 *Official Narratives*, II, 436 (Bulletin) and 440 (Ney).

261 'Proclamation Addressed by Field Marshal Prince Blücher to the Army of the Lower Rhine, to Be Read at the Head of Every Battalion', in *Authenticated Documents*, 31–32.

262 Ibid., 253–54.

263 Caulaincourt, *Napoleon and His Times*, II, 173–74. This early version of Caulaincourt's memoirs is often suspect, but there is plenty of evidence to support this statement.

264 Fleury, II, 320.

265 Marchand, 285–86.

266 Ibid., 285.

PART SIX

SAINT HELENA
AND IMMORTALITY

THE ROAD
TO EXILE

O n 15 July 1815, at seven o'clock in the morning, Napoleon boarded the *Bellerophon*. He was accorded due honours, including the Captain's quarters, in a reception worthy of an Emperor and it gave hope for the future to him and his entourage. That hope would soon be dashed.

Maitland did everything possible to make Napoleon comfortable. He treated him with immense respect, which Napoleon greatly appreciated and returned. The two of them had lengthy and friendly conversations. Napoleon chatted with the crew and the other officers. Maitland's opinion of Napoleon is best stated in the preface to his journal:

> It may appear surprising, that a possibility could exist of a British officer, being prejudiced in favour of one who had caused so many calamities to his country; but to such an extent did he possess the power of pleasing, there are few people who could have sat at the same table with him for nearly a month, as I did, without feeling a sensation of pity, allied perhaps to regret, that a man possessed of so many fascinating qualities, and who had held so high a station in life, should be reduced to the situation in which I saw him.[267]

Napoleon's charm had always been one of his strengths. In this case, however, it would work to his disadvantage. Convinced that even a few minutes with the Prince Regent would suffice to charm the Prince – as it had Alexander at Tilsit – and obtain permission to remain in England, the government was determined to prevent that meeting from ever taking place. To Napoleon's great despair, they were successful.

The problem of what to do with him now was not an easy one. There were many in Great Britain who thought it would be quite legitimate to allow him to settle in England. Some felt he should be sent back to France, where he would have probably been shot by Louis XVIII. Others felt that he should be allowed to go to the United States and thus become the Americans' problem. Those in power, however, were determined that he should remain closely confined, but not so close as to give him too sympathetic an image to the public. He would remain in British hands, but not in England.

While he was aboard the *Bellerophon* at anchor off the southern coast of England, he became the object of considerable curiosity to the local inhabitants. The waters around his ship were crowded with boat-loads of people anxious for a glimpse of the man against whom their country had fought for so long. Napoleon was happy to appear on deck for their benefit. The British officials were not pleased, but apart from moving the ship several times, there was little they could do to diminish the curiosity of the crowds. At one point, for the benefit of the sightseeing throng a large chalkboard was set up on which were written Napoleon's current activities and his whereabouts in the ship.

The British government had a dilemma in regard to the status of their illustrious prisoner. Napoleon had been recognised the world over as the Emperor of France and, afterwards, as the Emperor of Elba. By some tortured logic, the British had never officially recognised him as Emperor of France (their ambassadors to his court notwithstanding) and they decided that he had renounced his Elba title when he reclaimed the French crown.

In that case, he should have been considered still the First Consul of France and, thus, still head of state. But no, he was said to have resigned that office when he became Emperor (which in their eyes, of course, he never became). The fact that the people of France had voted him in first as Consul and then as Emperor was of no consequence.

Napoleon, of course, had been a general. In British eyes he evidently had not resigned *that* post, and thus it was as a general that he would be received. This was needlessly insulting; no one in the world would have considered Napoleon a mere general. To add to the insult, they insisted on reverting to the old spelling of his name, *Buonaparte*. It was as if history had stopped in 1799 and picked up again in 1815.

The question of where to put him was resolved fairly early. The island of St. Helena was a thousand miles from nowhere. There he would be gone from European politics forever, but able to live out his days in relative comfort. He would be allowed a small contingent of followers and staff.

Denied the chance to talk to the man who was presumably the head of government, namely the Prince Regent, Napoleon was instead dealing with people who, understandably, were not favourably disposed toward him. Indeed, they could have dealt with him more harshly than they did. To his credit, Wellington argued for leniency, and Wellington prevailed. Napoleon argued for his freedom, promising to ignore France forever and to move to the United States. If they insisted he was a general and a prisoner of war, then he asked to be treated as such and be allowed, as all officers were, to live on parole in England. Moreover, prisoners of war are released once hostilities end. If he was a prisoner of war, he should now be released. No matter: St. Helena it would be.

There was one last gambit available to Napoleon, and it held great potential. He was a master politician and he had studied British politics well. He knew that many liberal British officials, nobles and Members of Parliament were opposed to his confinement and might take action to prevent it. There was a move for Napoleon to use the protection of *habeas corpus*, which is a legal protection against arrest and confinement without benefit of a judicial hearing. Efforts in this direction were blocked by the government.

There was, as it happened, a libel trial taking place for which three witnesses had been summoned. One of them was Napoleon Bonaparte. At the time, he had been in France and the summons was little more than an amusing sidelight to the case. Now, however, it could serve as a weapon to force the government to allow him to leave the ship and appear before the court.

If that happened, public opinion might become enamoured of his personality and further legal actions might well prevent his removal from England. The government knew this, and Admiral Lord Keith had been given orders that under no circumstances whatsoever was he to allow Napoleon to reach shore. A subpoena was issued and, in accordance with law, an effort was made to deliver it either to Admiral Lord Keith or Napoleon himself. In a rather comical set of scenes, this effort failed and Napoleon set sail for St. Helena in the *Northumberland* on 8 August 1815.

The British government is often criticised for their treatment of Napoleon. Some of that criticism is justified, including the refusal to acknowledge his status as Emperor, the decision to send him to St. Helena instead of a more hospitable place and certainly his treatment while there. But it must be said that his hopes of living out his life in luxury in England or the United States, were not entirely realistic. The British government had good reason for fearing his influence in England or on the continent. Nor can they be blamed for distrusting his pledge to renounce politics. The pledge was undoubtedly sincere, but given the recent events of the time, their attitude was understandable.

It is also possible that they wished to isolate him for his own protection.

Napoleon's entourage included Grand Marshal of the Palace General Henri-Gatien Bertrand, his wife Fanny and their three children; Colonel Charles Tristan, comte de Montholon, his wife Albine and their youngest son; General Gaspard Gourgaud; Emmanuel August Dieudonné, marquis de Las Cases (whose command of the English language was invaluable to Napoleon); and Barry Edward O'Meara, a British naval surgeon who had agreed to go as Napoleon's physician. There were also, of course, Napoleon's faithful valet Marchand and numerous other valets, servants and other staff members.

The long, tedious and at times quarrelsome voyage to St. Helena ended on 15 October. Napoleon had spent a great deal of time playing cards, his favourite game being *vingt-et-un* (twenty-one). He would sometimes cheat but would never keep the winnings from such play. He spent a great deal of his time in discussions with Rear-Admiral Sir George Cockburn, whose diary gives one of the first insights into Napoleon's view of his own life.[268] He talked with the soldiers on board with him and met a young Irish military doctor named James Verling.

NOTES

267 Maitland, *Narrative*, v–vi.
268 Cockburn, *Voyage to St. Helena*.

THE
ISLAND PRISON

Yes, where is he, the champion and the child
Of all that's great or little, wise or wild,
Whose table earth, whose dice were human bones?
Behold the grand result, in yon lone isle,
And, as thy nature urges, weep or smile.

Byron

The British banished Napoleon to St. Helena to prevent him from becoming directly involved in the politics of the day. Had they handled him more carefully, they might have succeeded. He certainly never returned to Europe, but his influence continued even so. They also unwittingly gave him what he wanted most of all: a chance to shape his legend, to set his image on the stage of immortality and to show the world his worth. The more petty his treatment, the grander his image.

St. Helena is a small rock of an island, about eighty-five square miles, that had been used by the East India Company. It lies over eleven hundred miles from South Africa, seven hundred from the island of Ascension and four thousand four hundred miles from England. Even today, the voyage by ship takes a week, and there is no airport. No ship could approach unseen, and escape by means of a small craft was out of the question. In any case, a British squadron was stationed offshore and the island was garrisoned by about 1,400 soldiers.

Napoleon could have been given one of several possible residences, most notably Plantation House, which would have provided a pleasant climate and home for the deposed Emperor. No less than the Prince Regent had instructed the government to make Napoleon's life as comfortable as possible, always with the imperative that he didn't leave the island.

Nevertheless, the British government insisted that Napoleon stay in a rather dilapidated house called Longwood, high on a wind-swept, shadeless plateau, where he could be more easily observed. Some additions were to be made before Napoleon could move in, but this would eventually become his home. Improvements were made, but the house proved to be inadequate and rat-infested. Napoleon deserved better. Marchand described the situation:

> There are pleasant residences such as Plantation House, Rosemary Hall and Sandy Bay. The cottages of The Briars, Dewton and Mason present them with fine hospitality and cool shade to rest from the hot sun. These advantages were non-existent at Longwood. This land possessed no more than a plateau on which a few unsuccessful attempts had been made to establish grain plantations. That part of the island was constantly beaten by south-easterly winds. As good as it might appear to travellers who have just completed a long crossing, the climate of St. Helena is generally unhealthy, particularly in the area occupied by the Emperor.
>
> Therefore nothing that the admiral was projecting in the way of improvements on the Longwood plateau could appear attractive to the Emperor: it was simply a matter of making additions to a dilapidated, single-storey house of stone that had served as residence for the lieutenant-governor.[269]

Napoleon was to be put in the worst possible place on the island and eventually governed by the worst possible person who could have been assigned to the job. Before that happened, however, he would have a brief period of happiness. He was given the chance to stay with the Balcombe family, whose home was known as The Briars. There he got to know the 14-year-old Betsy Balcombe and they took to each other instantly. Her informal ways and playful nature delighted the Emperor, and she was the only person allowed to interrupt him when he was at a meeting. No doubt missing his son and Joséphine's children when they were younger, Napoleon showered attention on his young friend. He was saddened when he had to leave their home for Longwood; still more when she and her family left the island.

Napoleon's life at Longwood was routine and boring, but he tried to make the best of it. He went riding and enjoyed various guests. His health was excellent. Admiral Cockburn was serving as governor. The two of them had got along well in the ship, but their relationship began to sour as the British insisted on closer and closer control of Napoleon's movements. Various restrictions, such as having to be always accompanied by a British escort if he went beyond certain boundaries – boundaries that over the years became more and more restrictive – grated on the man who had once been master of Europe. He rightfully pointed out that there was no way that he could escape; they responded that they were just following orders and that in any event at least he was not in a prison.

They were both right, of course, but to Napoleon it *was* becoming more and more of a prison.

This might have been easier to tolerate, except for the insulting refusal of the British to refer to him as anything but General. For this, there can be no excuse, no understanding – what purpose could it have possibly served? Perhaps Napoleon could have just shrugged it off as an example of pettiness, but all things considered, they should have called him anything he wished.

NOTE

269 Marchand, 346–47.

SIR HUDSON LOWE

Sir Hudson Lowe, Sir Hudson *Low*,
  (By name, and ah! By nature so)
As thou art fond of persecutions,
  Perhaps thou'st read or heard repeated,
How Captain Gulliver was treated,
  When thrown among the Lilliputians.

They tied him down – these little men did –
  And having valiantly ascended
Upon the Mighty Man's protuberance,
  They did so strut! – Upon my soul,
It must have been extremely droll
  To see their pigmy pride's exuberance!

And how the doughty mannikins
  Amused themselves with sticking pins,
And needles in the great man's breeches;
  And how some *very* little things
That pass'd for Lords on scaffoldings
  Got up, and worried him with Speeches.

Alas, alas! that it should happen,
  To mighty men to be caught napping! –
Though different, too, these persecutions;
  For Gulliver *there*, took the nap,
While *here* the *Nap*, oh sad mishap,
  Is taken by the Lilliputians!

Thomas Moore, 1816

I t is quite possible to defend Great Britain's treatment of Napoleon;
that has, to some extent, been done here. It is virtually impossible to
defend their assignment of Sir Hudson Lowe as the new governor.
Lowe arrived at St. Helena in April 1816. He was a career military man,
generally popular with his soldiers and successful in his endeavors. He
was somewhat lacking in the social graces but was well meaning. He was,

however, unimaginative and a stickler for following instructions precisely, without any modifications based on the circumstances of the moment. It was this characteristic that would lead to the now famous difficulties between the two men.

From the beginning, Lowe was told, at least indirectly, that he would have *some* leeway in his treatment of Napoleon. His initial letter from Lord Bathurst on the subject specifically uses the word *spirit* rather than the more restrictive word *letter* in describing Lowe's requirements to follow the directives of Parliament:

> Herewith you will receive the King's Warrant under my Grant and Seal authorising you to detain keep and treat Napoleon Bonaparte as a Prisoner of War; and you will receive at the same time the Act of Parliament lately passed giving powers to the above effect. You will be pleased to regulate your conduct according to the spirit of the above Instruments.[270]

Lowe must be given his due. He arrived determined to establish a good relationship with his famous guest – for *guest* is how they referred to Napoleon in written communication on the island. When he was presented to Napoleon, he was proper and friendly. The two spoke Italian, and Lowe was clever enough not to fall into any verbal traps set by Napoleon. Lowe soon agreed to build a new house in a better location for Napoleon; there were, after all, no orders from London forbidding this.

One thing Lowe would not do was to reduce the restrictions on Napoleon's freedom of movement. From the very beginning, he was obsessed with the fear that Napoleon might somehow escape the island, however absurd that fear might be. Add that to his general inflexibility regarding regulations and you have a recipe for trouble.

Trouble indeed came, but it was not entirely Lowe's fault. It would have been reasonable to suppose that Napoleon might have accepted the restrictions, for the moment at least, and hoped for better things as he and Lowe established a longer-term relationship. Once the new house was built, perhaps things would change.

But this was against Napoleon's nature. He had already developed the image of a martyr, an image which suited his plans for his legend quite well, and Lowe was playing right into that image.

Napoleon was the prisoner and relatively powerless. Lowe had virtually all the power, including the power to be lenient, to bend rules, to interpret regulations; in short, to make Napoleon's life – and his own – more comfortable. This was not in the nature of the man. He was clearly the wrong man for the job, but he was there none the less.

Over the years, the two men engaged in a petty and demeaning war of attrition. When Hobehouse, a British admirer of Napoleon, sent a book inscribed to *The Emperor Napoleon*, Lowe used the regulation requiring him to be addressed as *General* as an excuse to seize the book. When Napoleon needed a new doctor, O'Meara having been forced out by Lowe, the best one available was Dr. James Verling, who was one of the few surgeons with a medical degree. Over the objections of his staff, Napoleon refused to accept Verling as his doctor. Why? Because he had been recommended by Sir Hudson Lowe. Verling was far more qualified than any other doctor who saw Napoleon and it is interesting to speculate on the possibility that Napoleon might have lived longer had he been under Verling's care.

Unbelievably, the British soon expected Napoleon to help pay for his own imprisonment. Napoleon humiliated them by publicly selling some of his silver. When they were out of wood, he had some furniture burned. These outrages were discussed in Europe and public sympathy for Napoleon increased. The *Ogre* was quickly becoming the *martyr*, and Lowe could not see it.

Lowe's obsession with a possible escape deepened and the restrictions increased. A marble bust of Napoleon's son arrived but was withheld for fear it contained a message inside. Eventually, Lowe relented and sent it to Napoleon, but the damage to his image had already been done.

Before leaving for Elba, Napoleon had sworn to write his memoirs but had not done so. On St. Helena – indeed, during his passage to the island – he dedicated much of his time to them. He would spend hours dictating to Baron Gourgaud. The other members of his staff would also write down what he would tell them; others would keep their memoirs. Those which were published were instant hits; Las Cases' work, *Mémorial de Saint Hélène* raced through numerous editions, it was almost instantly translated into English and was a monumental best seller.

Ironically, it is Marchand's diary that gives us the best description of his life in exile, as well as of earlier events beginning in 1811. It was not published until 1952. In 1998, Proctor Patterson Jones had it translated into English. At almost eight hundred pages, it is a monument to the fidelity of Marchand and to the many contributions to the study of Napoleon made by Proctor Jones, who died in 1999.

The battle between Napoleon and Lowe continued. Soon, Napoleon would virtually refuse to leave his home, peering out through small holes in the shutters. Lowe, for his part, became even more obsessed and fearful that Napoleon was going to escape and insisted on sending sentries to confirm that he was still there. In time, this began to break Napoleon's spirit.

His physical health, which had been excellent upon his arrival, soon began to deteriorate. In early 1819, he had taken seriously ill and the British surgeon John Stokoe had been sent to offer treatment. Lowe did not like the diagnosis, which seemed to confirm Napoleon's constant complaint that the climate was unhealthy. Worse, Stokoe had agreed to serve as Napoleon's personal physician, in a way that did not conflict with his military duties. Napoleon needed a doctor, but Lowe was furious and had Stokoe court-martialled.

Later in the year, Dr. François Antommarchi arrived. Lowe, anxious not to be seen by the public – and by history – as the man who withheld proper medical care from Napoleon, had allowed him to arrange for a doctor to be sent. Unfortunately, Antommarchi was inept and Napoleon knew it. He never trusted him, which naturally enough limited Antommarchi's effectiveness. By then, Napoleon had seemingly lost much of his will to live and did not, therefore, worry about the quality of his health care.

NOTE

270 Letter to Lowe from Bathurst 13 April
1816, Lowe Papers, MS15,729 (19).

OF DEATH
AND MURDER

We do not curse thee, Waterloo!
  Though Freedom's blood thy plain bedew:
There 'twas shed, but is not sunk. –
  Rising from each glory trunk,
Like a strong and growing motion –
  It sours and mingles in the air,
With that of lost Labédoyère –
  With that of him whose honoured grave
Contains the 'bravest of the brave'.

. . .

The chief has fallen! but not by you,
Vanquishers of Waterloo!

Byron, *Ode From the French*

Napoleon's health continued to worsen. Nothing seemed to bring any relief. He suffered sharp pains in his side and severe vomiting attacks. All soon began to realise that the end must be near and a general gloom settled on them all. He began to make his will, asking for his ashes to be put 'on the banks of the Seine, amongst the French people, whom I have loved so well'. Napoleon had, at least in theory, great personal wealth and he distributed that to friends and family: 400,000 francs to Marchand, 500,000 to Bertrand – and two million to Montholon.

On 5 May 1821, at a few minutes before six in the evening, Napoleon I, Emperor of the French, King of Italy, Protector of the Confederation of the Rhine, died on an obscure little island in the middle of nowhere. It was an ignominious end. His last words are said to have been 'France, my son, the army', with some also hearing 'Joséphine'. By all accounts, it was really just about impossible to be sure what he said. That, however, was just one of the controversies that would stem from his death.

Even after Napoleon's death, pettiness would reign supreme, and this time blame must fall on the people who had one last chance to humiliate him. He was to be buried in a pleasant spot on the island where he used to go to relax; the British would not allow his return to France even in death. Napoleon's staff wanted the gravestone to read 'Emperor Napoleon'. A dead man's wishes are usually followed when it comes to the inscription on his tomb: not so Napoleon's. Lowe would only allow 'Napoleon Buonaparte'. As a result, there would be no inscription. Napoleon would be buried in an unmarked grave.

> *I die prematurely, murdered by the English*
> *oligarchy and its hired assassin.*
> Napoleon's will

The official cause of death was cancer. That made some sense, as there was cancer in Napoleon's family. It also suited the political concerns of the British, still fearful that posterity would assign them guilt for having brought the great man to a poor climate. There seemed to be little reason to challenge the belief that Napoleon died of cancer.

Until recently, if you suggested to serious historians that Napoleon had been murdered on St. Helena *and* that he was murdered by one of his most trusted French companions in exile, no one would have believed you. Times change and with them knowledge of the past. Beginning with the research of amateur Swedish toxicologist Sten Forshufvud in the 1950s, the idea that Napoleon was murdered began to become a respectable theory.

With the publication of Ben Weider and David Hapgood's book *The Murder of Napoleon*[271] in 1982, the theory had become a serious assertion. In 1995, Ben Weider and Sten Forshufvud, who has since died, wrote a sequel designed to convince the sceptics.[272] Publication of this book coincided with the release of new arsenic tests of two of Napoleon's hairs by the Chemistry and Toxicology unit of the United States Federal Bureau of Investigation (FBI). They used Graphite Furnace Atomic Absorption Spectroscopy to determine the levels of arsenic remaining in the hairs. These hairs, given to the young Betsy Balcombe in 1818, three years before Napoleon's death on St. Helena, showed levels of arsenic that were, in the words of the FBI, 'consistent with arsenical poisoning'.

Napoleon, of course, always felt that the British were going to poison him. Weider, however, does not lay the blame upon the British. He concludes that the murderer of Napoleon was one of his most trusted

French aides on St. Helena, Count Charles-Tristan de Montholon, acting under the direction of the French king Louis XVIII's brother, the comte d'Artois (later to become Charles X, one of France's worst kings), who wanted to ensure that Napoleon would never be able to return to reclaim his throne.

Briefly, here is Weider's hypothesis of what happened on St. Helena. Over a period of some six years (Napoleon was there from 1815 to 1821), Napoleon was given dosages of arsenic. It was not the arsenic, however, that Weider believes killed him. The arsenic was given to weaken his system and to give the world the impression of numerous bouts of sickness, either brought on by the poor climate of the island or by cancer, that would eventually lead to his demise. Death itself was brought on by a combination of other common ingredients that produced deadly mercurial salts in the stomach. The stomach's natural defences had been weakened by the periodic ingestion of arsenic, potassium tartrate, orgeat and calomel, all toxic poisons. These produced mercury cyanide, which eventually proved fatal.

This method of poisoning was commonly used in those times. Moreover, the autopsy performed on Napoleon found conditions in his stomach that were consistent with those that would be expected from an administration of this type of poisoning.

What kind of evidence does Weider produce to support these assertions, almost 200 years after the fact? The evidence is found in a combination of modern technology and eye-witness accounts on St. Helena. The most important of these accounts are the published memoirs of Louis Marchand and, to a lesser extent, Henri Bertrand. Marchand's work is especially useful, providing day by day accounts of Napoleon's condition and virtually everything that he ate or drank. These two memoirs were not published until the 1950s.

Technology can show varied degrees of intake in different time periods by measuring arsenic levels in the hair. This testing, using irradiation testing procedures, was done by Dr. Hamilton Smith at the University of Glasgow. The real detective work begins when the indications of high arsenic content are matched to symptoms reported by various eye-witnesses on St. Helena, especially Marchand. Weider presents strong evidence that Napoleon exhibited symptoms of arsenical poisoning at the same time that the hair samples indicated high arsenic content. And for example, when Napoleon's tomb was re-opened in July 1840, his body was perfectly preserved, a state consistent with a high arsenic level.

Murder, but by whom? Montholon is the most likely suspect. He was the least understandable of all Napoleon's companions in his final exile. An aristocrat, Montholon had been out of favour with Napoleon and rallied to his cause only at the last moment, after Waterloo. It was Montholon who ultimately controlled the food and drink given to the Emperor, a level of control necessary if one is to poison someone over a long period. Weider suggests that Montholon's motive may have been blackmail, or loyalty to the king.

If Napoleon was to be murdered, why not do it right away? Because Napoleon was still very popular with many of the French, especially the army, and an obvious murder might well have sparked an uprising. Napoleon's son was still alive and in Austria; Napoleon's immediate death in captivity might lead many to rally to his cause against an increasingly unpopular Louis XVIII.

Not surprisingly, the idea that Napoleon was murdered has sparked significant controversy. Some scholars disagree with Weider's theory, a few quite vehemently. But his evidence is strong and his arguments difficult to refute. Those who disagree, will need to counter with research of equal quality and arguments of equal strength.

In his foreword to Weider's book, the notable British historian David Chandler says that Weider and company's research is 'more than enough to provide justification for careful thought and reconsideration'. He has subsequently stated, 'It is now almost certain that Napoleon died by foul means and that Count Montholon was guilty of murder.'[273] Perhaps more importantly, an increasing number of French historians are beginning to accept Weider's argument.

The debate continues, however. In October of 2002, a new study of arsenic levels in Napoleon's hair was published and given broad media attention. Commissioned by the French magazine *Science et Vie* (Science and Life), it looked at hairs taken from Napoleon in 1805, 1814 and 1821 and found high levels of arsenic in all the samples. These investigators suggest that this proves arsenic poisoning could not have been the cause of death. Weider, of course, does not suggest that. How this new study will influence the debate is yet to be determined, but the widespread interest in its findings is a clear indication of continued fascination with Napoleon.

DIGNITY AT LAST

Napoleon's body was clothed in his favourite uniform of the Chasseurs of the Imperial Guard and placed in a tin casket lined with white satin. The casket was placed in a mahogany casket, which was placed in a lead casket, which was then placed in a fourth and final mahogany casket. A masonry tomb was constructed; by 9 May all was ready.

After Mass, twelve grenadiers carried the casket to the hearse. Then the procession passed by the troops of the garrison, who were under arms in respect for the fallen soldier. Sir Hudson Lowe, in one final gesture, was giving Napoleon the burial to which he was entitled and as much as could be mustered on the tiny island.

The garrison fell in behind the procession, while bands played funeral music. Guns from the flagship in the harbour and various forts fired salutes as the procession continued.

After prayers at the gravesite, Lowe asked Bertrand if he wished to say anything. He did not. Nearby artillery fired three honour salvos of fifteen rounds each, and the casket was lowered. A large stone was then lowered to cover the tomb, which would be under constant guard. Marchand recorded 'the scene was overwhelming in its sorrow and grief'.[274]

NOTES

271 Weider and Hapgood, *Murder.*
272 Weider, *Assassination.*
273 'Napoleon and Death', in *Napoleonic Scholarship*, I, 1, April 1997, 59.
274 Marchand, 709.

EPILOGUE: THE EAGLE RETURNS
The Final Road to Glory

They say that the body of the Emperor will not remain there for long.[275]

The last words of Bertrand's diary would prove prophetic. In July 1840, the Prince de Joinville, son of King Louis-Philippe of France, led a delegation that included Bertrand, Marchand, Las Cases' son and others to St. Helena to recover the body of the Emperor. When the coffin was opened, his body was found to be perfectly preserved; he looked as though he had been asleep all those years. The body was returned to France and then sent on its final journey to Paris.

The body of the Emperor slowly made its way by steamship along the Seine. Everywhere the crowds gathered to pay their respects. At Rouen, the boat passed through an Arch of Triumph as a one-hundred cannon salute was fired. At Courbevoie, Marshal Soult came to pay his respects. He would be followed by the great surgeon Larrey, whom Napoleon once called 'the most virtuous man I have ever known'.

On 15 December, the casket was placed upon a huge funeral chariot more than ten metres high. As the procession inched its way down the Champs-Elysées in Paris, massive crowds of people from all walks of life lined the street on this cold day with temperature well below freezing to pay tribute to the man who had become a legend.

Behind the casket marched members of his Grande Armée, his Old Guard, joyous at the return of their leader, reliving the glory of Austerlitz. Behind the casket also was the young Prince de Joinville. When the Emperor passed, shouts of 'Vive l'Empereur!' rang out. Long live the Emperor! Cannon fired salutes, flags were dipped in honour. The bells of Notre-Dame were joined by bells throughout Paris.

The Emperor passed through the Arc de Triomphe, accompanied by another twenty-one cannon salute. Then he slowly made his way to Les Invalides. There, the king's son presented the Emperor to the King. Gourgaud placed the Emperor's hat on the coffin.

The ceremony over, it was the people's turn. For weeks they lined up in the bitter cold. Napoleon had always been popular with the common people. Then, as they do today, they paid their respects by visiting his tomb.

The return of Napoleon's body was unlike any other event in history. This was only appropriate, for there has been no person like Napoleon in history. The German poet Goethe wrote, 'It could be said that he was in a permanent state of enlightenment, which is why his fate was more brilliant than the world has ever seen or is likely to see after him.' Even Talleyrand said his career was 'the most extraordinary that has occurred for one thousand years'.

On 2 April 1861, after completion of his tomb under the gilded dome of Les Invalides, Napoleon was laid to his final resting place 'on the banks of the Seine, amongst the French people, whom I have loved so well'.

NOTE

275 Bertrand, *Napoleon at St. Helena*, 244.

WORKS CITED

PRIMARY SOURCES

Authenticated Documents, British and Foreign, Relative to the Battle of
Waterloo, published in *The Battle of Waterloo*, containing the accounts
published by authority, British and foreign and other relative documents, with circumstantial details, previous to and after the battle,
from a variety of authentic and original sources. To which is added, an
alphabetical list of the officers killed and wounded, from 15th to 26th
June, 1815, and the total loss of each regiment, with an enumeration of
the Waterloo honours and privileges, conferred upon the men and officers, and lists of regiments, &c. entitled thereto. Illustrated by a
panoramic sketch of the battlefield, and a plan of the positions and
movements, with those of the Prussians, traced By a Near Observer.
Fourth edition, to which is added the Hanoverian, Spanish, and Dutch
Accounts, &c. London, 1815

Bennigsen, General Levin, Count. *Benningsen to the Tsar, 31 January
1807.* (In French) Original letter in The David Markham Collection

Berthier, Marshal Louis Alexandre. *Order of 6 September 1812 to General
Lefevbre, commander of the infantry of the Imperial Guard.* (In French)
Original order in The David Markham Collection

Bertrand, comte Henri Gratien. *Napoleon at St. Helena: Memoirs of
General Bertrand, Grand Marshal of the Palace, January to May 1821,
Deciphered and Annotated by Paul Fleuriot de Langle.* Trans. Frances
Hume. Garden City, 1952

Beyle, Henri (Stendhal). *The Private Diaries of Stendhal.* Ed. and trans.
Robert Sage. New York, 1954

— *To the Happy Few: Selected Letters of Stendhal.* Trans. Norman
Cameron. John Lehmann, 1952; London, 1986

Botta, Carlo. *History of Italy During the Consulate and Empire of Napoleon
Buonaparte.* Trans. from the Italian of Carlo Botta, by the Author of
'The Life of Joanna, Queen of Naples'. In Two Volumes. London, 1828

Bourrienne, Louis Antoine Fauvelet de. *Private Memoirs of Napoleon
Bonaparte, During the Periods of The Directory, The Consulate, and the*

Empire. 4 vols. Henry Colburn and Richard Bentley, London, 1830. First English edn.

Browning, Oscar (ed.). *England and Napoleon in 1803, Being The Despatches of Lord Whitworth and Others. Now first printed from the originals in the record office. For the Royal Historical Society*. London and New York, 1887

Cambridge Modern History. Planned by the Late Lord Acton, eds. Sir A. W. Ward, Sir G. W. Prothero, Sir Stanley Leathes. V. IX, Napoleon. Cambridge, 1907

Campbell, Major-General Sir Neil. *Napoleon at Fontainebleau and Elba, Being A Journal of Occurrences in 1814–1815*. London, 1869

Caulaincourt, General Armand Augustin Louis, marquis de, duc de Vicence. *With Napoleon in Russia*. From orig. edn. by Jean Hanoteau. Abridged, edited, and with an Introduction by George Libaire. New York, 1935

— *No Peace With Napoleon!* New York, 1936

— *Napoleon and His Times*. 2 vols. Philadelphia, 1838

Chaboulon, Pierre Alexandre Edouard, baron Fleury de. *Memoirs of the Private Life, Return, and Reign of Napoleon in 1815*. 2 vols. London, 1820

Cockburn, Rear-Admiral Sir George. *Buonaparte's Voyage to St. Helena; Comprising the Diary of Rear-Admiral Sir George Cockburn, During His Passage From England to St. Helena, in 1815. From the Original Manuscript, in the Handwriting of his Private Secretary*. Boston, 1833

Copies of Original Letters From the Army of General Bonaparte in Egypt, Intercepted by the Fleet Under the Command of Admiral Lord Nelson. London, 1798

Copies of Original Letters From the Army of General Bonaparte in Egypt, Intercepted by the Fleet Under the Command of Admiral Lord Nelson, Part the Second. London, 1799

Copies of Original Letters From the Army of General Bonaparte in Egypt, Intercepted by the Fleet Under the Command of Admiral Lord Nelson, Part the Third. London, 1800

Davidov, Denis. *In the Service of the Tsar Against Napoleon: The Memoirs of Denis Davidov, 1806–1814*. Trans. and ed. Gregory Troubetzkoy. London, 1999

Dumas, comte Mathieu. *Memoirs of His Own Time; Including the Revolution, the Empire, and the Restoration*. 2 vols. London, 1839

Durdent R. J. *Campagne de Moscow en 1812; ouvrage composé d'Après la collection des pièces officielles sur cette campagne mémorable, où plus de trois-cent mille braves Français furent victimes de l'ambition et de l'aveuglement de leur chef* (Work composed from a collection of official documents on this memorable campaign where more than three hundred thousand brave Frenchmen were the victims of the ambition and blindness of their chief). 2nd edition. Paris, 1814

Ebrington, Viscount Hugh. *Two Conversations with Napoleon at Elba.* (No details of pubn. but presumed London, *c.*1958)

Fain, Baron John. *The Manuscript of 1814. A History of Events which led to the Abdication of Napoleon. Written at the Command of the Emperor.* London, 1823

—*Napoleon: How He Did It. The Memoirs of Baron Fain, First Secretary of the Emperor's Cabinet.* First complete English edn. of orig. MS (1829). San Francisco, 1998

Fouché, Joseph. The Minister of the General Police of the Republic, to her Citizens, 9 November, 1799. (In French, with notes.) Original document in The David Markham Collection

Gourgaud, Baron General Gaspard. *Talks of Napoleon at St. Helena with General Baron Gourgaud, together with the Journal Kept by Gourgaud on their Journey from Waterloo to St. Helena.* Trans. and annotated by Elizabeth Wormeley Latimer. Chicago, 1903

Hortense, queen consort of Louis, King of Holland. *The Memoirs of Queen Hortense.* Published by arrangement with Prince Napoleon, ed. Jean Hanoteau, trans. Arthur K. Griggs. 2 vols. New York, 1927

Klingberg, Frank J., Sigurd B. Hustvedt (eds.). *The Warning Drum: The British Home Front Faces Napoleon, Broadsides of 1803.* Berkeley, 1944

La Bédoyère, Charles, comte de. *Memoirs of the public and private life of Napoleon Bonaparte; with copious historical illustrations and original anecdotes from the manuscript of comte de La Bédoyère. Interspersed with extracts from M. V. Arnault, Counts Rapp, Montholon, Las Cases, Gourgaud, Ségur, &c. Preceded by an interesting analysis of the French Revolution.* 2 vols. 1st English ed. London, 1839

Las Cases, E. A., comte de. *Mémorial De Sainte Hélène.* Journal of the Private Life and Conversations of The Emperor Napoleon at St. Helena. 4 vols. Boston, 1823

Lavallette, A. M. C., comte de. *Memoirs of Count Lavallette, Written by Himself.* 2nd edn. 2 vols. London, 1831

Lawrence, James Henry, Knight of Malta. *A Picture of Verdun, or the English Detained in France, From the Portfolio of A Détenu.* 2 vols. London, 1810

Le Registre de L'Ile D'Elbe: Lettres et Ordres Inédits de Napoléon Ier (28 mai 1814–22 fèvrier 1815). Paris, 1897

Lowe Papers, British Library. Letters and other documents of Sir Hudson Lowe in St. Helena

Macdonald, Jacques Etienne Joseph Alexandre, duc de Tarente. *Recollections of Marshal Macdonald, Duke of Tarentum.* Ed. Camille Rousset, trans. Stephen Louis Simeon. 2 vols. London, 1892

Macirone, Colonel Francis. *Interesting Facts Relating to the Fall and Death of Joachim Murat, King of Naples; the Capitulation of Paris in 1815; and the Second Restoration of the Bourbons; Original letters from King Joachim to the Author; with some account of the Author and his persecution by the French Government. By Francis Macirone, Late Aide-de-Camp to King Joachim; Knight of the Order of the Two Sicilies.* 3rd edn. with Additions. London, 1817

Maitland, Captain Frederick Lewis. *Narrative of the Surrender of Buonaparte and of His Residence on Board H.M.S. Bellerophon; with a Detail of the Principal Events that Occurred in that Ship, Between the 24th of May and the 8th of August, 1815.* London, 1826

Marchand, Louis-Joseph. *In Napoleon's Shadow: Being the First English Language Edition of the Complete Memoirs of Louis-Joseph Marchand, Valet and Friend of the Emperor 1811–1821. Produced by Proctor Jones, J. D.., D. F. A., including the original notes of Jean Bourguignon, Académie Des Beaux Arts, and Henry Lachouque: An Eyewitness Account of: the Tuileries, Elba, the Hundred Days, Waterloo, Sainte Helena.* Preface by Jean Tulard. San Francisco, 1998

Melito, André François, comte Miot de. *Memoirs of Count Miot de Melito, minister, ambassador, councillor of state and member of the Institute of France between the years 1788 and 1815.* Ed. General Fleischmann, from the French by Mrs. Cashel Hoey and Mr. John Lillie. 2 vols. London, 1881

Mikhailofsky-Danilefsky, Alexander (Aleksandr Ivanovich Mikhailovski-Danilevskii). *History of the Campaign in France in the Year 1814.* London, 1839

Molé, Mathieu Louis, comte. *The Life and Memoirs of Count Molé.* Ed. marquis de Noailles. 2 vols. London, 1923

Montholon, Charles Jean Tristan, marquis de. *Memoirs of the History of France During the Reign of Napoleon, Dictated by the Emperor at Sainte Hélène to the Generals Who Shared His Captivity; and Published from the Original Manuscripts Corrected by Himself.* 3 vols. London, 1823

Napoleon I, Emperor of the French. *Bulletins Officiels de la Grande Armée, dictés par L'Empereur Napoléon; et Recueillis par Alexandre Goujon, Ancien Officier D'Artillerie Légère, Membre de la Légion d'Honneur.* 2 vols. Paris, 1822

—*The Confidential Correspondence of Napoleon Bonaparte with His Brother Joseph, Sometime King of Spain. Selected and Translated With Explanatory Notes, From The 'Mémoires du Roi Joseph'.* 2 vols. New York, 1856

—*Confidential correspondence of the Emperor Napoleon and the Empress Joséphine: including letters from the time of their marriage until the death of Joséphine, and also several private letters from the emperor to his brother Joseph, and other important personages. With numerous illustrative notes and anecdotes.* Ed. and trans. John S. C. Abbott. New York, 1857

—*Correspondance de Napoléon Ier; Publiée par ordre de l'Empereur Napoléon III.* 32 vols. Paris, 1858–69

—*A Selection from the Letters and Despatches of the First Napoleon, with Explanatory Notes. Compiled by Captain The Honourable D. A. Bingham.* 3 vols. London, 1884

—*Letters of Napoleon to Joséphine.* Ed. Léon Cerf, Trans. Henry Bunn. New York, 1931

—*Letters of Napoleon.* Selected, trans., and ed. J. M. Thompson. Oxford, 1934

—*The Mind of Napoleon; a selection from his written and spoken words.* Ed. and trans. J. Christopher Herold. New York, 1955

—*My Dearest Louise: Letters of Marie-Louise and Napoleon, 1813–1814.* Collected and annotated by C. F. Palmstierna, Private Secretary to H.M. the King of Sweden, trans. E. M. Wilkinson. London, 1958

—*Letters and Documents of Napoleon, Volume One: The Rise to Power.* Ed. and trans. John Eldred Howard. London, 1961

New-England Palladium (Boston) Tuesday, 20 September 1803, XXII:1

Odeleben, Ernst Otto Innocenz, freiherr von. *A Circumstantial Narrative of the Campaign in Saxony in the Year 1813.* 2 vols. Trans. Alfred John Kempe. London, 1820

Official Narratives of the Campaigns of Buonaparte, Since the Peace of Amiens, Being a Complete Collection of the Whole of the Bulletins Published by Buonaparte to His Abdication. London, 1817, 43. Published in *Original Journals of the Eighteen Campaigns of Napoleon Bonaparte; Comprising All Those In Which He Personally Commanded In Chief; Translated From The French. To Which Are Added All The Bulletins Relating To Each Campaign, Now First Published Complete.* 2 vols. London, n.d. (1817)

O'Meara, Barry E. *Napoleon in Exile; or, A Voice From St. Helena. The Opinions and Reflections of Napoleon on the Most Important Events in His Life and Government, in His Own Words.* 2nd. edition. 2 vols. Philadelphia, 1822

Pelet, Baron (De La Lozère). *Napoleon in Council, or, The Opinions Delivered by Bonaparte in the Council of State.* Translated from the French of Baron Pelet (De La Lozère) member of the Chamber of Deputies, and late Minister of Public Instruction, by Captain Basil Hall, R.N., Robert Cadell, Edinburgh, 1837

Pelet, Jacques. *The French Campaign in Portugal 1810–1811: An Account by Jean Jacques Pelet.* Ed. trans. and annotated by Donald D. Horward. Minneapolis, 1973

Rapp, General Jean, comte. *Memoirs of General Count Rapp, First Aide-de-Camp to Napoleon, Written by Himself and Published by His Family.* London, 1823

Smith, Sir William Sidney. *The Life and Correspondence of Admiral Sir William Sidney Smith, G.C.B., In Two Volumes.* Ed. John Barrow. London, 1848

Rémusat, Claire Elisabeth Jeanne Gravier de Vergennes, comtesse de. *Memoires of Madame de Rémusat, 1802–1808.* With a preface and notes by her grandson, Paul de Rémusat, Senator. Ed. Paul de Rémusat, trans. from the French by Mrs. Cashel Hoey and Mr. John Lillie. 3 vols. New York, 1880

Savary, General A. J. M. R., duc de Rovigo. *Memoirs of the Duke of Rovigo, (M. Savary), Written by Himself: Illustrative of the History of the Emperor Napoleon.* 4 vols. London, 1828

Ségur, Philippe Paul, comte de. *History of the Expedition to Russia, Undertaken by the Emperor Napoleon, In the Year 1812. 'Sixth Edition, Revised and Corrected, to which is prefixed a Biographical Sketch of the Author.'* 2 vols. London, 1827

Talleyrand-Périgord, Charles Maurice de, prince de Bénévent. *Memoirs of Prince Talleyrand*. Ed. duc de, Broglie. Trans. Raphael Ledos de Beaufort. With an introduction by Whitelaw Reid. Imperial Edition, No. 3 of 10. 5 vols. New York and London, n.d. (1896)

Thiébault, Paul, Baron. *The Memoirs of Baron Thiébault, Late Lieutenant-General in the French Army*. Trans. Arthur John Butler. 2 vols. New York, 1896

SECONDARY SOURCES

Alison, Archibald, *History of Europe From the Commencement of the French Revolution in M.DCC.LXXXIX to the Restoration of the Bourbons in M.DCCC.XV.* 10 vols. Edinburgh and London, 1843

Ambrose, Stephen E. *Undaunted Courage: Meriwether Lewis, Thomas Jefferson, and the Opening of the American West*. New York, 1996

Bainville, Jacques. *Napoleon*. Boston, 1933

Battesti, Michèle. 'La bataille d'Aboukir et ses implications', Paper presented to *The International Congress: Napoleon and the French in Egypt and the Holy Land 1798–1801*. Tel Aviv, 5 July 1999

Bernard, H. *Education and the French Revolution*. Cambridge, 1969

Beyle, Marie Henri (Stendhal). *A Life of Napoleon*. Trans. Roland Gant. London, 1956

— *The Life of Henri Brulard*. Trans. Stewart, Jean, and Knight, B. Chicago, 1958

— *The Charterhouse of Parma*. Trans. Margaret Shaw. London, 1958

Britt, Albert Sidney. *The Wars of Napoleon*. Wayne, NJ, 1985

Bussey, George Moir. *History of Napoleon. Illustrated by Horace Vernet*. 2 vols. London, 1840

Byrd, Melanie. 'The Napoleonic Institute of Egypt', *Napoleonic Scholarship, in The Journal of the International Napoleonic Society*, ed J. David Markham, I: 2, December 1998

Carrington, Dorothy. *Napoleon and His Parents: On the Threshold of History*. New York, 1990

Chandler, David G. *The Campaigns of Napoleon*. New York, 1966

— *Dictionary of the Napoleonic Wars*. New York, 1979

— *Waterloo, The Hundred Days*. London, 1980, 1987

— 'Napoleon and Death', *Napoleonic Scholarship*, ed J. David Markham, I: 1, April 1997

Chappet, Alain, Pigeard, Alain, and Robe, André. *Répertoire mondial des souvenirs napoléoniens*. Paris, 1993

Connelly, Owen. *Blundering to Glory: Napoleon's Military Campaigns*. Rev. ed., Wilmington, 1999

Cronin, Vincent. *Napoleon Bonaparte: An Intimate Biography*. New York, 1972

Dempsey Guy C. 'The Peninsular War: A Reputation Tarnished', in *Napoleon: The Final Verdict*. London, 1996

Doyle, William. *The Oxford History of the French Revolution*. Oxford, 1989

Eidhal, Kyle. 'Marshal Nicolas Charles Oudinot "Le Bayard de l'armée française"', *Napoleonic Scholarship*, ed J. David Markham, I: 1, April 1997

Farrington F. *French Secondary Schools: an account of the origin, development and present organisation of secondary education in France*. New York, 1910

Fisher, Herbert. *'Bonapartism': Six Lectures Delivered in the University of London*. London, 1913

Gallaher John G. *The Iron Marshal: A Biography of Louis N. Davout*. Carbondale and Edwardsville, 1976

— *General Alexandre Dumas: Soldier of the French Revolution*. Carbondale and Edwardsville, 1997

Gichon, Mordechai. 'Jaffa, 1799', in *Napoleonic Scholarship*, ed. J. David Markham, I: 2, December, 1998.

— 'The Peculiarities of Napoleon's Near Eastern Campaign': Paper presented to *The International Congress: Napoleon and the French in Egypt and the Holy Land 1798–1801*. Tel Aviv, 4 July 1999

Houssaye, Henry. *Napoleon and the Campaign of 1814: France*. Tyne and Wear, 1994. Facsimile edn. of 1914 edition

— *The Return of Napoleon*. London, 1934

Jefferson, Thomas. *The Political Writings of Thomas Jefferson*. Ed. Merrill D. Peterson. Annapolis Junction, Maryland, 1993

Jones, Proctor Patterson, 'From Glory to Treachery: The Story of the Duc d'Enghien': *Selected Papers of the Consortium on Revolutionary Europe*, 1999

Josephson, Matthew. *Stendhal, or The Pursuit of Happiness*. Garden City, 1946

Lefebvre, Georges. *The French Revolution from 1793 to 1799*. Trans. J. Hall and J. Friguglietti. New York, 1964

—*Napoleon from 18 Brumaire to Tilsit, 1799–1807*. Trans. H. Stockhold. New York, 1969

—*Napoleon from Tilsit to Waterloo,1807–1815*. Trans. J. Anderson. New York, 1969

Lewis, Michael. *Napoleon and his British Captives*. London, 1962

Lloyd, Peter A. *The French Are Coming! The Invasion Scare 1803–5*. Tunbridge Wells, 1991

McErlean John. 'The Napoleonic Recapture of Corsica in 1796: A Necessary Preliminary for the Egyptian Expedition': Paper delivered to *The International Congress: Napoleon and the French in Egypt and the Holy Land 1798–1801*. Tel Aviv, 5 July 1999

Malone, Dumas. *Jefferson the President: First Term 1801–1805*. Boston, 1970

Markham, Felix. *Napoleon*. New York, 1963

Nafziger, George. *Napoleon's Invasion of Russia*. Novato, CA., 1988

Paris, Francklyn. *Napoleon's Legion*. New York, 1927

Polowetzky Michael. *A Bond Never Broken: The Relations Between Napoleon and the Authors of France*. London and Toronto, 1993

Ratcliffe, Bertram. *Prelude to Fame: An Account of the Life of Napoleon Bonaparte From His Arrival in France to the Battle of Montenotte*. London, 1981

Schur, Nathan. *Napoleon in the Holy Land*. London, 1999

Sloan, William Milligan. *Life of Napoleon Bonaparte*. New York, 1896

Soboul, A. *Understanding the French Revolution*. Trans. A. Knutson. New York, 1988

Thiers, Adolphe. *History of the Consulate and the Empire of France Under Napoleon*. Trans. D. Forbes Campbell and H. W. Herbert. 5 vols. Philadelphia, 1893

Tulard Jean. *Napoleon: The Myth of the Saviour*. Trans. Teresa Waugh. London, 1984

Tulard, Jean, and Garros, Louis. *Itinéraire de Napoléon au jour le jour 1769–1821*. France, 1992

Vignery, R. *The French Revolution and the Schools*. Madison, Wisconsin, 1966

Weider, Ben. *Assassination at St. Helena Revisited*. New York, 1995

— 'Napoleon and the Jews': *Napoleonic Scholarship*, ed. J. David Markham, I:2, December 1998

Weider, Ben, and Hapgood, David. *The Murder of Napoleon*. New York, 1982

Wilkinson, Spenser. *The Rise of General Bonaparte*. Oxford, 1930

Woloch, Isser. *Napoleon and His Collaborators: The Making of a Dictatorship*. New York, 2001

Young, Norwood. *Napoleon in Exile at St. Helena (1815–1821)*. 2 vols. Philadelphia, 1915

INDEX

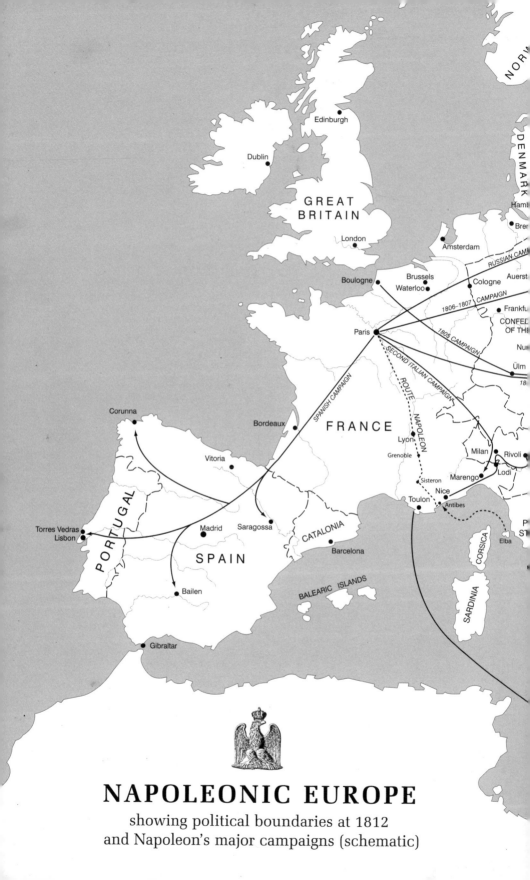

NAPOLEONIC EUROPE

showing political boundaries at 1812
and Napoleon's major campaigns (schematic)